First World War
and Army of Occupation
War Diary
France, Belgium and Germany

38 DIVISION
Divisional Troops
Royal Army Medical Corps
130 Field Ambulance
3 December 1915 - 10 June 1919

WO95/2549/2

The Naval & Military Press Ltd
www.nmarchive.com
Published in association with The National Archives

Published by

The Naval & Military Press Ltd

Unit 10 Ridgewood Industrial Park,

Uckfield, East Sussex,

TN22 5QE England

Tel: +44 (0) 1825 749494

www.naval-military-press.com

www.nmarchive.com

This diary has been reprinted in facsimile from the original. Any imperfections are inevitably reproduced and the quality may fall short of modern type and cartographic standards.

© **Crown Copyright**
Images reproduced by permission of The National Archives, London, England, 2015.

Contents

Document type	Place/Title	Date From	Date To
Heading	WO/95/2549/2 130 Field Ambulance		
Heading	38th Division Medical 130th Field Ambulance Dec 1915-1919 Jun		
Heading	130th. F.A. Vol I December 1915		
War Diary	Winchester	03/12/1915	03/12/1915
War Diary	Havre	04/12/1915	06/12/1915
War Diary	Enguingatte	07/12/1915	08/12/1915
War Diary	Glomenghem	09/12/1915	20/12/1915
War Diary	Calonne	21/12/1915	31/12/1915
War Diary	Glomenghem	16/12/1915	16/12/1915
War Diary	Estaires	17/12/1915	24/12/1915
Heading	38th Div F/201/2 130th F.a. Vol 2 Jan 1916		
War Diary	Calonne	01/01/1916	23/01/1916
War Diary	Mesplaux	24/01/1916	31/01/1916
War Diary	Calonne	31/01/1916	31/01/1916
War Diary	Locon	04/01/1916	10/01/1916
War Diary	Calonne	06/01/1916	06/01/1916
War Diary	Green Barn	07/01/1916	14/01/1916
War Diary	Calonne	26/12/1915	26/12/1915
War Diary	Vieille Chapelle	27/12/1915	02/01/1916
Heading	130th Field Ambulance Feb 1916		
Heading	130th F.a. Vol 3		
War Diary	Mesplaux	01/02/1916	29/02/1916
Heading	130 F Amb Vol 4 March 1916 April 1916		
War Diary	Mesplaux	01/03/1916	18/04/1916
War Diary	La Gorgue	19/04/1916	30/04/1916
Heading	130th (St. John) F. A. May 1916 38th (Welsh) Div		
War Diary	La Gorgue	01/05/1916	31/05/1916
Heading	War Diary Of 130th (St John) Field Ambulance For June 1916		
War Diary	La Gorgue	01/06/1916	10/06/1916
War Diary	Busnes	11/06/1916	12/06/1916
War Diary	Auchel	13/06/1916	13/06/1916
War Diary	Villers Chatel Mingoval	14/06/1916	26/06/1916
War Diary	Ransart	27/06/1916	27/06/1916
War Diary	St Hilaire	28/06/1916	30/06/1916
Heading	War Diary Of 130th (St John) Field Ambulance From 1st July 1916 To 31st July 1916		
War Diary	Val De Maison	01/07/1916	01/07/1916
War Diary	Puchevillers	02/07/1916	03/07/1916
War Diary	Franvillers	04/07/1916	04/07/1916
War Diary	Heilly.	05/07/1916	05/07/1916
War Diary	Morlancourt	06/07/1916	07/07/1916
War Diary	Morlancourt Minden Post Cater Pillar Wood	07/07/1916	08/07/1916
War Diary	Morlancourt Minden Post Triangle Loop Caterpillar Wood	07/07/1916	07/07/1916
War Diary	Morlancourt Minden Post Caterpillar Wood	07/07/1916	07/07/1916
War Diary	Morlancourt	07/07/1916	10/07/1916
War Diary	Morlancourt Mindon Post Triangle	10/07/1916	10/07/1916
War Diary	Morlancourt Mindon Post Sapper Corned Triangle	11/07/1916	11/07/1916

War Diary	Morlancourt	10/07/1916	12/07/1916
War Diary	Longpre	13/07/1916	13/07/1916
War Diary	Bellancourt	13/07/1916	14/07/1916
War Diary	Le Pluoy	15/07/1916	15/07/1916
War Diary	Thievres	19/07/1916	30/07/1916
War Diary	Thievres Arques Volkerinckhove	31/07/1916	31/07/1916
War Diary	War Diary Of 130th (St John) Field Ambulance From 1st August 16 To 31st August 16 Vol 9		
War Diary	Volkerinckhove	01/08/1916	03/08/1916
War Diary	C11c.3.2 Sheet 27		
War Diary	Wormhoudt Herzeele	03/08/1916	24/08/1916
War Diary	Proven	24/08/1916	24/08/1916
War Diary	Wormhoudt		
War Diary	Proven	25/08/1916	31/08/1916
Heading	War Diary Of 130th (St John) Field Amb From 1st Sept 16 To 30th Sept 16		
Miscellaneous	A. D. M. S. 38th Div.	30/09/1916	30/09/1916
War Diary	Proven	01/09/1916	30/09/1916
Heading	War Diary Of 130th (St John) Field Ambulance 38th (Welsh) Division From October 1st 1916 To October 31st 1916		
War Diary	Proven	01/10/1916	31/10/1916
Heading	War Diary Of 130th (St John) Field Ambulance 38th (Welsh) Division From November 1st 1916 To November 30/1916		
War Diary	Proven	01/11/1916	30/11/1916
Heading	War Diary Of 130th (St John) Field Ambulance Dec 1st 1916 To Dec 31st 1916 Vol 13		
War Diary	Proven	01/12/1916	13/12/1916
War Diary	Herzeele	13/12/1916	31/12/1916
Heading	War Diary Of 130th. (St. John) Field Ambulance. From January 1st. 1917 To January 31st. 1917 Vol 14		
War Diary	Herzeele	01/01/1917	14/01/1917
War Diary	Essex Farm Sussex Farm and Main Dressing Station at A23C 2.9	15/01/1917	15/01/1917
War Diary	A23.C.2.9	16/01/1917	31/01/1917
Heading	War Diary Of The 130th (St John) Field Ambulance 38th (Welsh) Division. From February 1st To February 28th 1917 Vol 15		
War Diary	A23.c 2.9	01/02/1917	28/02/1917
War Diary	War Diary Of 130th (St John) Field Ambulance 38th (Welsh) Division From March 1st 1917 To March 31st 1917 Vol 16		
War Diary	A23.C.2.9	01/03/1917	31/03/1917
Heading	War Diary Of 130th (St John) Field Amb. From 1st April 17 To 30th April 17 Vol 17		
War Diary	A23 C 2.9	01/04/1917	30/04/1917
Heading	War Diary Of The 130th (St John) Field Ambulance 38th (Welsh) Division From May 1st 1917 To May 31st 1917 Vol 18		
War Diary	A23 C 2.9	01/05/1917	31/05/1917
Heading	War Diary Of 130th. (St. John) Field Ambulance. From 1st. June 1917 To 30th. June 1917 Vol 19		
Miscellaneous	B.E.F. Summary of Medical War Diaries for 130th F.A., 38th Divn., 14th Corps, 5th Army. Western Front June 1917		

War Diary	B.E.F. 130th F.A. 38th Div. 14th Corps, 5th Army. O.C. Lt. Col. J.E.H. Davies. Western Front June 1917.		
War Diary	Headquarters		
War Diary	Medical Arrangements		
War Diary	Operation R.A.M.C.		
War Diary	Operation Enemy.	26/06/1917	26/06/1917
War Diary	Medical Arrangements	28/06/1917	28/06/1917
War Diary	Moves	30/06/1917	30/06/1917
Miscellaneous	B.E.F. Summary of Medical War Diaries for 130th F.A., 38th Divn., 14th Corps, 5th Army. Western Front June 1917.		
War Diary	Headquarters.		
War Diary	Transfer.		
War Diary	Medical Arrangements		
War Diary	Operations R.A.M.C.	11/06/1917	25/06/1917
War Diary	Operations Enemy.	26/06/1917	26/06/1917
War Diary	Medical Arrangements	28/06/1917	28/06/1917
War Diary	Moves	30/06/1917	30/06/1917
War Diary	A23 C 2.9	01/06/1917	09/06/1917
War Diary	Gwalia Farm	10/06/1917	14/06/1917
War Diary	Gwalia Farm A22 C 2.9	15/06/1917	15/06/1917
War Diary	Gwalia Farm A23c 2.9	16/06/1917	25/06/1917
War Diary	Gwalia Farm	25/06/1917	30/06/1917
Heading	War Diary Of 130th (St John) Field Ambulance From July 1st 1917 To July 31st 1917 Vol 20		
Miscellaneous	B.E.F. 130th F.A. 38th Div. 14th Corps, 5th Army. O.C. Lt. Col. J.E.H. Davies. Western Front June '17.		
War Diary	Operations R.A.M.C.	01/07/1917	15/07/1917
War Diary	Moves	16/07/1917	18/07/1917
War Diary	Moves Detachment	19/07/1917	19/07/1917
War Diary	Moves	21/07/1917	21/07/1917
War Diary	Casualties R.A.M.C.		
War Diary	Casualties Gas.		
War Diary	Moves	28/07/1917	28/07/1917
War Diary	Moves Detachment		
War Diary	Moves Transport.		
War Diary	Moves Detachment	30/07/1917	30/07/1917
War Diary	Operations.	31/07/1917	31/07/1917
War Diary	Casualties R.A.M.C.		
War Diary	Moves Detachment		
War Diary	Moves	06/07/1917	06/07/1917
War Diary	Decorations	15/07/1917	15/07/1917
War Diary	Headquarters.		
War Diary	Operations R.A.M.C.	01/07/1917	15/07/1917
War Diary	Moves	16/07/1916	18/07/1916
War Diary	Moves Detachment	19/07/1916	19/07/1916
War Diary	Moves	21/07/1916	21/07/1916
War Diary	Casualties R.A.M.C.		
War Diary	Casualties Gas.	26/07/1917	26/07/1917
War Diary	Moves	28/07/1917	28/07/1917
War Diary	Moves Detachment		
War Diary	Moves Transport		
War Diary	Moves Detachment	30/07/1917	30/07/1917
War Diary	Operations	31/07/1917	31/07/1917
War Diary	Casualties R.A.M.C.		
War Diary	Moves Detachment		

War Diary	La Tirmand	01/07/1917	12/07/1917
War Diary	La Tirmond	12/07/1917	16/07/1917
War Diary	Steen Becque	17/07/1917	17/07/1917
War Diary	Hondeghem	18/07/1917	18/07/1917
War Diary	Proven	19/07/1917	20/07/1917
War Diary	Proven Camp F6a	21/07/1917	21/07/1917
War Diary	Camp F6a Sheet 27	22/07/1917	22/07/1917
War Diary	Camp F6a	23/07/1917	23/07/1917
War Diary	Camp F6a Sefton	24/07/1917	27/07/1917
War Diary	Coppernolle A17a 2.9 (Sheet 28)	28/07/1917	28/07/1917
War Diary	Coppernolle A17a 2.9	29/07/1917	31/07/1917
Heading	War Diary Of 130th (Ft John) Field Ambulance From 1st August 1917 To 31st August 1917 Vol 21		
Miscellaneous	B.E.F. Summary of Medical War Diaries for 130th F.A., 38th Divn. 14th Corps, 5th Army. to 11th Corps, 1st Army from 13.9.17. Western Front Aug 1917.		
War Diary	Moves	18/08/1918	18/08/1918
War Diary	Decorations.		
War Diary	Casualties R.A.M.C.	19/08/1917	19/08/1917
War Diary	Medical Arrangements.	21/08/1917	21/08/1917
War Diary	Decorations.	22/08/1917	22/08/1917
War Diary	Moves	24/08/1917	24/08/1917
War Diary	Operations.	27/08/1917	27/08/1917
War Diary	Evacuation Casualties	28/08/1917	28/08/1917
War Diary	Coppernolle A17a 2.9	01/08/1917	04/08/1917
War Diary	Coppernolle	05/08/1917	06/08/1917
War Diary	Priory Camp F10 C8.6	07/08/1917	18/08/1917
War Diary	Sussex A.D.S. (e19 C 2.6) Fusiliers Ads. (c13.c1.2) St John Ads (c13.a.2.3)	19/08/1917	19/08/1917
War Diary	Sussex F (c19c2.6)	20/08/1917	21/08/1917
War Diary	Sussex ADS	22/08/1917	24/08/1917
War Diary	Sussex ADS C13c 1.2	25/08/1917	25/08/1917
War Diary	Fusilier ADS C.13c 1.12	26/08/1917	26/08/1917
War Diary	Advanced Ads's at Gallwitz Fm Cement Fm		
War Diary	Fusilier Ads C13 C.1.12	27/08/1917	27/08/1917
War Diary	Fusilier Ads C13 C1.2	28/08/1917	28/08/1917
War Diary	Fusilier Ads Cement Fm Gallwitz Fm	28/08/1917	31/08/1917
War Diary	Fusilier Ads Cement Fm Gallwitz Fm Advanced Ads	28/08/1917	28/08/1917
War Diary	Fusilier Ads Cement Fm Gallwitz Fm	29/08/1917	31/08/1917
Heading	War Diary Of 130th. (St John) Field Ambulance From 1st September 1917 To 30th September 1917 Vol 22		
Miscellaneous	B.E.F.		
War Diary	Operation Enemy Casualties R.A.M.C.	02/09/1917	02/09/1917
War Diary	Operations Enemy.	03/09/1917	03/09/1917
War Diary	Casualties R.A.M.C.		
War Diary	Decorations	09/09/1917	09/09/1917
War Diary	Moves	10/09/1917	10/09/1917
War Diary	Moves And Transfer.	13/09/1917	13/09/1917
War Diary	Operations Enemy Casualties R.A.M.C.	02/09/1917	02/09/1917
War Diary	Operations Enemy.	03/09/1917	03/09/1917
War Diary	Casualties R.A.M.C.		
War Diary	Decorations	09/09/1917	09/09/1917
War Diary	Moves	10/09/1917	10/09/1917
War Diary	Moves And Transfer.	13/09/1917	13/09/1917
War Diary	Fusilier Ads	01/09/1917	04/09/1917
War Diary	Fusiliers Ads C13 C1.2	05/09/1917	09/09/1917

War Diary	Pellisser Fm	10/09/1917	10/09/1917
War Diary	Pellisser Fm Priory Camp F10c8.6	10/09/1917	10/09/1917
War Diary	Priory Camp F10 C8.6	11/09/1917	13/09/1917
War Diary	Eecke	14/09/1917	14/09/1917
War Diary	Morbecque	15/09/1917	16/09/1917
War Diary	Estaires	16/09/1917	16/09/1917
War Diary	Sailly G17a8.4	17/09/1917	27/09/1917
War Diary	Sailly Sur La Lys G17a8.4	28/09/1917	30/09/1917
Heading	War Diary Of 130th (Ft John) Field Ambulance From 1st October 1917 To 31st October 1917 Vol 23		
War Diary	Sailly Sur La Lys G17a8.4	01/10/1917	01/10/1917
War Diary	Sailly San La Lys	02/10/1917	07/10/1917
War Diary	Sailly Sur La Lys G17a8.4	08/10/1917	08/10/1917
War Diary	Sailly Sur La Lys	09/10/1917	31/10/1917
Heading	War Diary Of 130th (Ft John) Field Ambulance From 1st November 1917 To 30th November 1917 Vol 24		
War Diary	Sailly Sur La Lys	01/11/1917	30/11/1917
War Diary	War Diary Of 130th (St John) Field Ambulance From 1st December 1917 To 31st December 1917 Vol 25		
War Diary	Sailly Sur La Lys	01/12/1917	09/12/1917
War Diary	Estaires L29 G 6.6	10/12/1917	11/12/1917
War Diary	Estaires	12/12/1917	31/12/1917
Heading	War Diary Of 130th (St John) Field Ambulance 1st January 1918 To 31st January 1918 Vol 26		
War Diary	Estaires L29g 6.6	01/01/1918	01/01/1918
War Diary	Estaires & 54 Ads Say Map	02/01/1918	02/01/1918
War Diary	Estaires	03/01/1918	15/01/1918
War Diary	Estaires L29b.6.6	16/01/1918	28/01/1918
War Diary	Estaires	29/01/1918	31/01/1918
Heading	War Diary Of 130th (St John) Field Ambulance From 1st February 1918 To 28th February 1918 Vol 27		
War Diary	Estaires Z29b 6.6	01/02/1918	12/02/1918
War Diary	Estaires L'Estrade A30b 2.9 Map 36	13/02/1918	13/02/1918
War Diary	L'Estrade A30b 2.9	13/02/1918	22/02/1918
War Diary	L'Estrade A30 b.2 9 Ads Pont de Nieppe B23b 6.0	23/02/1918	28/02/1918
Heading	130 Field Ambulance March 1918		
Heading	War Diary Of 130th (St John) Field Ambulance From 1st March 1918 To 31st March 1918		
War Diary	L'Estrade A30b 2.9	01/03/1918	12/03/1918
War Diary	L'Estrade A306 2.9 Ads's at B23b 6.0 C 26b 8.1	13/03/1918	31/03/1918
Heading	War Diary 130th (St John) Field Ambulance From 1st April 1918 To 30th April 1918 Vol 29		
War Diary	La Vicogne M21a 6.0	08/04/1918	11/04/1918
War Diary	Rubempre T14.c 4.0	12/04/1918	23/04/1918
War Diary	Rubempre Herissart	24/04/1918	24/04/1918
War Diary	T10a 4.4 Herissart	25/04/1918	30/04/1918
Heading	War Diary Of 130th (St John) Field Ambulance From 1st May 1918 To 31st May 1918 Vol 30		
War Diary	Herissart T10a5.6	01/05/1918	01/05/1918
War Diary	Domqueur (Le Plouy)	02/05/1918	03/05/1918
War Diary	St Lot. N Hiermont	04/05/1918	04/05/1918
War Diary	St Lot	05/05/1918	06/05/1918
War Diary	St Lot Lens 11 4a7.5	07/05/1918	23/05/1918
War Diary	Toutencourt U1d 3.1 Sheet 57.D	24/05/1918	25/05/1918
War Diary	Toutencourt U1d 3.1	25/05/1918	31/05/1918

Heading	War Diary Of 130th (St John) Field Ambulance From 1st June 1918 To 30th June 1918 Vol 31		
War Diary	Toutencourt U1d 3.1	01/06/1918	02/06/1918
War Diary	Toutencourt	03/06/1918	04/06/1918
War Diary	Toutencourt Clairfaye	05/06/1918	05/06/1918
War Diary	Clairfaye O 29b 5.6	06/06/1918	11/06/1918
War Diary	Clairfaye O29 B 5.6 Gas Center	12/06/1918	23/06/1918
War Diary	Clairfaye	24/06/1918	30/06/1918
Heading	War Diary Of 130th (St John) Field Ambulance From 1st July 1918 To 31st July 1918 Vol 32		
War Diary	O 29b 5.6	01/07/1918	12/07/1918
War Diary	Clairfaye	12/07/1918	17/07/1918
War Diary	Toutencourt U1a 2.1	18/07/1918	23/07/1918
War Diary	Toutencourt	26/07/1918	31/07/1918
Heading	War Diary Of 130th (St John) Field Ambulance From 1st August 1918 To 31st August 1918 Vol 33		
War Diary	Toutencourt U1d3.1	01/08/1918	06/08/1918
War Diary	O27b 8.9	07/08/1918	19/08/1918
War Diary	Mds O27b.8.9 Nr Lealvillers Ads Hedauville Forward Ads Bouzincourt	20/08/1918	20/08/1918
War Diary	Also Ads. Englebelmer	21/08/1918	22/08/1918
War Diary	Hedauville	23/08/1918	24/08/1918
War Diary	Hedauville Martinsart	25/08/1918	25/08/1918
War Diary	La Boisselle		
War Diary	Martinsart Ads La Boisselle Ads Contalmaison	26/08/1918	26/08/1918
War Diary	Mds La Boisselle Ads Contalmaison Ads Bazentin-Le Grande	27/08/1918	27/08/1918
War Diary	Mds Contalmaison Ads Bazentin-Le Grande	28/08/1918	28/08/1918
War Diary	Mds. Bazentin-Le Grande Ads Ginchy	29/08/1918	31/08/1918
Heading	War Diary Of 130th (St John) Field Ambulance From 1st September 1918 To 30th September 1918 Vol 34		
War Diary	MDS HQ Bazentin-Le Grande Ads Ginchy	01/09/1918	02/09/1918
War Diary	T13c 8.9 MDS Ginchy ADS Morval-Les. Boeufs R T4d2.4	03/09/1918	03/09/1918
War Diary	H Q To U8a6.8 Sailly-Saillisel	04/09/1918	04/09/1918
War Diary	MDS Sailly Saillisel ADS Governments ADS Mesnil Rd ADS Sailly Saillisel U8c2.0	05/09/1918	05/09/1918
War Diary	HQ Gas Centre Beaulancourt	06/09/1918	06/09/1918
War Diary	Beaulancourt	07/09/1918	10/09/1918
War Diary	Bus O23d 3.4	10/09/1918	10/09/1918
War Diary	Bus	11/09/1918	29/09/1918
War Diary	Bus Fins V12.c1.9	30/09/1918	30/09/1918
Heading	1130th F.a. Oct 1918		
War Diary	Fins V12c.1.9 Sheet 57c	01/10/1918	09/10/1918
War Diary	Fins Aubencheul Aux Bois	10/10/1918	10/10/1918
War Diary	Aubencheul Aux Bois Malincourt	11/10/1918	11/10/1918
War Diary	Malincourt Bertry	12/10/1918	12/10/1918
War Diary	Bertry P8d5.6	13/10/1918	14/10/1918
War Diary	Bertry	15/10/1918	31/10/1918
Heading	War Diary Of 130th (St John) Field Ambulance From 1st November 1918 To 30th November 1918 Vol 36		
War Diary	Bertry	01/11/1918	04/11/1918
War Diary	Bertry Moulin D'Harpies	05/11/1918	05/11/1918
War Diary	Moulin D'Harpies	06/11/1918	06/11/1918
War Diary	Foret De Mormal Berlaimont Pot-Devin	07/11/1918	07/11/1918
War Diary	Berlaimont Ads Pot Devin	08/11/1918	08/11/1918

War Diary	Berlaimont Pot De Vin Wattignies La Victoire W30b.1 (ADS)	09/11/1918	09/11/1918
War Diary	Pot-De Vin HQ Wattignies La Victoire ADS	10/11/1918	10/11/1918
War Diary	Wattignies HQ	11/11/1918	11/11/1918
War Diary	Wattignies	12/11/1918	23/11/1918
War Diary	Berlaimont 426 D4.9	24/11/1918	26/11/1918
War Diary	Berlaimont	27/11/1918	30/11/1918
Heading	War Diary Of 130th (St John) Field Amb. From 1st Dec 1918 To 31st Dec 1918		
War Diary	Berlaimont	01/12/1918	31/12/1918
Heading	War Diary Of 130 (St John) Field Ambulance. From January 1st 1919 To January 31st 1919 Vol 37		
War Diary	Englefontein	01/01/1919	01/01/1919
War Diary	Querrieu	02/01/1919	10/01/1919
War Diary	Bussy	11/01/1919	31/01/1919
Heading	No 130 Field Ambulance Feb 1919		
War Diary	Bussy	01/02/1919	28/02/1919
Heading	130th F.a. Mar 1919		
War Diary	Bussy	01/03/1919	19/03/1919
War Diary	Bussy Les Daours.	20/03/1919	31/03/1919
Heading	130th F.a. April 1919		
War Diary	Bussy-Les-Daours	01/04/1919	07/04/1919
War Diary	Lamotte Brebiere	08/04/1919	30/04/1919
Heading	No. 130 Field Ambulance May 1919		
War Diary	La Motte Brebiere	01/05/1919	30/05/1919
War Diary	130th F.a. June 1919		
War Diary	La. Motte Brebiere	01/06/1919	10/06/1919

WO/95/2549/2

130 Field Ambulance

38TH DIVISION
MEDICAL

130TH FIELD AMBULANCE
DEC 1915 - DEC 1918
1919 JUN

38TH DIVISION
MEDICAL

130th F.A.
Vol: I

12/7936

38th Div

F/20/11

130 F.A.

December 1915.

Dec '15
Dec '18

Army Form C. 2118.

WAR DIARY
INTELLIGENCE SUMMARY

(Erase heading not required.) 130th (St John) Field Ambulance, 39th Welsh Division

Instructions regarding War Diaries and Intelligence Summaries are contained in F. S. Regs., Part II. and the Staff Manual respectively. Title pages will be prepared in manuscript.

Place	Date	Hour	Summary of Events and Information	Remarks and references to Appendices
WINCHESTER	3/12/15	6 a.m.	Left FLOWERDOWN CAMP, WINCHESTER and marched to SOUTHAMPTON arriving at 12.30 p.m. Embarked on S.S. "KARNAK". Staff of 115th Brigade, 332nd Coy. A.S.C. and Captain and details on board. Strength of Unit on embarkation 230 all ranks. JSHD	
HAVRE	4/12/15	6 a.m.	Arrived off HAVRE. Disembarked by 12.30 p.m. Delay on account of weak crane, each wagon having to be unloaded. Left Harbour 12.30 p.m. for No 6 Dock Rest Camp. Reported on arrival at 1.15 p.m. to Commandant. JSHD	
"	5/12/15	11 a.m.	Left Rest Camp. Entrained at GARE DES MERCHANDISES departing therefrom at 2.20 p.m. Acted as O.C. Train. A Company of South Wales Borderers were also on the train. No casualties occurred on the journey. JSHD	
"	6/12/15	1 p.m.	Arrived at AIRE. — before arriving, our own R.T.O. boarded train at St Omer, supplied maps and directions. All transport had to be side unloaded as there was only one platform of about 15 yards and such does were at the sides; this took about an hour. Notified the A.D.M.S. immediately on our arrival by Cyclist Orderly. We were met	

WAR DIARY
of
INTELLIGENCE SUMMARY.
(Erase heading not required.)

Army Form C. 2118.

Place	Date	Hour	Summary of Events and Information	Remarks and references to Appendices
			met at AIRE and had no guide or Interpreter. The Unit marched to ENGUINGATTE in very bad weather leaving AIRE at 2.30 p.m. and arriving at our destination by 6 p.m. Billeting Officer with party went on in front but had great difficulty in finding billets for men and horses, as the Wiltshire Yeomanry were also stationed at ENGUINGATTE. The O.C. Wiltshire Yeomanry helped us in every way possible, and allowed us to the use of his Interpreter to find Billets. Billets were eventually found but they were very poor and crowded. J.S.H⊃	
ENGUINGATTE	9/12/15		The morning was spent in rearranging Billets to the men and fatigue duties. Visited by the A.D.M.S. in the afternoon. Received Orders from Headquarters of Brigade to proceed to GLOMENGHEM on the following day at 9 a.m. B.H⊃	
"	6/12/15	9 a.m.	The Unit marched out of ENGUINGATTE and upon arrival at GLOMENGHEM at 1 p.m. the men were shewn their Billets which were in barns and stables. The Headquarters were established in a Chateau, and the remainder of the day was spent in getting settled. Lieut. Douglas Charles Murray Page R.A.M.C. reported himself for duty and is	

WAR DIARY
or
INTELLIGENCE SUMMARY.
(Erase heading not required.)

Army Form C. 2118.

Place	Date	Hour	Summary of Events and Information	Remarks and references to Appendices
G.L. OMENGHEM	9/12/15		Taken on the strength of the Unit. Visited by the A.D.M.S. JS NR A.S.C. Motor transport reported for duty — 4 Lieutenants, 2 Fords, 2 Motor Cycles. Received orders to collect sick from the 113th and 114th Brigades and convey them to Hospital of 129th Field Ambulance at CLARQUES. JS NR	
"	10/12/15		Company went for a route march and the usual collecting of sick was carried on. Informed arrangements had been made for Field Cashier to be at Brigade Headquarters by 10 a.m. Captain Anderson of this Unit attended at Headquarters at this hour to draw money for Unit, and after waiting an hour a telephone message came through saying that the Cashier would not be able to come, and that Captain Anderson should proceed to Division Headquarters at ROQUETOIRE for the money. On arrival there found that the Field Cashier had no money left. The Field Cashier then advised Captain Anderson and other Officers requiring money to proceed to MEREVILLE a distance of 25 kilos for the money — this was done and the money obtained by 6 p.m. JS NR	

Army Form C. 2118.

WAR DIARY
or
INTELLIGENCE SUMMARY.
(Erase heading not required.)

Instructions regarding War Diaries and Intelligence Summaries are contained in F. S. Regs., Part II. and the Staff Manual respectively. Title pages will be prepared in manuscript.

Place	Date	Hour	Summary of Events and Information	Remarks and references to Appendices
G. LOMENGHEM	11/12/15		Men received their pay to-day — first payment made them in this country.	J.S.H.R
"	12/12/15		Instructions this day received to open a hospital, and a suitable site was formed. A section were detailed to proceed to hospital to clean same down. Orderlies were immediately informed and handed in for necessary chair etc; by 6 pm hospital was ready to receive patients. Captain A.J. Andrew was placed in charge.	J.S.H.R
"	13/12/15		Sent sub-division of A section sent to hospital for duty the remainder of the Company going a route march or doing fatigues.	J.S.H.R
"	14/12/15		Fatigue work e.g. laying roads for motor Ambulances at Headquarters and at the Hospital.	J.S.H.R
"	15/12/15		Similar work as that done on the 14th inst. was carried on today.	J.S.H.R
"	16/12/15		Lieut. Elliott of this Unit took on the duties of Lieut. Rennard Medical Officer of the	J.S.H.R

T2134. Wt. W708—776. 500000. 4/15. Sir J. C. & S.

Army Form C. 2118.

WAR DIARY
or
INTELLIGENCE SUMMARY.
(Erase heading not required.)

Instructions regarding War Diaries and Intelligence Summaries are contained in F. S. Regs., Part II. and the Staff Manual respectively. Title pages will be prepared in manuscript.

Place	Date	Hour	Summary of Events and Information	Remarks and references to Appendices
			13th Welsh Regiment who had been sent to Hospital. Instructions received for A Section to proceed to 9th Field Ambulance for instructional purposes. Nothing to report	Please see diary of A section attached. J.S.↑↓
GLOMENGHEM	17/12/15			
"	18/12/15		Orders were received in the morning of a possible sudden move of the Unit in the following day. In the evening orders received from the A.D.M.S. to send forward on the following day a party consisting of one Officer and 18 men to take over Field Hospital at CALONNE and also that this party were to arrange for the billeting of the Personnel of the 129th and 130th Field Ambulances.	J.S.↑↓
"	19/12/15		Lieut. Elliott returned to duty with the 13th Welsh Regiment. Orders received from Brigade Headquarters for billeting party of one Officer and two men to meet Staff Captain at ST FLORIS to arrange about billeting. This party was sent off, also the party to take over Hospital. Orders received late at night that the Unit was to march to CALONNE next day and to leave the starting point by 9 a.m. The A.D.M.S. visited Unit.	J.S.↑↓

Army Form C. 2118.

WAR DIARY
or
INTELLIGENCE SUMMARY.
(Erase heading not required.)

Instructions regarding War Diaries and Intelligence Summaries are contained in F. S. Regs., Part II. and the Staff Manual respectively. Title pages will be prepared in manuscript.

Place	Date	Hour	Summary of Events and Information	Remarks and references to Appendices
GLOMENGHEM	20/12/15		The Unit marched out of GLOMENGHEM at 7.30am and proceeded by route as directed, but were blocked by 113th Brigade owing to their having got on wrong roads; the blocking however passed by 9.5am. the Unit arriving at CALONNE by 2.30 pm. Wagons had to be left on road as no park had been obtained for them. Received 31 patients into Hospital this day.	JSHD
CALONNE	21/12/15		Billets were rearranged and standings and park obtained for horses and transport. Fatigue duties performed by the men. Ambulances collected patients from the 114th Brigade. Visit by the D.A.D.M.S.	JSHD JSHD
"	22/12/15		Fatigue duties by the men.	JSHD
"	23/12/15		Visit by the A.D.M.S.	JSHD
"	24/12/15		"A" Section returned to Headquarters at CALONNE, arriving at 11.30am. Visited by A.D.M.S. 11th Division.	JSHD
"	25/12/15		In accordance with the request expressed by the Major General Commanding the 38th Division in his circular Memo dated 22.12.'15 the men were permitted to observe	

Army Form C. 2118.

WAR DIARY
or
INTELLIGENCE SUMMARY.
(Erase heading not required.)

Instructions regarding War Diaries and Intelligence Summaries are contained in F.S. Regs., Part II. and the Staff Manual respectively. Title pages will be prepared in manuscript.

Place	Date	Hour	Summary of Events and Information	Remarks and references to Appendices
CALONNE	26/12/15		The day as a day of rest and recreation, so far as exigencies would permit. A number of fatigues were however necessary on this day. Visit by A.D.M.S. 38th Division.	JSHD
			In accordance with the Major Generals request to-day was also observed as a holiday and day of rest as far as possible, a number of fatigues were however necessary on this day. "B" Section composed of 60 N.C.O's and men under Capt: Hawkes, Lieut Burke and Lieut. Page with a limber wagon for Blankets left at 6 am for VIEILLE CHAPELLE to be attached to the 57th Field Ambulance for instructional purposes. Ambulance Cars were to-day marked with two textile white lines on the radiator. Horse transport were also marked in the same way on the Tail Boards in accordance with Divisional Routine Order No 99.	JSHD
"	27/12/15		On this 9 am Parade the O.C. read out to the Unit His Majesty the Kings Christmas Message to the troops. Kings Regulations paras: 461 and 462 regarding Discipline were also read on Parade.	JSHD

Army Form C. 2118.

WAR DIARY
or
INTELLIGENCE SUMMARY.
(Erase heading not required.)

Instructions regarding War Diaries and Intelligence Summaries are contained in F. S. Regs., Part II. and the Staff Manual respectively. Title pages will be prepared in manuscript.

Place	Date	Hour	Summary of Events and Information	Remarks and references to Appendices
CALONNE			The A.D.M.S. visited the Unit and in company with the O.C. inspected the Hospital, Stables, Baths and arrangements were made with the representative of the Mayor to take over the remaining class room of the School from Wednesday night the 29th inst. for a week for hospital purposes and for a further period if absolutely necessary.	JSHD
"	28/12/15		Nothing to report this day.	JSHD
"	29/12/15		The remaining class room of the School was taken over to be converted into further accommodation for hospital purposes.	JSHD
"	30/12/15		Visit by the A.D.M.S. who in company with the O.C. inspected the Hospital.	JSHD
"	31/12/15		A and B sections paraded for bathing at 8.15 am and 9.15 am respectively after which the men were detailed off to carry on their daily duties. Visited by the D.A.D.M.S. 38th Division.	JSHD

John H Prosser
Lieut.-Colonel,
R.A.M.C.

Army Form C. 2118.

WAR DIARY
of
"A" SECTION
INTELLIGENCE SUMMARY.
(Erase heading not required.)

Instructions regarding War Diaries and Intelligence Summaries are contained in F. S. Regs., Part II. and the Staff Manual respectively. Title pages will be prepared in manuscript.

Place	Date	Hour	Summary of Events and Information	Remarks and references to Appendices
GLOMENGHEN	16/12/15		On instructions from the A.D.M.S. "A" Section proceeded by Motor Bus at 1.30 hrs to be attached to the 9th Field Ambulance at ESTAIRES for instructional purposes, arriving at Headquarters of 9th Field Ambulance at 4.15 hrs. A Sergeant and 12 stretcher bearers proceeded to Advance Dressing Station at LAVENTIE for instruction under Lieut. Buckley.	JSNR
ESTAIRES	17/12/15		At 9 a.m. the N.C.Os and men of "A" Section remaining at Headquarters of 9th Field Ambulance were told off to be attached to their respective corresponding departments for instruction.	JSNR
"	18/12/15		The men at advanced dressing station were to-day exchanged for 12 more men from "A" Section. The O.C. also proceeded to Advanced Dressing Station.	JSNR
"	19/12/15		Instruction of the men proceeded in the various departments and the O.C. visited the Aid Post at Red House and also the Advance Aid Post in the trenches. Included several visits off RUE TILLEROY	JSNR
"	20/12/15		Instruction proceeded with. The O.C. returned to ESTAIRES and Captain Andrew went to	

Army Form C. 2118.

WAR DIARY
or
INTELLIGENCE SUMMARY.
(Erase heading not required.)

Instructions regarding War Diaries and Intelligence Summaries are contained in F. S. Regs., Part II. and the Staff Manual respectively. Title pages will be prepared in manuscript.

Place	Date	Hour	Summary of Events and Information	Remarks and references to Appendices
ESTAIRES	21/12/15		LAVENTIE Advanced Dressing Station. Indiriduals furnished with.	93 HD
"	22/12/15		attended Hospital and orderly room with O.C. 9th Field Ambulance.	93 HD
"	23/12/15		Visited Grain Barn, Advanced Dressing station of 3rd Field Ambulance with Captain Fraser acting as O.C. 9th Field Ambulance.	93 HD
"	24/12/15		Left ESTAIRES at 9 am and arrived Mess at CALONNE at 11.30 am. Visited by D.D.M.S. 1st Division.	93 HD

John R H Booth
Lieut.-Colonel,
R.A.M.C.

3rd Div
F/201/2.

130 Bde F.A.
Vol: 2

Jan 1916

Army Form C. 2118.

WAR DIARY

~~INTELLIGENCE SUMMARY.~~

(Erase heading not required.)

130TH (ST. JOHN) FIELD AMBULANCE, 38TH (WELSH) DIVISION.

Instructions regarding War Diaries and Intelligence Summaries are contained in F. S. Regs., Part II. and the Staff Manual respectively. Title pages will be prepared in manuscript.

Place	Date	Hour	Summary of Events and Information	Remarks and references to Appendices
CALONNE	1/1/16		Lieut. J. J. Buckley R.A.M.C. of this Unit went to relieve Lieut. Macmillan R.A.M.C. Medical Officer of the 14th Welsh Regiment in accordance with instructions received from the A.D.M.S. 38th Division. Lieut. Macmillan being sent to the Hospital for Officers at ROBECQ.	JS.KD
"	2/1/16		Lieut. Elliott R.A.M.C. of this Unit has this day relieved Lieut. Tennant 13th Welsh Regiment. The G.O.C. of the Division visited and inspected the Hospital in company with the A.D.M.S. 38th Division. B Section returned to Headquarters from the 59th Field Ambulance where they had been for instructional purposes. Lieut Page R.A.M.C. of this Unit proceeds for duty as M.O. to the 13th Battalion, Welsh Regiment to replace Lieut Elliott R.A.M.C. who had been acting as M.O. Lieut Burke R.A.M.C. of this Unit proceeds to the 14th Battalion Welsh Regiment for duty as M.O. in place of Lieut Buckley R.A.M.C.	JS.KD JS.KD JS.KD
"	3/1/16		"C" Section (3 Officers and 60 men) under Capt. Audinwin R.A.M.C. left at 9am to be attached for a period of one week to the 59th Field Ambulance for	(See Diary of "C" Section attached)

WAR DIARY
INTELLIGENCE SUMMARY.
(Erase heading not required.)

Army Form C. 2118.

Place	Date	Hour	Summary of Events and Information	Remarks and references to Appendices
CALONNE	4/1/16		instructional purposes; a limber wagon carried the blankets and officers' valises. Visited by the D.A.D.M.S. 38th Division. JNT	
"	5/1/16		The O.C. attended with other O.C's at office of A.D.M.S at 3.0 pm with reference to a move of Section B. JNT	
"			Two Horse Ambulances were detailed to follow the 10th and 15th Battalions the Welsh Regiment to pick up stragglers from the march. Lieut Bateman R.A.M.C. of 131st F.Amb reported for duty (temporarily) JNT	
"	6/1/16		"B" Section composed of 2 Officers and 61 other ranks under Capt M Fforelles left Section B left Headquarters at 9.0 am to proceed by Caute Minch to GREEN BARN for the purpose of taking over an advanced Dressing Station arriving at their destination at 12.15 pm. Lieut Bateman RAMC reported sick and on examination he was found to be suffering from a fracture of left Fibula which occurred when riding to this station. He was conveyed by Ambulance Car to Pobecq	Army attached JNT

Army Form C. 2118.

WAR DIARY
of
INTELLIGENCE SUMMARY.
(Erase heading not required.)

Instructions regarding War Diaries and Intelligence Summaries are contained in F. S. Regs., Part II. and the Staff Manual respectively. Title pages will be prepared in manuscript.

Place	Date	Hour	Summary of Events and Information	Remarks and references to Appendices
CALONNE	7/1/16		Hospital. This left only one Medical Officer vz Capt Andrews at Headquarters. Lieut Burke, returned from duty with 114th 25 Field Reg. Lieut Anderson R.A.M.C. returned to Headquarters for duty from "C" Section. Two Horse ambulances were detailed to follow the 10th and 15th Battalions Welsh Regiment to pick up stragglers. Visited by D.A.D.M.S.	JZAD
"	8/1/16		Visited by A.D.M.S. Received Telegram from Headquarters 114th Brigade 9.45 p.m. for the 4 chaplains attached to this Unit to report at Headquarters of Brigade at LAVENTIE.	JZAD
"	9/1/16		Capt J Alban Davies C.F. reported sick suffering from Colic, and was conveyed to Hospital for Officers at ROBECQ. The 3 other Chaplains proceeded to LAVENTIE at 1/30 p.m. in accordance with above mentioned instructions.	JZAD
"	10/1/16		Lieut M Howells of this Unit gazetted Captain as and from 1st December 1915. Section "C" of this Unit returned to Headquarters at 12/30 p.m. from the 59th Field	

Army Form C. 2118.

WAR DIARY

INTELLIGENCE SUMMARY.

(Erase heading not required.)

Instructions regarding War Diaries and Intelligence Summaries are contained in F. S. Regs., Part II. and the Staff Manual respectively. Title pages will be prepared in manuscript.

Place	Date	Hour	Summary of Events and Information	Remarks and references to Appendices
CALONNE	11/1/16		Ambulance where they had been attached for instructional purposes. Visited by the A.D.M.S. 38th (Welsh) Division. JSH	
"	12/1/16		Nothing to report this day. JSH	
			Received instructions from A.D.M.S. to collect sick of 56th Brigade who were to-day exchanging billets with the 1st Guards Brigade in this area. JSH	
CALONNE	13/1/16		Lieut Elliott R.A.M.C. proceeded to the 13th Welsh Regiment to take on the duties of Regimental M.O. in place of Lieut Gage R.A.M.C. who returned to the Headquarters of this Unit to duty. JSH	
CALONNE	14/1/16		Section "B" under Capt M Plowdew returned to Headquarters from the Advanced Dressing Station at Green Barn, the Advanced Dressing Station being taken over by a Section of the 131st Field Amb. JSH	

WAR DIARY or INTELLIGENCE SUMMARY.

(Erase heading not required.)

Army Form C. 2118.

Place	Date	Hour	Summary of Events and Information	Remarks and references to Appendices
CALONNE	15/1/16		Nothing to report to-day. JSHD	
CALONNE	16/1/16		Hospital visited by the A.D.M.S. 38th (Welsh) Division. JSHD	
CALONNE	17/1/16		The Hospital was visited by D.D.M.S XIth Corps who expressed his satisfaction with same. JSHD	
CALONNE	18/1/16		Hospital visited by the O.C. 59th Field Ambulance for the purpose of discussing exchange of hospitals. JSHD	
"	19/1/16		Nothing to report this day JSHD	
"	20/1/16		Hospital visited by the D.A.D.M.S. 38th Division JSHD	
"	21/1/16		Nothing to report this day JSHD	

Army Form C. 2118.

WAR DIARY
~~INTELLIGENCE SUMMARY~~
(Erase heading not required.)

Place	Date	Hour	Summary of Events and Information	Remarks and references to Appendices
CALONNE	22/1/16		Nothing to report this day. JSHR	
"	23/1/16		On instructions from the A.D.M.S. 38th Division a Section in charge of Capt Forbes proceeded to Advanced Dressing Station at 8.30 a.m. at RUE DE BOIS to take same over from the 59th Field Ambulance. JSHR	
MESPLAUX	24/1/16		The remainder of the Unit proceeded by route march to MESPLAUX leaving CALONNE at 10 a.m. to take over Field Hospital from the 59th Field Ambulance, arriving at MESPLAUX at 1.30 p.m. JSHR Lieut Burke of this Unit on instructions from the A.D.M.S. proceeded on duty as Regimental Medical Officer to the 10th Royal Welsh Fusiliers. JSHR	
"	25/1/16		The day was spent in fatigues and cleaning up the premises. The first wounded case to pass through the Hospital after being taken over by this Unit arrived at 7.45 p.m. from the 13th Royal Welsh Fusiliers. JSHR	

Army Form C. 2118.

WAR DIARY
INTELLIGENCE SUMMARY.
(Erase heading not required.)

Instructions regarding War Diaries and Intelligence Summaries are contained in F. S. Regs., Part II. and the Staff Manual respectively. Title pages will be prepared in manuscript.

Place	Date	Hour	Summary of Events and Information	Remarks and references to Appendices
MESPLAUX	26/1/16		The day was spent in fatigues and carrying out improvements generally. Visit by A.D.M.S. 98TD	
"	27/1/16		Instructions were received to prepare for the reception of a large number of wounded. Everything was prepared in readiness but only one case was received up to midnight. 98TD	
"	28/1/16		The Hospital was visited by Major General Lord Phillips G.O.C. commanding 38th (Welsh) Division. The C.C. visited the Advance Dressing Station. 98TD	
"	29/1/16		The Hospital was visited by the D.D.M.S. II Corps accompanied by the A.D.M.S. 38th Division. The C.C. visited the Advance Dressing Station. 98TD	
"	30/1/16		Nothing to report this day. 98TD	
"	31/1/16		Nothing to report this day. 98TD	

John N Beard Lieut.-Colonel,
R.A.M.C.

Army Form C. 2118.

WAR DIARY
or
INTELLIGENCE SUMMARY
(Erase heading not required.) 130" Field Amb: "C" Section

Instructions regarding War Diaries and Intelligence Summaries are contained in F. S. Regs., Part II. and the Staff Manual respectively. Title pages will be prepared in manuscript.

Place	Date	Hour	Summary of Events and Information	Remarks and references to Appendices
CALONNE	3/1/16	9.0am	Acting upon instructions received from 2OMS 38th Welsh Division "C" Section proceeded on foot, commencing at 9.0 a.m., to LOCON to be attached to the 59th Field Ambulance for instructional purposes arriving there at	
		11.45 am	Captain Ors Anderson, one sergeant and 28 stretcher bearers proceeded to the Advanced Dressing Station at the Rue de Bois for instruction. Lieut Robinson & Lieut Elliott remained at Headquarters AWA.	
LOCON	4/1/16	9.0am	Part Section left at Hospital of 59th Field Ambulance paraded and all duties were told off for attachment to corresponding departments for instruction AWA.	
LOCON	5/1/16		Capt Anderson was relieved at the Advanced Dressing Station by Lieut Anderson, and returned to Headquarters. Instruction of the men proceeded in the various departments AWA	
LOCON	6/1/16		Instruction proceeded with AWA	

Army Form C. 2118.

WAR DIARY
or
INTELLIGENCE SUMMARY.
(Erase heading not required.)

"C" Section.

Instructions regarding War Diaries and Intelligence Summaries are contained in F. S. Regs., Part II. and the Staff Manual respectively. Title pages will be prepared in manuscript.

Place	Date	Hour	Summary of Events and Information	Remarks and references to Appendices
LOCON	7/1/16		Lieut Anderson was relieved at the Advanced Dressing Station by Lieut Elliott and, acting under instructions received was returned to Headquarters at CALONNE to duty. Party from Advanced Dressing Station returned and remainder of Section under Lieut Elliott proceeded to the Advanced Dressing Station for duty and instruction.	A.D.S.
LOCON	8/1/16		Instruction proceeded with. A.D.S.	
LOCON	9/1/16		Instruction proceeded with. A.D.S.	
LOCON	10/1/16		Party under Lieut Elliott relieved from Advanced Dressing Station at 9.0 am. Whole Section under Capt Anderson left Locon at 9.45 am and rejoined Unit at CALONNE at 11.30 am A.W.Anderson Capt RAMC	

WAR DIARY

INTELLIGENCE SUMMARY

150" (½th) Field Amb. "B" Section

Army Form C. 2118.

Place	Date	Hour	Summary of Events and Information	Remarks and references to Appendices
CALONNE	4/1/16	9.30 AM	B. Section (Two Officers, 56 N.C.Os & men) proceeded to LA GORGUE to report to A.D.M.S. Guards Division. Reported at 11.45 AM and received instructions to proceed to GREEN BARN (Sheet 36 M 27 d 6.2). This point reached at 1 P.M. and the A.D.S. taken over from the Officer in charge. All transport with the exception of 2 Motor Ambulances and water cart and one limbered waggon was returned to CALONNE.	
GREEN BARN		2.30 P.M.	Six men carrying rations were detailed as bearers for 24 hours and taken to following Regimental aid posts — EBENEZER FARM (Sheet 36 M 26 d 7.5) STIRLING CASTLE (5504.7). One wheeled stretcher was left at last mentioned post. One casualty treated in the evening and sent to No. 7 Field Ambulance ESTAIRES. h. 2f. Routine Orders were issued. Bearers at Regimental Aid Post were relieved at 2 A.M. daily, and Aid visits daily by M.O. on duty for the day. Nursing Section Aid on duty at the dressing room and one man on night duty. h. 2f.	
GREEN BARN	5/1/16	2.30 P.M.	Fatigue parties attached daily to clean town and entrenched and approved A.D.S. Reported at Headquarters 114th Brigade, LAVENTIE and arranged those field telephone connected Divisional ← Regimental Aid Post. h. 2f.	

Army Form C. 2118.

WAR DIARY
or
INTELLIGENCE SUMMARY
(Erase heading not required.)

Instructions regarding War Diaries and Intelligence Summaries are contained in F.S. Regs., Part II. and the Staff Manual respectively. Title pages will be prepared in manuscript.

Place	Date	Hour	Summary of Events and Information	Remarks and references to Appendices
GREEN BARN	9/1/16	2 P.M.	Visit from A.D.M.S. 35th Division and accompanied him to EBENEZER FARM which was the Headquarters of the 13th Batt. Welsh Regt. h.J.	
GREEN BARN	10/1/16		Nothing to report.	
GREEN BARN	11/1/16	5 P.M.	Instructions from A.D.M.S. Guards Division that bombardment of enemy's front was contemplated between 8-5 P.M. 12/1/16 and therefore few heavy casualties in view of possible retaliation on part of enemy. h.J.	
GREEN BARN	12/1/16		Strength of stretcher bearers doubled with each Regimental Aid Post, also accommodation made for reception of wounded in barns and dug outs. Visit from D.A.D.M.S. Guards Division. h.J.	
GREEN BARN	13/1/16		Number of casualties treated not greater than usual. Instructions to return to CALONNE on 14.1.16 when we would be relieved by a Section of the 131st Field Ambulance. h.J.	
GREEN BARN	14/1/16	2.30 P.M.	Handed over to Major Davis 131st Field Ambulance and visited Regimental Aid Posts with Lieut. G. Jones. h.J. "B" Section in charge of Lieut. Buckley proceeded for CALONNE at 3.30 P.M. arriving at 5.30 P.M. Route GREEN BARN – PONT DU HEM – BOUT DEVILLE – RIEZ BAILLEUL –	

Army Form C. 2118.

WAR DIARY
or
INTELLIGENCE SUMMARY.
(Erase heading not required.)

Place	Date	Hour	Summary of Events and Information	Remarks and references to Appendices
PONT RIQUEUL - LESTREM - CALONNE			Motor Ambulances in charge of Capt Jonkers reached CALONNE at 6 p.m. One wheeled stretcher destroyed by shell fire. One left at STIRLING CASTLE	

M. Jonkers Capt. R.A.M.C.

Army Form C. 2118.

WAR DIARY
or
INTELLIGENCE SUMMARY. 130 (1st/1st John) Field Amb. "B" Section

(Erase heading not required.)

Instructions regarding War Diaries and Intelligence Summaries are contained in F. S. Regs., Part II. and the Staff Manual respectively. Title pages will be prepared in manuscript.

Place	Date	Hour	Summary of Events and Information	Remarks and references to Appendices
CALONNE	26/11/15	9.30 AM	"B" Section (3 officers and 60 N.C.Os men) proceeded to VIEILLE CHAPELLE to be attached for instructional purposes to the 67th Field Ambulance. Owing to the flooded condition of the roads the march was too prolonged and the section did not reach its destination until 1 P.M. h.J.	
VIEILLE CHAPELLE	27/11/15	10 A.M.	Lieut J. Burke with a party of 1 N.C.O. and 12 men proceeded to the Advanced Dressing Station at ST VAAST for two days' instruction. The remainder of the section was employed in various ways at the hospital. The nursing section took duties in the wards, the bearer section helping in the conveyance of sick and wounded to the hospital. Convoy. h.J.	
VIEILLE CHAPELLE	28/11/15		Nothing to report. h.J.	
VIEILLE CHAPELLE	29/11/15	10AM	Capt. M. Frankles with a party of 13 men proceeded to the A.D.S. Orchard Lieut. Burke, the Six men carrying rations were detailed as bearers and proceeded to the Regimental Aid Posts. The wounded were brought to the A.D.S. for treatment and conveyed by ambulance to the hospital at VIEILLE CHAPELLE. Lieut. D.C.M. Page acted as orderly medical officer for the day at the hospital h.J.	
VIEILLE CHAPELLE	30/11/15		Remained Regimental Aid Posts relieved. h.J.	

Army Form C. 2118.

WAR DIARY
or
INTELLIGENCE SUMMARY.
(Erase heading not required.)

Instructions regarding War Diaries and Intelligence Summaries are contained in F. S. Regs., Part II. and the Staff Manual respectively. Title pages will be prepared in manuscript.

Place	Date	Hour	Summary of Events and Information	Remarks and references to Appendices
VIEILLE CHAPELLE	31/1/15	10 A.M.	Lieut D.C.M. Page with a party of 13 men proceeded to the A.D.S. Krelière. Capt. M. Fowlkes Lieut J. Burke acted as orderly medical officer for the day at the hospital.	
VIEILLE CHAPELLE	1/2/16		Nothing of interest to report. h.2f	
VIEILLE CHAPELLE	2/2/16	11:30 A.M.	Lieut. Page and his party returned from the A.D.S. h.2f	
		2 P.M.	B Section proceeded on its return to CALONNE. Route VIEILLE CHAPELLE - ZELOBES - PARADIS - CALONNE. The destination was reached at 4.30 P.M. h.2f	

h. Fowlkes Capt. R.A.M.C.

130th Field Ambulance

Feb 1916

130th F.A.
Vol: 3

Army Form C. 2118.

WAR DIARY
or
INTELLIGENCE SUMMARY.

130TH (ST. JOHN) FIELD AMBULANCE.
38TH (WELSH) DIVISION

(Erase heading not required.)

Instructions regarding War Diaries and Intelligence Summaries are contained in F. S. Regs., Part II. and the Staff Manual respectively. Title pages will be prepared in manuscript.

Place	Date	Hour	Summary of Events and Information	Remarks and references to Appendices
MESPLAUX	1.2.'16		Advanced Dressing Station and Hospital visited by A.D.M.S. 38th Division when he made an inspection of the Boths and Records of the Unit.	
"	2.2.'16		Nothing to report this day.	
"	3.2.'16		The C.O. visited the First Aid Post at TUBE STATION also the Advanced Dressing Station	
"	4.2.'16		All men who were not employed on Hospital Duties were on fatigue work carrying out improvements in and around the premises viz, making paths, levelling off the ground, whitewashing etc. Visit by the A.D.M.S.	
"	5.2.'16		The A.D.M.S. & D.A.D.M.S. 38th Division and the C.O. visited the Advanced Dressing Station and Aid Post at TUBE STATION and inspected same.	
"	6.2.'16		Nothing to report this day.	

Army Form C. 2118.

WAR DIARY
or
INTELLIGENCE SUMMARY.
(Erase heading not required.)

130th (ST. JOHN) FIELD AMBULANCE
38th (WELSH) DIVISION

Instructions regarding War Diaries and Intelligence Summaries are contained in F. S. Regs., Part II. and the Staff Manual respectively. Title pages will be prepared in manuscript.

Place	Date	Hour	Summary of Events and Information	Remarks and references to Appendices
MESPLAUX	7.2.16		The C.C. visited the Advanced Dressing Station and upheld same	J.C.↑D
"	8.2.16		The A.D.M.S. visited the Hospital and gave instructions for 4 men to be billeted at TUBE STATION and No.1 and 2 at the junction of CADBURY CORNER and PRINCES ROAD but on ascertaining that there was no accommodation at CADBURY CORNER, 2 men were posted at PATH HOUSE POST.	J.C.↑D J.C.↑D
"	9.2.16		The following Officers attended a Gas Lecture at the Recreation Room LESTREM, Officer Commanding, Captain Anderson, Captain Forster, Lieut Anderson, Lieut Elliot	J.C.↑D
"	10.2.16		The C.C. visited the Advanced Dressing Station at 11 a.m. and found everything in order and everyone on the alert.	J.C.↑D
"	11.2.16		The Hospital was visited by the A.D.M.S. 38th Division	J.C.↑D
"	12.2.16		Nothing to report this day	J.C.↑D

T2134. Wt. W708—776. 500000. 4/15. Sir J. C. & S.

Army Form C. 2118.

WAR DIARY
or
INTELLIGENCE SUMMARY.
(Erase heading not required.)

130TH (ST. JOHN) FIELD AMBULANCE.
38TH (WELSH) DIVISION.

Instructions regarding War Diaries and Intelligence Summaries are contained in F. S. Regs., Part II. and the Staff Manual respectively. Title pages will be prepared in manuscript.

Place	Date	Hour	Summary of Events and Information	Remarks and references to Appendices
NESPLAUX	13.2.16		The O.C. visited the Advanced Dressing Station.	82
"	14.2.16		Nothing to report this day.	82
"	15.2.16		Mr. Gwen Gwen Secretary Welsh Army Corps visited the Hospital and also the Advanced Dressing Station. In accordance with instructions received from the A.D.M.S. the O.C. together with Captain Andrews proceeded to RUE D'EPINETTE and visited Aid Post of 13th Essex Regiment situated at S.9.B.04 and from thence to BREWERY CORNER with a view of ascertaining the practicability of evacuating from Aid Posts thus to RUE DE BOIS Advanced Dressing Station. They then proceeded via DANGER CORNER to FESTUBERT to view the Aid Posts of the 5th Field Ambulance and 1st Herts are situated to ascertain the best route for evacuating cases from 7.25d and 7 Central to NESPLAUX when it was found that via GORRE was the most suitable.	82
"	16.2.16		Hospital inspected by the A.D.M.S.	82

WAR DIARY
or
INTELLIGENCE SUMMARY.

(Erase heading not required.)

130TH (ST. JOHN) FIELD AMBULANCE.
38TH (WELSH) DIVISION.

Army Form C. 2118.

Place	Date	Hour	Summary of Events and Information	Remarks and references to Appendices
MESPLAUX	17.2.16		In accordance with instructions from the A.D.M.S. the Advanced Dressing Station at RUE DE BOIS and the Aid Posts at TUBE STATION and PATH HOUSE POST were handed over to a party from the 131st Field Ambulance. Major Mackie of the 2/1st Field Ambulance 61 (S.M.) Division reported for the purpose of receiving 24 hours instruction.	J.S. H?
"	18.2.16		The O.C. in company with Major Hopkin D.A.D.M.S. 61st Division and Major Mackie also of the 61st Division visited the Advanced Dressing Station of the 5th Field Ambulance at MARAIS also the Aid Posts at FESTUBERT.	J.S. H?
"	19.2.16		Visited by A.D.M.S. Advance Party 1 Officer (Captain Forbes) proceeded with 12 other ranks, with cart to MARAIS leaving 8.30 a.m. to take over Advanced Dressing Station.	J.S. H?
"	20.2.16		Party for Advanced Dressing Station completed and left for Advanced Dressing Station at MARAIS at 6.30 a.m. Served in Barn.	J.S. H?

Army Form C. 2118.

WAR DIARY
or
INTELLIGENCE SUMMARY.
(Erase heading not required.)

130TH (ST. JOHN) FIELD AMBULANCE
38TH (WELSH) DIVISION.

Instructions regarding War Diaries and Intelligence Summaries are contained in F. S. Regs., Part II. and the Staff Manual respectively. Title pages will be prepared in manuscript.

Place	Date	Hour	Summary of Events and Information	Remarks and references to Appendices
MESPLAUX			Lieut Col Walter, O.C. 107th Field Ambulance arrived with 3 officers and 5 other ranks who are attached for instructional purposes. O.C. in company with Lieut Col Walter visited the Advanced Dressing Station at MARAIS and aid posts at FESTUBERT which were being heavily shelled.	JSND
"	21/2/16		General Pike D.M.S. after his inspection of Field Ambulance and Hospital and Advanced Dressing Station, congratulated the Officer Commanding on behalf of the Unit and stated he had known this farm for a good many months and it had always appeared to him to be a hopeless place to convert into a Field Ambulance but he could state it was now one of the best, if not the best kept Field Ambulance in the First Army.	JSND
"	22/2/16		Heavy fall of snow in the morning. Nothing of any importance to report.	JSND
"	23/2/16		The following routine order received from the A.D.M.S. 38th Division.	JSND

Army Form C. 2118.

129TH (ST. JOHN) FIELD AMBULANCE
35TH (WELSH) DIVISION.

WAR DIARY
or
INTELLIGENCE SUMMARY.
(Erase heading not required.)

Instructions regarding War Diaries and Intelligence Summaries are contained in F. S. Regs., Part II. and the Staff Manual respectively. Title pages will be prepared in manuscript.

Place	Date	Hour	Summary of Events and Information	Remarks and references to Appendices
NESPLAUX	28/2/16		"I have pleasure in communicating to all Ranks R.A.M.C. 38th (Welsh) Division the appreciation of the Results of Medical Service 1st Army of the excellent results attained by all Medical Units of this Division in reorganising the Ambulance Stations and Sanitary arrangements of the area now occupied. The long months of training and hard work show results of which all ranks may be proud. "Officers Commanding will please read the foregoing on Parade. (signed) T. J. Morgan Colonel A.D.M.S. 38th (Welsh) Division.	
	22.2.16		The following letter was also received from the A.D.M.S. "35th (Welsh) Division No. A 1305 22.2.'16 2347 "To A.D.M.S. 38th (Welsh) Division "I have heard with great pleasure that the D.M.S. 1st Army has given a very good report on the Field Ambulances and has expressed his pleasure generally with the high state of efficiency of the medical arrangements of the	

T2134. Wt. W708—776. 500000. 4/15. Sir J. C. & S.

Army Form C. 2118.

WAR DIARY
or
INTELLIGENCE SUMMARY.
(Erase heading not required.)

130TH (ST. JOHN) FIELD AMBULANCE.
38TH (WELSH) DIVISION

Instructions regarding War Diaries and Intelligence Summaries are contained in F.S. Regs., Part II. and the Staff Manual respectively. Title pages will be prepared in manuscript.

Place	Date	Hour	Summary of Events and Information	Remarks and references to Appendices
MESPLAUX	23/2/16		"Division. "Will you kindly convey to all the officers & C.O.s and men of the three "Field Ambulances and of the Sanitary Section and Bacteriological Laboratory "my congratulations. I have watched their work since they have been in "France with much interest and have noted their steady progress. I hope no "satisfactory report will be an incentive to all ranks for further efforts "that the Field Ambulances of the 38th Division may eventually be held as "second to none in the Army." (Signed) Ivor Philipps, Major General Commanding 38th (Welsh) Division.	92 H.R.
"	24/2/16		The C.O. visited the Advanced Dressing Station and inspected same. A.D.M.S. and D.A.D.M.S. visited the Hospital.	98 H.R.
"	25/2/16		The A.A. & Q.M.G. 38th Division and other Staff Officers together with a number of American Journalists visited the Hospital.	98 H.R.

WAR DIARY or INTELLIGENCE SUMMARY

Army Form C. 2118.

130TH (ST. JOHN) FIELD AMBULANCE
38TH (WELSH) DIVISION

Place	Date	Hour	Summary of Events and Information	Remarks and references to Appendices
NESPLAUX	26/2/16		Nothing to report this day.	
"	27/2/16		Section C of the 107th Field Ambulance which has been attached to this Unit for instruction for one week returned to your their Unit today. A Section of the 106th Field Ambulance composed of 3 Officers and 59 other Ranks have today been attached to this Unit for one weeks instruction.	
"	28/2/16		Nothing to report this day.	
"	29/2/16		Capt. Anderson R.A.M.C. and Capt. Foulkes R.A.M.C. departed on leave from 29.2.16 to 14.3.16. Lieut Page R.A.M.C. proceeded to the 14th Welsh Regiment to act as Regimental Medical Officer in place of Lieut McMillan reported sick.	

John H. David Wallis
R.A.M.C.

130 f Amb
Vol. 4
38th Div

March 1916
April 1916

COMMITTEE FOR THE
MEDICAL HISTORY OF THE WAR
Date 9 - JUN. '25

WAR DIARY
or
INTELLIGENCE SUMMARY

(Erase heading not required.) 130th (St John) Field Ambulance

Army Form C. 2118.

Place	Date	Hour	Summary of Events and Information	Remarks and references to Appendices
MESPLAUX	1/3/16		Hospital visited by the A.D.M.S and D.A.D.M.S. 38th Division who inspected same. Large number of men employed making new horse standing	8 AD
"	2/3/16		Nothing to report this day	9 AD
"	3/3/16		Nothing to report this day	9 AD
"	4/3/16		Further accommodation was today obtained at Headquarters, a Granary being obtained giving accommodation for 40 men. Heavy fall of snow in the morning.	9 AD
"	5/3/16		"A" Section of the 105th Field Ambulance who have been attached to this Unit for the past week for instructional purposes left for their Headquarters at 10 a.m.	9 AD
"	6/3/16		O.C. visited the Advanced Dressing Station and inspected same.	9 AD

Army Form C. 2118.

WAR DIARY
or
INTELLIGENCE SUMMARY.
(Erase heading not required.)

Instructions regarding War Diaries and Intelligence Summaries are contained in F. S. Regs., Part II. and the Staff Manual respectively. Title pages will be prepared in manuscript.

Place	Date	Hour	Summary of Events and Information	Remarks and references to Appendices
MESPLAUX	7/3/16		A Junior's shop was today erected	29th
"	8/3/16		Nothing to report this day	28th
"	9/3/16		Horse standing was today provided with.	29th
"	10/3/16		C.C. visited and inspected Advanced Dressing Station	28th
"	11/3/16		Nothing to report this day.	28th
"	12/3/16		C.C. visited the Advanced Dressing Station and inspected same	28th
"	13/3/16		Instructions received to make arrangements at the Bearer Post FESTUBERT to dry the socks of the 2 Battalions in the trenches, and to massage the feet of any men who required such treatment with Whale Oil. The necessary arrangements were made accordingly.	29th

WAR DIARY or INTELLIGENCE SUMMARY

Army Form C. 2118.

Place	Date	Hour	Summary of Events and Information	Remarks and references to Appendices
MESPLAUX	14/3/16		The Horse transport of this Unit was today inspected by the O.C. 38th Divisional Train who after inspection stated it was the best kept transport he had yet seen in the Division.	85 HD
"	15/3/16		Nothing to report this day	29 HD
"	16/3/16		The D.A.D.M.S. 11th Corps visited the Hospital also the D.A.D.M.S. 38th Division	85 HD
"	17/3/16		Lieut Elliott R.A.M.C. of this Unit proceeded to the 13th R.W.F. to act temporarily as M.O. also Lieut Burke R.A.M.C. of this Unit proceeded to 232nd Coy Royal Engineers to temporarily act as Medical Officer	85 HD
"	18/3/16		Nothing to report this day	28 HD
"	19/3/16		Hospital visited by the D.A.D.M.S. 38th Division.	29 HD

Army Form C. 2118.

WAR DIARY
or
INTELLIGENCE SUMMARY.
(Erase heading not required.)

Instructions regarding War Diaries and Intelligence Summaries are contained in F. S. Regs., Part II. and the Staff Manual respectively. Title pages will be prepared in manuscript.

Place	Date	Hour	Summary of Events and Information	Remarks and references to Appendices
MESPLAUX	19/3/16		Lieut Taylor R.A.M.C. reported for one months instruction.	38 MD
"	20/3/16		Lieut Buckley R.A.M.C. of this Unit proceeded to the 10th South Wales Borderers to act temporarily as Medical Officer to that battalion	38 MD
"	21/3/16		Nothing to report this day	38 MD
"	22/3/16		Colonel Elliott A.D.M.S. 41st Division together with the D.A.D.M.S. 38th Division visited the Hospital.	38 MD
"	23/3/16		The A.D.M.S. 38th Division and A.D.M.S. 41st Division visited Advanced Dressing Station and Aid Posts at MARAIS and FESTUBERT	38 MD
"	24/3/16		The O.C. visited the Advanced Dressing Station and inspected same	38 MD
"	25/3/16		Nothing to report this day	38 MD

T2134. Wt. W708—776. 500000. 4/15. Sir J. C. & S.

WAR DIARY or INTELLIGENCE SUMMARY.

Army Form C. 2118.

Place	Date	Hour	Summary of Events and Information	Remarks and references to Appendices
MESPLAUX	26/3/16		Major W. Bickerton Edwards R.A.M.C. reported for duty	38 FA
"	27/3/16		The O.C. visited the Advanced Dressing Station and inspected same. 96 of the Personnel of the Unit were today inoculated	38 FA
"	28/3/16		Nothing to report this day.	38 FA
"	29/3/16		Hospital visited and inspected by the A.D.M.S. 38th Division	38 FA
"	30/3/16		Nothing to report this day.	38 FA
"	31/3/16		Major W. Bickerton Edwards was today attached to the 129th Field Ambulance for duty. The A.A. & Q.M.G. 38th Division visited and inspected the Hospital.	

John Davies Lt Col R.A.M.C.
O.C. 130th (ST. JOHN) FIELD AMBULANCE,
38th (WELSH) DIVISION.

Army Form C. 2118.

WAR DIARY
or
INTELLIGENCE SUMMARY.
(Erase heading not required.)

130TH (ST. JOHN) FIELD AMBULANCE,
38TH (WELSH) DIVISION

130 FAMO
Vol 5

Place	Date	Hour	Summary of Events and Information	Remarks and references to Appendices
MESPLAUX	1/4/16		On instructions from the A.D.M.S. 38th Division Major M. Bickerton Edwards R.A.M.C. was to-day struck off the strength of this Unit; also Capt: A.J. Andrew R.A.M.C. was to-day struck off the strength of this Unit.	JSJR
"	2/4/16		Nothing to report this day.	JSJR
"	3/4/16		The O.C. departed on leave. Capt: A. M Andrew R.A.M.C. taking over charge of the Unit during his absence.	JSJR
			The A.D.M.S. 38th Division visited the Hospital and inspected same.	
			Lieut. Welch R.A.M.C. returned to duty from the 13th Royal Welsh Fusiliers with whom he has been acting as Regimental Medical Officer.	
"	4/4/16		"A" Section of the 132nd Field Ambulance 39th Division have to-day been attached to this Unit for instructional purposes.	
			Lieut: Buckley R.A.M.C. of this Unit to-day proceeded to the 10th South Wales Borderers to act temporarily as Medical Officer in place of Lieut: J.B. Evans R.A.M.C. who has been attached	

Army Form C. 2118.

WAR DIARY
or
INTELLIGENCE SUMMARY.
(Erase heading not required.)

Instructions regarding War Diaries and Intelligence Summaries are contained in F. S. Regs., Part II. and the Staff Manual respectively. Title pages will be prepared in manuscript.

Place	Date	Hour	Summary of Events and Information	Remarks and references to Appendices
MESPLAUX	4/4/16		to this Unit temporarily for Light Duty. AWA.	
"	5/4/16		Nothing to report this day. AWA.	
"	6/4/16		A Clinical afternoon was held at this Hospital a number of R.A.M.C. Officers being present including the A.D.M.S. and D.D.M.S. 38th Division. Papers were read by Capt. Day R.A.M.C. on the arrangements and work carried out at Aid Posts, and by Lieut. Andrew R.A.M.C. on the treatment of wounds as carried out at this Hospital. These papers were followed by a most interesting discussion in which views of the different Medical Officers were expressed. AWA.	
"	7/4/16		The D.D.V.S. 1st Army inspected the Horses of this Unit and expressed satisfaction in the condition in which they were in. AWA.	
"	8/4/16		Lieut. F.A. Andrew R.A.M.C. and Lieut. J. Barber R.A.M.C. of this Unit attended Lecture by the Chemical Adviser 1st Army at AIRE. AWA.	

T2134. Wt. W708—776, 500000, 4/15. Sir J. C. & S.

Army Form C. 2118.

WAR DIARY
or
INTELLIGENCE SUMMARY.
(Erase heading not required.)

Place	Date	Hour	Summary of Events and Information	Remarks and references to Appendices
MESPLAUX	8/4/16		Lieut: R.C.M. Page R.A.M.C. of this Unit proceeded to the 13th Welsh Regiment to act as Medical Officer in place of Lieut. Watkins R.A.M.C. who was conveyed to Hospital. AWA	
"	9/4/16		Church Parade was held at 9.15 am for the Church of England and at 11.15 am for the Nonconformists. AWA	
"	10/4/16		Nothing to report this day. AWA	
"	11/4/16		The A.D.M.S. 38th Division visited and inspected the Hospital. AWA	
"	12/4/16		Capt. A.W. Anderson R.A.M.C. on instructions from the A.D.M.S. 38th Division visited the Hospital now occupied by the 59th Field Ambulance at L.34.b.2 LA GORGUE and the Advanced Bearing Station at M.10.c.7.1 LA FLINQUE which this Unit is shortly to take over. AWA	
"	13/4/16		The A.D.M.S. 39th Division visited and inspected the Hospital in company of	

WAR DIARY
or
INTELLIGENCE SUMMARY.
(Erase heading not required.)

Army Form C. 2118.

Place	Date	Hour	Summary of Events and Information	Remarks and references to Appendices
MESPLAUX	13/4/16		A.D.M.S. 35th Division.	
			Capt. A.M. Boyce R.A.M.C. delivered a lecture at this Hospital during the afternoon on the subject of Lectures being delivered by the Chemical Adviser, the A.D.M.S. 38th Division and several other Medical Officers of the Division were present.	
"	14/4/16		Lieut. Page R.A.M.C. returned to duty with this Unit from the 13th Welch Regiment where he has been acting as Medical Officer in place of Lieut. Watkins R.A.M.C. Sd. Anderson Capt. RAMC	
"	15/4/16		The O.C. returned to duty from leave today. Sd. Anderson Capt. RAMC	
"	16/4/16		A party consisting of 2 Officers and 36 other ranks of this Unit proceeded to LAVENTIE at 8 a.m. to take over the Advanced Dressing Station run from the 105th Field Ambulance arriving 12.30 p.m.	Sd AD
			Our advance party of the 134th Field Ambulance took over the Advanced Dressing Station at MARAIS from this Unit and the section of this Unit who have been stationed there returned to Headquarters at MESPLAUX.	Sd AD

WAR DIARY
or
INTELLIGENCE SUMMARY.
(Erase heading not required.)

Army Form C. 2118.

Place	Date	Hour	Summary of Events and Information	Remarks and references to Appendices
MESPLAUX	17.4/16		A Party consisting of 2 Officers and 36 other ranks of this unit proceeded to LA FLINQUE to take over the Advanced Dressing Station there from the 59th Field Ambulance	B+D
"	18.4/16		On instructions from the A.D.M.S. 38th Division the Dressing Station at MESPLAUX was this morning handed over to the 134th Field Ambulance after which this Unit proceeded by route march to LA GORGUE and took over the Dressing Station at L.34.6.2 from the 59th Field Ambulance.	B+D
LA GORGUE	19.4/16		The remainder of the personnel who were sent in Hospital Ruts were put on fatigue work cleaning up the Hospital and adjacent premises. The O.C. visited and inspected the two Advanced Dressing Stations at LAVENTIE and LA FLINQUE. The A.D.M.S. 38th Division also the D.A.D.M.S. visited and inspected the Advanced Dressing Station at LAVENTIE. Lieut. J.B. Evans R.A.M.C. was this day transferred to 131st Field Ambulance	B+D B+D B+D

Army Form C. 2118.

WAR DIARY
or
INTELLIGENCE SUMMARY.
(Erase heading not required.)

Instructions regarding War Diaries and Intelligence Summaries are contained in F. S. Regs., Part II. and the Staff Manual respectively. Title pages will be prepared in manuscript.

Place	Date	Hour	Summary of Events and Information	Remarks and references to Appendices
LA GORGUE	20/4/16		The A.D.M.S. 38th Division visited and inspected the Hospital	JLR
"	21/4/16		Special Church Parades were held for the Church of England and Nonconformists at 9.30am and 11.30am respectively. O.C. visited and inspected the Advanced Dressing Station at LAVENTIE and also the Aid Posts at RED HOUSE M.b.3.1 and HOUGAMONT M.12.c.3.6	JLR JLR
"	22/4/16		Orders received from A.D.M.S. to make arrangements to handover Advanced Dressing Station at LA FLINQUE to the 129th Field Ambulance on the 23rd inst.	JLR
"	23/4/16		Advanced Dressing Station at LA FLINQUE handed over to a Section of the 129th Field Ambulance at 11.30am, the Section of this Unit who had been on duty there returning to Headquarters	JLR
"	24/4/16		Nothing to report this day.	JLR

Army Form C. 2118.

WAR DIARY
or
INTELLIGENCE SUMMARY.
(Erase heading not required.)

Place	Date	Hour	Summary of Events and Information	Remarks and references to Appendices
LA GORGUE	25/4/16		O.C. visited and inspected the Advanced Dressing Station at LAVENTIE also the Aid Posts at G.5.c.8.9.	95*R
"	26/4/16		Commenced building of new Latrines for men also hospital and whitewashed Receiving Room and Dispensary	95*R
"	27/4/16		The Horse Lines being in a very insanitary condition when taken over by this Unit a fatigue party was today put in to clean same and remove manure which had accumulated round the lines	95*R
"	28/4/16		Hospital visited by A.D.M.S. and inspected by him. Work continued on Mens Latrines and Horse Lines.	95*R
"	29/4/16		Nothing to report this day.	—
"	30/4/16		Instructions received from the A.D.M.S. for an Officer and 30 men to	95*R

WAR DIARY
or
INTELLIGENCE SUMMARY.
(Erase heading not required.)

Army Form C. 2118.

Place	Date	Hour	Summary of Events and Information	Remarks and references to Appendices

Parade near Divisional Headquarters from LA GORGUE at 11.30 a.m. when Genl Sir Charles Monro presented Medal Ribbons to officers N.C.O.s and men who have been awarded decorations in the 38th Division. O.C. visited and inspected the Advanced Dressing Station at LAVENTIE also Aid Post at RED HOUSE.

John B. Davies
Lieut. Colonel, R.A.M.C.
O.C. 130th (ST. JOHN) FIELD AMBULANCE,
38TH (WELSH) DIVISION

37ᵈ (Welsh) Div.

130ᵗʰ (St. John) F. a.

May 1916

COMMITTEE FOR THE
MEDICAL HISTORY OF THE WAR
Date 26 JUN. 1915

Army Form C. 2118.

VOL 6

WAR DIARY
or
INTELLIGENCE SUMMARY.
(Erase heading not required.)

130TH (ST. JOHN) FIELD AMBULANCE.
38TH (WELSH) DIVISION.

Instructions regarding War Diaries and Intelligence Summaries are contained in F. S. Regs., Part II. and the Staff Manual respectively. Title pages will be prepared in manuscript.

Place	Date	Hour	Summary of Events and Information	Remarks and references to Appendices
LA GORGUE	1/5/16		Number of Cases admitted 8 AM 30/4/16 - 8 AM 1/5/16 Sick 29 Officer Otherranks, 1 Wounded - 5 other ranks	J E H D
LA GORGUE	2/5/16		Number admitted 8 AM 1/5/16 - 8 AM 2/5/16. Sick 2 - 21 Wounded. 1 Visited by DADMS - in reference to 100 tons (estimate) of old manure in horse lines, left by 19th Division. - Arrangements made with Farmer owner of LA GORGUE to allow this to be placed on his land. A.D.M.S. visits A.D.S. at LAVANTIE	J E H D
LA GORGUE	3/5/16		Number admitted 8 AM 2/5/16 - 8 AM 3/5/16. Sich 1, 16 Wounded 1 - Men inspected in full marching order by A.D.M.S. - Gas helmets, Goggles, Contents of Kit Valises, Haversacks - Clothing & Boots of Personnel. Scrunned - most satisfactory.	J E H D
LA GORGUE	4/5/16		Cases admitted 3/5/16 - 4/5/16. Wounded Officers 3, Other ranks 4. Sick Officers Nil, other ranks 15. Visits LAVENTIE, A. D. S. -	J E H D
LA GORGUE	5/5/16		Cases admitted. 4/5/16 - 5/5/16 (8 am) Wounded 3 Officers, 4 other ranks, Sick 15 other ranks.	J E H D
LA GORGUE	6/5/16		Cases admitted 5/5/16. - 6/5/16.(8 am) Wounded 1 Officer 11 other ranks Sick 30. Other ranks Field Ambulance Works.	J E H D

Army Form C. 2118.

WAR DIARY
or
INTELLIGENCE SUMMARY.
(Erase heading not required.)

John Dooly
Lieut Col
136th Field Ambulance
38t Division

Instructions regarding War Diaries and Intelligence Summaries are contained in F.S. Regs., Part II. and the Staff Manual respectively. Title pages will be prepared in manuscript.

Place	Date	Hour	Summary of Events and Information	Remarks and references to Appendices
LA GORGUE	6/5/16		(Continued) — 6/5/16. D.D.M.S. XI Corps. also inspected 16 Hospital, in company with A.D.M.S. 38t Divn.	8 M D
LA GORGUE	7/5/16		Cases admitted 6/5/16 – 7/5/16 (8am) Wounded Officers Nil, Other Ranks 15. Sick 23 other ranks.	8 M D
LA GORGUE	8/5/16		7/5/16 – 8/5/16. 8am Cases admitted Officers 1 Sick other ranks 21 sick, 10 wounded – run by a Bug. Clothing Steriles at A.D.S. LAVENTIE unstocks	8 M D
LA GORGUE	9/5/16		8/5/16 – 9/5/16. 8am cases admitted Officers Nil, other ranks 7 wounded, 14 Sick Evacuated to C.C.S. 30 sick Inspection Clothing board held at Headquarters.	8 M D
LA GORGUE	10/5/16		9/5/16 – 10/5/16. 8am to 8 AM cases admitted. Officers wounded. Nil Sick, Officers Sick 1 other ranks wounded 1 S.C.R. 19, Evacuated Officers wounded Nil S.C.P, 1 other Ranks wounded 6 Sick 15	8 M D
LA GORGUE	11/5/16		10/5/16 – 11/5/16. 8am to 8 AM, Cases admitted Officers wounded Nil S.C.P, Nil other Ranks wounded 3. Sick 14 Evacuated Officers wounded Nil Sick, Nil other Ranks wounded 1 Sick 13	8 M D
LA GORGUE	12/5/16		11/5/16 – 12/5/16. 8am to 8am Cases admitted Officers Nil, Other Ranks wounded 1, Sick 16, Evacuated 12 body 2.	8 M D

WAR DIARY
or
INTELLIGENCE SUMMARY.
(Erase heading not required.)

Army Form C. 2118.

JOU 2HD coul hunst Rume

130TH (ST. JOHN) FIELD AMBULANCE,
38TH (WELSH) DIVISION.

Place	Date	Hour	Summary of Events and Information	Remarks and references to Appendices
LA GORGUE	13/5/16	12.15 a.m. – 13/5 8 a.m.	Cases admitted 12.15 a.m. – 13/5 8 a.m. Officers nil, Other ranks 26 Evacuated 11 wounded	JS4HD
			" Evacuated 19 Sick 6 wounded. Duty 1 Sick, 1 wounded	
			Lieut T. J. Buckley RAMC returned from leave and reported for duty.	
LA GORGUE	14/5/16	13/5 8 a.m. – 14/5 8 a.m.	Cases admitted 13/5 8 a.m. – 14/5 8 a.m. Officers 1 Sick, Other ranks 24 Sick. Evacuated Officers 2 Sick, Other ranks 15 Sick	99 HD
LA GORGUE	15/5/16	14/5 8 a.m. – 15/5 8 a.m.	Cases admitted 14/5 8 a.m. – 15/5 8 a.m. Officers nil, Other ranks 33 Sick, 3 wounded. Evacuated Officers nil, Other ranks 37 Sick	Extra
			3 wounded. Duty two – nil. Visited A.D.S. and Advanced Post. Capt. Anderson RAMC took over A.D.S. from Capt. Forshee RAMC who is acting M.O. 13th Welsh. Lieut Reynolds RAMC reported for duty. (instructional)	
LA GORGUE	16/5/16	15/5 8 a.m. – 16/5 8 a.m.	Cases admitted 15/5 8 a.m. – 16/5 8 a.m. Officers Sick 1, Other ranks Sick 15, wounded 11. – Evacuated Officers nil, Other ranks Sick 23, wounded 5. Lieut Pope RAMC acting M.O. 19th Pioneers holds Regimental	JS4HD
			Aid Post. Capt Anderson RAMC of this unit proceeded on leave. Lieut Reynolds RAMC proceeded to A.D.S. Lieut Burke RAMC of this unit proceeded on leave, in exchange with Capt Audraw RAMC 19th Pioneers Welsh Regiment whose leave was cancelled owing to outbreak of Small Pox in Cardiff.	
			Lieut Elliott RAMC took over temporary duties as M.O. 255 Tunnelling Co. vice Lieut Audraw Capt. Jones RAMC took over duties at Indian Hospital vice Lieut Burke	

T2134. Wt. W708—776. 500000. 4/15. Sir J. C. & S.

WAR DIARY or INTELLIGENCE SUMMARY

Army Form C. 2118.

(Erase heading not required.)

John H. Rawes
Lt Col RAMC
OC 130 (S/Pom) Field Ambce

Place	Date	Hour	Summary of Events and Information	Remarks and references to Appendices
LA GORGUE	17/5/16		Cases admitted Officers nil, other ranks Sick 18, Wounded 3. Evacuated Sick 15, Wounded 5. Pte Read Preparator of lions, heart held "Summer time Standing" Completed patrols. nae -	99/AD
LA GORGUE	18/5/16		Inspection by ADMS 8 Field Ambulance, Billets, horse lines. Admitted Officers nil - Other ranks Sick 17, Wounded 14. Evacuated other ranks Sick 14, Wounded 5. - No Officers - rides A.D.S.	92/AD
LA GORGUE	19/5/16		Admitted Officers nil, Other ranks Sick 18. Wounded 2. Evacuated Officers nil, other ranks Sick 10, Wounded 3	92/AD
LA GORGUE	20/5/16		Admitted Officers nil other ranks Sick 23 Wounded 5. Evacuated Officers Nil Other Ranks Sick 23 Wounded 4 (This includes Divl Casn Evacuated)	92/AD
LA GORGUE	21/5/16		Admitted Officers. Sick 1 Wounded 1. - Evacuated Wounded 1. Other ranks Admitted 25 Sick 5 Wounded. - Evacuated 19 Sick 5 Wounded. 10 July 5. (Labourunders Divl Casn)	92/AD
LA GORGUE	22/5/16		Admitted Officers Sick 1, Wounded 2. Evacuated Sick 1 Wounded 2. Other Ranks Admitted	99/AD

WAR DIARY
or
INTELLIGENCE SUMMARY.
(Erase heading not required.)

Army Form C. 2118.

Place	Date	Hour	Summary of Events and Information	Remarks and references to Appendices
LA GORGUE	22/5/16		1 Can'l S.ct 23 wounded N.C. Evacuated S.ct 17 wounded nil. Totals one — A number of improvements to billets, rations at A.D.S. 3+ G.C.7.3, about at LAVENTIE EAST, were Sand bagging, repairs to the roofs, making of new roads, Steel Shelters to the property.	A.D.M.S.
LA GORGUE	23/5/16		Admitted: Officers S.cle 3. other ranks S.cle 13. wounded 5. Evacuated to C.C.S, other ranks S.cle 12. wounded 3. To-day, Officers 2, other ranks 1. — To CRS (13)	A.D.M.S.
LA GORGUE	24/5/16		(Others) Admitted: 25 S.cle 5 wounded, Evacuated to C.C.S. Officers(sy) H other Ranks S.cle 11, wounded 3, To CRS (11) wards A.D.S.	A.D.M.S.
LA GORGUE	25/5/16		Admitted: Officers Nil. — Other Ranks 19 S.cle 7 wounded, Evacuated to CCS, 6 S.cle 3 wounded 16 CRS Rank 16 S.cle 2 Health Inspector. Inspected ASC rifles	A.D.M.S.
LA GORGUE	26/5/16		Lieut.Col. D.E. Evans RAMC (Temporal 2/3 Bn/46 Field Ambulance) reported his Officer was shown through, inspected units the Stoves at the Main Dressing Station, LA. GORGUE, Divisional Baths, Divisional Laundry, Labour Corps. Hospital, the ADS's at LAVENTIE, MARAIS, the Main Dressing Station previously occupied by the unit at MESPLAUX	

WAR DIARY
or
INTELLIGENCE SUMMARY.
(Erase heading not required.)

Army Form C. 2118.

Place	Date	Hour	Summary of Events and Information	Remarks and references to Appendices
LA GORGUE (Continued)	26/5/16		This Officer was also shown the Sieve Shelter now completed, with window door — throughout Sandbagged with Reinforced bracing to same — also the works of this unit at LAVENTIE EAST POST, the AID POSTS at RED HOUSE, the AID POST at HOUGEMONT POST. When the two of this unit are constructing a further shelter. The two Shelters previously erected by this unit at MARAIS were also inspected. — All records, returns, forms in use, were explained to this Officer, who has left LA GORGUE the same evening. Conveyances in Field Ambulance. — Officers Sick 2, wounded N.C. Officers & Men Sick 16, wounded 2, Evacuated to CCS Officers Sick 1, other ranks Sick 6, — to CRS Other Sick 7, wounded 2, to Fd Amb Sick 1.	J.P.H.R
La Gorgue	27/5/16		Conveyances Officers N.E. Other ranks Sick unknown(total) 24, wounded 2, Evacuated to CCS Officer 1 sick, other ranks 13 Sick 2 3 wounded CRS ranks (Duty 1 Officer Sick) Other ranks 7 Sick 1 wounded Noted O.R.S. Work of telling in Stokes at HOUGEMONT POST.	J.P.H.R

WAR DIARY
or
INTELLIGENCE SUMMARY.
(Erase heading not required.)

Army Form C. 2118.

130TH (ST. JOHN) FIELD AMBULANCE,
38TH (WELSH) DIVISION.

Place	Date	Hour	Summary of Events and Information	Remarks and references to Appendices
LA GORGUE	28/5/16		Lieut. BUCKLEY R.A.M.C. ill, posted for Temporary duty to 119 Bde. R.F.A.	
			Admissions. Sick, Officers Nil, Other Ranks 2, wounded Nil, Evacuated to 15 C.C.S. Officers Nil	
			Other Ranks 25 (Battle) Nil 4 Other Ranks Sick 22 (Battle) wounded 4	
			To C.R.S. Batty. Other Ranks 9 Sick	
			S.M. Shrond proceeded on leave (25th) Inst. UK —	
			Visited A.D.S.	
			Inspected Riding Horses, Pare tack Saddlery — found in good order.	
LA GORGUE	29/5/16		Admissions Other Ranks 12 sick, 3 wounded, Evacuated 6 C.C.S. 9 Sick 3 wounded	
			Lieuts. G. Gustafson & J. Burke & Nurse & Nurse unit returned to duty from leave.	
LA GORGUE	30/5/16		Admitted Officers 1 Sick, Other Ranks 19 Sick, 6 wounded, Evacuated to C.C.S. Officer 1 Sick	
			Other Ranks 4 Sick, 5 wounded, To C.R.S. 15 Sick, 2 wounded, To Duty, 1 Sick.	
			Visited Advanced Dressing Station at LAVANTIE, Divisional baths at LAVANTIE	

Army Form C. 2118.

WAR DIARY
or
INTELLIGENCE SUMMARY.
(Erase heading not required.)

John H. Passel
Lieut. Col. Raoul
OC 130 (S. Nat) Field Amb

Place	Date	Hour	Summary of Events and Information	Remarks and references to Appendices
LA GORGUE	31/5/16		Admitted Officers 1 wounded, Other ranks 16 Sick, 21 wounded. Other ranks 16 Sick, 8 wounded evacuated to CCS 11 Sick, 8 wounded. Transferred to C.R.S. 13 Sick, 2 wounded. Hospital and Wagon demens visited by G.O.C. 38th Div, who expressed his satisfaction with the arrangements and work carried out by this Field Ambulance which he wished to be intifed to the Officers and Other ranks in the unit.	JSMD JSMD

John H. Passel
Lieut. Col. Raoul
OC 130 (S. Nat) Field Amb
38th Div.

Confidential

War Diary

of

130ᵗʰ (St John) Field Ambulance

for

June 1916.

WAR DIARY
or
INTELLIGENCE SUMMARY.
(Erase heading not required.)

Army Form C. 2118.

Lt.Col. Rowe
J.D. Wright, 135th St John Ambulance

Place	Date	Hour	Summary of Events and Information	Remarks and references to Appendices
LA GORGUE	1/6/16		Admitted (a) Wounded 2 officers 9 other ranks (b) Sick 20 other ranks = 31. Died 1 Officer (at ADS) Evacuated CCS Wounded 1 Officer 7 other ranks (b) Sick 9 other ranks Transferred to CRS — other ranks 9., visited by acting ADMS & DADMS, Main ADS	ADMS
LA GORGUE	2/6/16		Casualties Wounded 1 Officer, 4 other ranks, Sick, 10 other ranks. Evacuated Wounded 1 officer, 9 other ranks, Sick, 14 other ranks. Visited ADS	ADMS
LA GORGUE	3/6/16		Casualties Wounded. 12 other ranks. Sick 1 Officer 26 other ranks. Evacuated Wounded 1 Officer 9 other ranks. Sick 1 Officer, 20 other ranks. Visited by acting ADMS & DADMS — visited ADS + Divisional Baths & laundry. Program of work has been concentrated on the New Stat Stretcher socket outline by Requisition at ADS at the back of M.O's Dug out at HOUGOMONT. The Engineers Supply material but the Stretcher this work.	ADMS

WAR DIARY
or
INTELLIGENCE SUMMARY.
(Erase heading not required.)

Army Form C. 2118.

John Barrax Lt Col
OC 138th St John Sgt Amb

Place	Date	Hour	Summary of Events and Information	Remarks and references to Appendices
LA GORGUE	4/6/16		Admitted Officers 2. Wounded. Other ranks 25 S.ick, 4 wounded. Evacuated Other ranks (CCS) 16 Sick, 6 wounded (CRS) 4 Sick, 4 wounded Iordets, 1 wounded. Other ADS. However Shed. Completed, LAVENTIE EAST. Steller Comforts completed. Visited ADS. However Shed. Completed.	
LA GORGUE	5/6/16		Admitted Officers 4 wounded. Other ranks 16 Sick. 16 wounded. Evacuated Officers 3 wounded. Other ranks (CCS) 7 Sick 3 wounded (CRS) 7 Sick 3 wounded. G.O.C. visited. Wounded Officers & Thigh in this area Stokes. Acting ADMS visited ADS.	B/HS
LA GORGUE	6/6/16		Headquarters of this Field Ambulance visited at 11.15 a.m. by Lt General Sir R.C.B. Haking KCB Commanding XI Army Corps, accompanied by the D.D.M.S. XI Army Corps and the following has passed from ADMS 38th (Welsh) Division. "The Corps Commander has expressed himself very well pleased with all he saw at your Field Ambulance & his Satisfaction." — Cases admitted. Officers Nil - Other ranks Sick 24, wounded 6. Evacuated to CCS. ———— Other ranks S.ick 15. wounded 10. Transferred to CRS. Other ranks Sick, wounded 1 ADS at LAVENTIE and Sgt Steller at LAVENTIE EAST. POST inspected by the OC.	AdMS (38D/W/20) 4/6/16

Army Form C. 2118.

WAR DIARY
or
INTELLIGENCE SUMMARY.
(Erase heading not required.)

Instructions regarding War Diaries and Intelligence Summaries are contained in F.S. Regs., Part II. and the Staff Manual respectively. Title pages will be prepared in manuscript.

[Signature] John Frost
Lieut Col RAMC
OC 130th (St John) Field Ambulance

Place	Date	Hour	Summary of Events and Information	Remarks and references to Appendices
LA GORGUE	7/6/16		Admitted Officers 1 Sick, Other ranks 18 Sick, 10 wounded.	
			Evacuated to CCS. Other ranks — 12 Sick 4 wounded	
			Transferred to CRS 12 Sick 2 wounded	JF
			Hospital visited by Deputy Director of Medical Services	
LA GORGUE	8/6/16		Admitted Officers 1 Sick. Other ranks 19 Sick, 5 wounded.	
			Evacuated to CCS Other ranks 7 Sick 2 wounded,	
			Transferred to CRS Other ranks 6 Sick 3 wounded	
			To Duty: Officers 2 wounded, Other ranks + Sick 1 wounded	
			Died: Other ranks 1 wounded —	JF
			Capt. M. Forbes Reane of this Unit reported from Duty at Temporary HQ of 13th Welsh	
			Lieut J. Reynolds (attached to this Unit for Instructional Purposes) posted to 13th Welsh Regt.	
LA GORGUE	9/6/16		Admitted Officers 1 wounded, Other ranks 15 Sick 6 wounded.	
			Evacuated to CCS Officers 1 wounded Other ranks 2 Sick 1 wounded	
			Transferred to CRS Other ranks 11 Sick 2 wounded, totals Other ranks 1 wounded	JF

WAR DIARY
or
INTELLIGENCE SUMMARY.
(Erase heading not required.)

Army Form C. 2118.

John 2/1 Basel Nigel Col. Rouse

Place	Date	Hour	Summary of Events and Information	Remarks and references to Appendices
LA GORGUE	10/6/16	1.30 P.M.	Unit paraded, marched via MERVILLE, CALONNE, ROBECQ to BUSNES arriving 8.30 P.M. - Billet in BUSNES-ROBECQ road Southestern. Small party of details left at LA GORGUE to hand over to (5/2/1 Field Amb.) to 61 Division laRang over	JJA
BUSNES	11/6/16		Cases oreilles 9(Syth) Seaworks 5CCS 9. - Coopers Beard & released for instructional purposes. Details from LA GORGUE & LAVENTE rejoined -	JJA
BUSNES	12/6/16		Advance party, under Lieut R.A.G. Elliott, left for AUCHEL 7am. Main Unit paraded 9, marches via LILLERS, BURBURE to AUCHEL arriving 2.30 P.M. - Very poor billets to Officers, warmed (ba) Shortage for Horses — Visited VILLERS CHATEL.	JJA
AUCHEL	13/6/16		Advance party under OC left to VILLERS CHATEL at 7.15am and relieved the 76th Field Ambulance 25 Division at 1 P.M.	

T2134. Wt. W708—776. 500000. 4/15. Sir J. C. & S.

Place	Date	Hour	Summary of Events and Information	Remarks and references to Appendices
AUCHEL	13/2/16		(Continued) Both at VILLERS CHATEL (12 beds (officers) 18 (ordinary) Officers & 40 Other ranks, and at MINGOVAL (156 beds (ordinary) Other ranks (Extraordinary) Both these are excellent Schools, Spoke to D.D. Ambulance both, the former containing ample accommodation for Officers (Sick) with a beautiful Catholic Church - the other at MINGOVAL spacious and a Small Chapel. The Billets were in an unsatisfactory state. Here at MINGOVAL unfit for occupation & verminous. No certificate re billets asked for or given -- The previous 2nd Amb - have built an excellent Sep lic tank which is most satisfactory, put up a RUSSIAN BATH. also at MINGOVAL a vis infectious Chamber, Cresoling of all with Brazier for burning Sulphur, a closely fitting Cover - the works Sapper Pauling -- The Chalet Chateau is owned by M. de Crespigny late La Comtesse 377/01 16515 and to SMs OC en 10/02 D.D.M.S. paid short visit before arrival OC of 76th Lt Col. HINDE after departure of 76th Fd Amb. of Lieut and	

WAR DIARY
or
INTELLIGENCE SUMMARY.
(Erase heading not required.)

Army Form C. 2118.

Place	Date	Hour	Summary of Events and Information	Remarks and references to Appendices
VILLERS CHATEL MINGOVAL	14/6/16		The Scottish (B) posted under Lt. Buckley Page at MINGOVAL. Fatigue work carried on. Route march, Drill	JSH2
VILLERS CHATEL MINGOVAL	15/6/16		Transferred from 76 F. Amb - 2 Officers Sick - 2 Officers Sick, Other ranks 36 Sick, 1 wounded (prisoner) to CCS - Other ranks 4 Sick. A large amount of Fatigue work done this day - behind at both hospitals	JSH2
VILLERS CHATEL MINGOVAL	16/6/16		New latrines for Patients + Pedestals constructed, with covers &c. Other ranks 11 sick. Astrulea 8 AM (15) - 8 AM (16)	JSH2
VILLERS CHATEL MINGOVAL	17/6/16		Drill + Physical exercises, Fatigues - Admitted 8 am (16) - 8 am (17) Officer 1 Sick, Other ranks 8 Sick. Evacuated CCS Officer 1 Sick Other ranks 4 Sick. To Amby. Other ranks 1 Sick	JSH2

Army Form C. 2118.

WAR DIARY
or
INTELLIGENCE SUMMARY.
(Erase heading not required.)

To O.C. 2nd Cavalry W.R. Rawa
OC 130th (St John) Field Ambce.

Instructions regarding War Diaries and Intelligence Summaries are contained in F.S. Regs., Part II. and the Staff Manual respectively. Title pages will be prepared in manuscript.

Place	Date	Hour	Summary of Events and Information	Remarks and references to Appendices
VILLERS CHATEL	18/6/16		Hospital visited and inspected by Brig. Gen. commanding 114th Brigade 36 Divn. Route March with Stretchers was Capt Foulkes.	
MINGOVAL			A large amount of Fatigue Duties carried out at this Station. Admitted 8 ain/18 (11 Officers & 1 sick other ranks) 10 Sick. Evacuated to hospital. Officers Nil other ranks 2 " remained Officers sick 3, OR st Sick 1 hospital 2 NTR	
VILLERS CHATEL	19/6/16	10.30 A.M. 3.30 P.M.	A.D.M.S. visited hospital. Board held on 7 T.B. was. 8, 10, 13, 14, 15 Bath with legs (102 Cases)	
MINGOVAL			VILLERS CHATEL visited by Commander XVII Corps (Sir Chas Ferguson Bart) who inspected the hospital. Route March with Stretchers under Capt. Anderson. Capt Foulkes Lieut Elliott (R.A.C) R.A.M.C. & this was successful on Brave (through 18-19') Admitted Officers 1 Sick. Other ranks 2. Discharged. Officers Nil other ranks Nil. To sick 1 other rank. 52 NTR	

T2134. Wt. W708—776. 500000. 4/15. Sir J. C. & S.

Army Form C. 2118.

WAR DIARY
or
INTELLIGENCE SUMMARY.
(Erase heading not required.)

Instructions regarding War Diaries and Intelligence Summaries are contained in F. S. Regs., Part II. and the Staff Manual respectively. Title pages will be prepared in manuscript.

Place	Date	Hour	Summary of Events and Information	Remarks and references to Appendices
VILLERS CHATEL Hospital	20/6/16		9am - 2.P.M. Route March with Stretchers. Worked by Coys. Arrivals Officers nil Other ranks 10 Sick Discharges Officers 1 Other ranks 1 Evacuated to C.C.S. 2 other ranks	GMR
VILLERSCHATEL MINGOVAL	21/6/16		Route march with Stretcher Drill. 9.12.30-2.4.30 Practice in loading turbury Stretchers. Carrying wounded over different Country, through woods, Examined by O.C. 57 Stal clear bearers in 1st Aid. 9 am - 5 P.M. Reconnoitering ground in area, selected for Motorbus jumper, 4 Officers & S.M. Rowe & S.M. &C. Arrivals Officers 4 sick Other ranks 9 Sick Discharges Officers 1 Sick Other ranks 17 Sick. Evacuated to C.C.S. other ranks 4. Sick.	GMR
VILLERSCHATEL MINGOVAL	22/6/16		Route March, Stretcher Drill, Hospital Duties Route march to Mauveysourd. Arrivals Officers 1 Sick. Other ranks 8 S.ick 8 Sick. Evacuated to C.C.S. 1 other ranks Sick. To Duly - other ranks 2. Sick	GMR

Army Form C. 2118.

WAR DIARY
or
INTELLIGENCE SUMMARY.
(Erase heading not required.)

1st & 3rd Board Lewllor [Rouse]
OC 1st & 3rd [John] Field Amb

Instructions regarding War Diaries and Intelligence Summaries are contained in F.S. Regs., Part II. and the Staff Manual respectively. Title pages will be prepared in manuscript.

Place	Date	Hour	Summary of Events and Information	Remarks and references to Appendices
VILLERS-CHATEL MINGOVAL	23/6/16		Staff Ride with 111th B.Ed. OC + Capt Honeres left 6 am, starting point N of MONCHY-BRETON, 9.30 am. Returned 7 P.M.	
			Admitted 1 sick officer, 10 other ranks	
			Evacuated to CCS, 2 sick other ranks to Duty 5 S.O.R	8 N.R.
VILLERS CHATEL MINGOVAL	24/6/16		111th Brigade Manoeuvres - ADS at MONCHY-BRETON. Capt Robinson in command of Unit visited by ADMS 37th Div. The Advanced Dressing Station was moved from in the afternoon to ROCOURT. Personnel Six Officers, 145 Other Ranks bivouacked out for the night. OC, Lieut Burke remained in charge of Hospital at VILLERS CHATEL, MINGOVAL.	
			Admitted 7 other ranks S.O.R.	
			Evacuated to CCS 1 Officer Sick, 6 other ranks S.O.R, to Duty, 1 officer sick, 11 other ranks	8 N.R.
VILLERS CHATEL MINGOVAL	25/6/16		DIVISIONAL MANOEUVRES - ADS under Capt Honeres. MONCHY-BRETON. Main Dressing Station & OSTREVILLE under Capt Anderson - OC after.	

Army Form C. 2118.

WAR DIARY
or
INTELLIGENCE SUMMARY.
(Erase heading not required.)

John 2nd Army, April 25
OC 138 (St John) Fd Amb

Place	Date	Hour	Summary of Events and Information	Remarks and references to Appendices
VILLERS CHATEL MINGOVAL	25/6/16		After visiting ADS + Main Bearing Station, resumed work, + moved forward with Bde Headquarters. Stretcher bearers under Capt A Jones, Lieut F.O. Anderson + Lieut Burton. ADS opened 9 AM closed Main Bearing Station opened 9 AM closed 1.30 P.M. 2 Tent Sub-division +3 bearer Sub-divisions took part. Subsidiary advanced Bearing Stations opened during the day, as an advance of the whole line took place. Had worked even very heavy, full of ground, carrying a very large number of "Sitting" wounded — on Shelter Wheeled Stretcher. The Collecting ground was exposed to enemies fire, so that motor Ambulances were not able to proceed a mile in for of ADS. Admitted at Villier chatel Frameric. The had returned from Maubure, found at 9 P.M. assistance of 10 miles after hard day in good condition, horses falling out	

Army Form C. 2118.

WAR DIARY
or
INTELLIGENCE SUMMARY.
(Erase heading not required.)

John Davis Lieut Col. RAMC
OC - 130th (St John, F.A.) Ambce

Place	Date	Hour	Summary of Events and Information	Remarks and references to Appendices
VILLERS CHATEL MINGOVAL	26/6/16		Talipes. Got inspection arranging to Evacuation of all cases. British hospitals closed VILLERS CHATEL later over as HQ 60 Div — Visit by ADMS 60 Div. Unit passed 5 P.M. Marched with 114th Brigade via Mingoval, Cary, BERLES (Starting Pt.) AMBRINES, DENIER, ETREE-WAMIN, IVERGNY, LE SOUICH, 16 RANSART arriving destination 4 A.M. distance - approximately 26 miles - Billeting Party had been sent on in advance, and we were accommodated in Barns. 197 Prisoners unable to march belonging to units "114" Bde. were collected from various billeting areas around VILLERS CHATEL and transferred by us to Ambulances (86), remainder by lorries to NSW Area Admissions 1 Officer Sick, 6 Other ranks Sick. Evacuations WCCS, 2 Officers Sick, 9 other ranks Sick to Duty 4 Officers Sick, 13 other ranks Sick BTR	
RANSART	27/6/16		Visited by DADMS during afternoon. Lieut/Collect RAMC reported from Base. Unit paraded 6 P.M. Marched with 114th Bde via HERISEE (starting point) HEM, ENVILLERS BERNEUIL to St HILAIRE arriving 3.15 AM 28/6/16, Billeting party had been sent on.	

WAR DIARY or INTELLIGENCE SUMMARY

Army Form C. 2118.

John E.A. Davis Lieut Col
OC 130 (St John) Fd. Amb.

Place	Date	Hour	Summary of Events and Information	Remarks and references to Appendices
RANSART (continued)	27/6/16		Dr. in advance, and was accommodated in barns, 110 men unable to march were collected and transferred to new area by Motor Ambulance Cars of this unit. 118 men still remained for removal. Admissions 1 Officer sick, 9 o/ranks sick. Evacuations 2 Officers sick, 23 other ranks sick.	
ST HILAIRE	28/6/16		Arrived 3.15. a.m. – at 11.a.m. reported to GOC 114th Bde. that 118 men of this Bgde. still required to be collected strong at New Area, instructions (verbal) given to cease further transferring, pending application being made for lorries. Preparations made to march this evening in accordance with Brigade orders No. 31, dated 3.25. Wire received 114th Rif Brig "Stand fast". At 11.45 P.M. orders received from Brigadier to continue to collect men left behind at RANSART area. Cars were immediately despatched to collect 8 men from 10th battn. at NEUVILLETTE, 50 of 11th battn. at BOUQUEMAISON, and 60 from 15th battn. at BARLY. – It was found that these men had moved & no information could be obtained. Bathing Parades, and Foot inspection by Med.	29/6/16

WAR DIARY
or
INTELLIGENCE SUMMARY.

Army Form C. 2118.

John H Dagood Lumley
OC Bd (S. John) Field Amb RAMC

(Erase heading not required.)

Place	Date	Hour	Summary of Events and Information	Remarks and references to Appendices
St HILAIRE	28/6/16		Admissions 5 other ranks SICK. Evacuations 10 CCS. 5 other ranks SICK.	
ST. HILAIRE	29/6/16		Parade 9.30 AM. Physical Drill 1 hour, foot Inspection. Visit D.C.M. Page R.A.M.C. of this Unit proceeds from leave. Admissions. 4 other ranks SICK. Evacuated 10CCS 4 other ranks SICK.	82HD
St HILAIRE	30/6/16		9 AM. Inspection of rifles ASC. 9.30 Inspection of Unit — men parade, gas helmets, goggles, — by OC — 10 AM. Instruction by Capt. Jonathan Lunt on wearing Gas helmets in front line trenches. (Pineto to front of Shirt —) A.D.M.S. visited 130th 2 and 4 San numbers of Cases for P13. of the 111th Brigade. Admitted 3 other ranks sick. Evacuated 10CCS 3 other ranks sick.	82HD

John H Dagood
Lieut Col.

Confidential.

War Diary

of

130th (St John) Field Ambulance

From 1st July 1916 to 31st July 1916

38th (Welsh) Div.

WAR DIARY
or
INTELLIGENCE SUMMARY.

Army Form C. 2118.

1st D.G. H Pros & 2nd Lieut.
OC. "Bo" 2nd Aubre

(Erase heading not required.)

Place	Date	Hour	Summary of Events and Information	Remarks and references to Appendices
VAL DE MAISON	1/7/16		Left ST HILAIRE 5 P.M. June 30/1916, arrived VAL DE MAISON 3.15AM & pitched hospitals for 114th Brigade, also Divisional Hospital for Scabies. Received memo" (A7H51/4) on and after noon July 1st 1916 be prepared to move at six hours notice "/- at 6.15 P.M. received orders from Brigade to prepare to march East" at 7 P.M. — The unit quickly packed up, and were ready, v Stood by, at 7 P.M. — (the whole of wagons packed, all canvas struck, cases evacuated, with exception of Scabies cases which marched with the unit), in 3/4 of an hour. Billeting Party was sent to H.Q. Brigade, and received orders to proceed to billeting area at PUNCHEVILLERS. — An officer from the unit who reported at the Headquarters of 114th Brigade, brought back verbal orders that the unit was to move off, at 10.5 P.M. to PUNCHEVILLERS arriving there 10.45 P.M. 1/7/16. Commissions, Other Ranks (SQR) 4. Evacuated RCCS other ranks 4. at PUNCHEVILLERS, the unit relieved 1st Roar, billets of 129th D'Aubre and took over 26 patients from that unit. JSNP	

Army Form C. 2118.

WAR DIARY
or
INTELLIGENCE SUMMARY.
(Erase heading not required.)

John S. Davy
Lt Col. RAMC o/c 130 (Field) 3rd Amb
o/c 3rd Amb

Place	Date	Hour	Summary of Events and Information	Remarks and references to Appendices
PUNCHEVILLERS	2/7/16		At 12.20 P.M. O.C. 3. C.C.S. PUNCHEVILLERS, called, and stated that a large number of wounded were being admitted into his hospital near Railway PUNCHEVILLERS. I proceeded with five Medical Officers & 50 men of this unit to No 3 C.C.S. to assist him – a large number of the casualties were machine gun wounds & limbs. From information gained, I learnt that 1400 cases passed thro' this CCS (from the evening of the 1/7/16 to evening 2/7/16. – A certain number of German wounded 15 (about) in number amongst. The Officers & other ranks of this unit' went for duty, were relieved by others of this unit' the same evening. – The O.C. of No 3 CCS was Lt. Col. Parr, R.A.M.C.(T). – An order received from A.D.M.S. to establish one Officer to 131 St F Amb Lord Elliott, R.A.M.C. Stores for this unit. Admissions. Officers Sick 3, other ranks 66. Evacuated W.C.S. Officers Sick 2, other ranks 14. To D.w Rot Station 12, the limb. Shew to recog to move, but no further order received.	

J.S.D

WAR DIARY or INTELLIGENCE SUMMARY

Army Form C. 2118.

J.O.W.S H Dec? / Lt Col R.A.M.C
O.C.

Place	Date	Hour	Summary of Events and Information	Remarks and references to Appendices
PUCHEVILLERS	3/7/16		5 Officers + about 55 other ranks reported mid-day to OC 3 CCS. with other N.C.Os me that they be moved bagged as a large number of Casualties were still known to be waiting in Convoys for admission to No 3 CCS. A large number of wounded waiting in Ambulances in the road, for admission to CCS. – were given food and drink by Orderlies & Men of this unit, after instruction by MO of this Unit. Orders received at 4. P.M from 14th Brigade that Unit would move that night to FRANVILLERS. The Unit marched out of PUCHEVILLERS at 7.55.P.M. and arrived FRANVILLERS 1.5 AM 4/7/16 — considerable delay caused to column by 11th & 13th Bde A.S.C. on arrival at FRANVILLERS by large column of artillery, were passing thro. Admissions Officers (w'd) Other Ranks (sick) 6 " (sick) " " (w'd) Evacuated: CCS Officers Sick 1 Other Ranks sick / To Div Rail Station - other ranks 20 (sick) To Corps Rest Station " " 6 037001 Dr ALDERSON A.S.C. attached to this Unit Evacuated to CCS Two Motor Ambulances reported in accordance with ADMS order to OC Motor ambe LES ALENCONS for temporary duty.	

Army Form C. 2118.

WAR DIARY
or
INTELLIGENCE SUMMARY.
(Erase heading not required.)

JoRus'n David
WGt Rawe

Instructions regarding War Diaries and Intelligence Summaries are contained in F.S. Regs., Part II. and the Staff Manual respectively. Title pages will be prepared in manuscript.

Place	Date	Hour	Summary of Events and Information	Remarks and references to Appendices
FRANVILLERS	4/7/16	1.5 A M	Arrived FRANVILLERS 1.5 AM	
			Following wire received 114th Bde:- "Brigade will move today, acc. Be prepared to move from about 10 am onward". – Unit at FRANVILLERS billets in scattered barns & lofts	
			at 4 P.M. orders received that billeting parties be sent to HEILLY. Lieut Buckley & Rhodes	
			for this duty.	
			Load of Brigade Column vehicles	
			Brigade transferred and starting point 9.5 PM 1369 (behind 114th CFA), arrived	
			HEILLY at 10.30 P.M.	
			Here the Unit was accommodated in Canvas huts	
			Orders received from A.D.M.S. that 13th Field Amb.ce comes close	
			Admitted, Officers (Sick) 1. Other ranks (Sick) 25	
			Evacuated to CCS. Officer 1.	
				15 C.F.S. other ranks sick 25
				Sd/HO
HEILLY.	5/7/16		In Marshy wood, under Canvas huts.	
			Attended 11.30 am Conference at A.D.M.S office at TREUX.	
			Unit now Acting Divisl. with A.D.M.S no longer attached to Brigade.	
			Orders received to proceed to MORLANCOURT that evening and take over ADS	
			at CITADEL from 23rd Field Ambulance, also main dressing station at St Church	

WAR DIARY
or
INTELLIGENCE SUMMARY.
(Erase heading not required.)

Army Form C. 2118.

John G.H. Dowd Lieut Col RAMC
OC 130th (St John) Field Amb Ce

Place	Date	Hour	Summary of Events and Information	Remarks and references to Appendices
HEILLY	5/7/16		(continued) Lt. MORLANCOURT, Capt Foster & Lieut Elliot to this Unit with a small advance party forces Threebarne to CITADEL Capt Anderson & Lieut Anderson, with Interpreter, Cook, Processor & 22nd Field Amb. Main Dressing Station, at Old Church, MORLANCOURT. Bearer Subdivision under Lieut Bickerton, Asst Page, moves from HEILLY 5.15. PM OC Capt Foster & Burke - left with 1st Subdivision + Transport 5.30.P.M. were accommodated in Billets: arrived 8.20 PM. Admitted: Nil. Evacuated to Brit. 16 (S.of R) Scabies, other ranks	
MORLANCOURT HEILLY	6/7/16		Took over main Dressing Station 23rd Field Amb. (OC Lt Col Smith) at 9.30 am. Their dressing station is opened in a Derelict Church, the chancel being used as dressing + dressing room, the Sacristy as entries through door of North aisle where they are Supplied to wait for RC. While waiting there room for dressing, and Parkarion taken & passed till can leave on FF 3210. after passing this Dressing Room, then particular are subdued in a R Boot	

Army Form C. 2118.

WAR DIARY
or
INTELLIGENCE SUMMARY.
(Erase heading not required.)

John H. Bazal Van Gl. RAMC
OC 130th (St John's Field) Ambulance

Place	Date	Hour	Summary of Events and Information	Remarks and references to Appendices
MORLANCOURT	6/7/16		Took over ADS at the Cease, in park, morning, and Main Dressing Station at 9.30 a.m. from the 23rd Field Amb - all casualties attended by them were evacuated before taking over with one exception.	
			The Main ADS consists of dug-outs, liable to form a good dressing room, and bunks have room for 20 cases.	
			The Main Dressing at MORLANCOURT is a derelict Church, dated 1741, which appears to have been altered to get into a replaced & deplorable condition – spinal. The roof – a plaster front of the ceiling has fallen in from repeated shell shock – There are two entrances on either side of tower on the West for casualties suitable for entrance door, which a cook house and Pack Stores was erected.	
			Cases on admission, one wash, and their socks & steel helmets removed & stored. They take the M. ade - their garments are taken on A.F. 3210 and beaten. The fears in that case, until they are fed on hot beef tea, cocoa, tea, bread, jam, butter, cheese &c - This Field Ambulance, in accordance with instructions from ADMS, is only	

Army Form C. 2118.

WAR DIARY
or
INTELLIGENCE SUMMARY.   John ?? Drew
(Erase heading not required.)   Lieut Col RAMC   OC 130/S/Sb Fd Amb

Place	Date	Hour	Summary of Events and Information	Remarks and references to Appendices
MORLANCOURT	6/7/16		(Continued) only Sitting Cases (Causalties) all Stretcher Cases go to 5th Fd Amb Back to the 129 4th Fd Amb. The Chancel is screened off, and used as an operating Dressing Room. Three Dressing Tables are laid out an M.O is posted to each, and has his Dressers. The Sergt. Dispenser on Duty is in Charge of Anti Tetanus Serum Table, Sterilizer & Fills the Serum Syringes + marks wrists of all patients wounded. The vestry is used as a Dispensary. "Dispensary Shoes" issued a 2nd Dispenser Sergt is posted by day - making solutions, prepared dressings, lotions, assisted by the Carpenter of the Unit, also sharping + Cutting Splints. After being Dressed, the patient passes in to the South Aisle, where Stretchers in Charge of A.T.D Boots is posted and taken further particulars - the Fatal Case is then dressed with a blanket supplied with food + cigarettes, + evacuated thro the door of the Southern Aisle or placed to lie on Stretchers in the Lower Room. The 1st Casualty admitted by this was Stretcher was at 9.40 a.m + the number up to day were as follows:- M.G. 10. 12. Noon. 16. 6/7/1916 12 noon + 9 P.M. 20. Total. 36. These Cases were largely G.S.W. of limbs, + a few Shell Shock Cases. JG AD	

T2134. Wt. W708—776. 500000. 4/15. Sir J. C. & S.

WAR DIARY or INTELLIGENCE SUMMARY

Army Form C. 2118.

John & Basil Sullot
OC 130(s)(C) 1/9th Aust. F. Ambe

Place	Date	Hour	Summary of Events and Information	Remarks and references to Appendices
MORLANCOURT	7/7/16		In accordance with Instructions from A.D.M.S. 4 Officers + 108 other ranks (Stretcher Squadron) left H.Q. of this unit and the A.D.S. at the CITADEL at 7.30 a.m. Capt. Ffoulkes in Command to report at 9.30 a.m. to the O.C. 131; Field Amb. at MINDEN POST and take orders from this O.C., taking rations, Shelters, Wheeled Stretchers + Cookers Wheeled. Six Motor Cars of this unit under charge of this MT ASC Sergt. had also reported at 9.30 a.m. to O.C. 131; 3/A	
		6 a.m		
		9.30 a.m	3 Horse Ambulances sent to report to O.C. 129th at Divisional Collecting Station. Capt FFOULKES, CAPT. JONES, LIEUT ELLIOTT, LIEUT BURRE with Web of Stretcher Bearers/Bers, orders to occupy the TRIANGLE (MAP ref.) MONTAUBAN – A 7.a 4.10. and get in touch with R.M.O's who had their Aid Posts in CATERPILLAR TRENCH, thus they quickly Es. and remained and Bearers the RMO's of the 11 Sussex +16 W. working between Aid Posts +	Capt Ffoulkes report Begins
			TRIANGLE – Capt FFOULKES reported as follows – "All walking cases evacuated, along CATERPILLAR TRENCH, LOOP TRENCH, and TRIANGLE, lying cases over the Open to R of CATERPILLAR TRENCH. Personally joining LOOP TRENCH."	
		7 PM	At 11.15 hours I reported to A.D.M.S. 38 Div at MINDEN POST, later Capt JONES and myself accompanied O.C Sanitary Section, to the TRIANGLE and remained on duty all night"	

Army Form C. 2118.

WAR DIARY
or
INTELLIGENCE SUMMARY.
(Erase heading not required.)

Instructions regarding War Diaries and Intelligence Summaries are contained in F. S. Regs., Part II. and the Staff Manual respectively. Title pages will be prepared in manuscript.

John Brown
Lieut Col. RAMC
OC 130th Field Ambce

Place	Date	Hour	Summary of Events and Information	Remarks and references to Appendices
MORLANCOURT	7/7/16		Capt FFOULKES report continues	
MINDEN POST			Bearers of 130th Field Ambulance brought cases to the TRIANGLE, and personnel of Sanitary Section carried them from there to MINDEN POST.	
CATERPILLAR WOOD		6 AM	Col A JONES RAMC 130th Field Amb? reports as follows:- "At 6AM on 7/7/16 - Left MORLANCOURT with Lt BURKE RAMC + Lt PAGE RAMC of the 130th with 70 bearers arriving MINDEN POST	
		9 AM	at 9 AM - here joined by Capt FFOULKES, Lt ELLIOTT (130) + 20 bearers - Thirty bearers were left at MINDEN POST, L? ELLIOTT, L? BURKE + 12 bearers posted at TRIANGLE, + 4 bearers at LOOP. The remaining Officers ← Men under Capt. F.FOULKES proceeded to CATERPILLAR WOOD - here he found the 11th S.W.B. + 16th Welsh Regt. attacking MAMETZ WOOD - a large number of Casualties had already occurred, we rendered assistance to the R.M.O.s - Dug outs were found on slope of CATERPILLAR WOOD in a protected position - These we cleaned out, and wounded were placed into them by Regimental + RAMC SB?s. Walking cases were directed along CATERPILLAR TRENCH, this was the only communicating hand carrying track to the LOOP it was too narrow for any Stretcher Cases.	

WAR DIARY or INTELLIGENCE SUMMARY

Army Form C. 2118.

JoRes & Beaves Lieut Col 12 AMC
OC 130 (St John) Fd Ambce

Place	Date	Hour	Summary of Events and Information	Remarks and references to Appendices
MORLANCOURT MINDEN POST CATERPILLAR WOOD	7/7/16	4 PM	CAPT. A. JONES Report Continues "At this hour, found that dug outs could not accommodate any further cases, additional ones had to be placed in open, as far as could be obtained in shelters position. Question of Search now a serious one. He surveyed the whole of CATERPILLAR WOOD. Together Sgt. HOPKINS, Sgt. RING of this Unit, discovered a good path through the wood. Five Squads selected & 5 Cases sent along this route with the two Sergts, this path necessitates on emerging from the wood being exposed to the Enemy - the cases who safely carried to TRIANGLE a distance of about 3 miles.	
		P.M. 5/30	Lieut Capt Stroulkes, and a number of Walking cases took along hence to MINDEN POST. Reported to A.D.M.S. Kent, obtained additional bearers returned to the TRIANGLE where he remained throughout the night - Dressing bearers & serving wounded. On account of the sodden condition of the ground, & the heavy stale Machine gun fire of the enemy, it was found impossible to convey all the cases from CATERPILLAR WOOD. Two bearers of this unit reported killed —	
	8/7/16	9 AM	Relieved by Officer of 131st Fd. Ambce, returned to MINDEN POST. Bearers of 130th withdrawn during day, & we returned to MORLANCOURT. Leaving 3 bearers of 130th to carry on during night, that as guide to brank stats to the wood. (Capt A Jones report ends)	J R MB

WAR DIARY or INTELLIGENCE SUMMARY

Army Form C. 2118.

John Basil Lanfear Maud
OC B Coy John Goldfinch

Place	Date	Hour	Summary of Events and Information	Remarks and references to Appendices
MORLANCOURT	7/11/16		Report of Sergt Hopkins N.C.O. in charge of S.B's -	
MINDEN POST		6 AM	left HdQts. arrived MINDEN POST. 9AM, Bearers told off in 3 parties, under 3 section Sergts.	
TRIANGLE			My party consisted of 30 men = 5 squads + 2 Wheeled Stretcher Squads. R proceeded to TRIANGLE. Each party.	
LOOP			All Wheeled Stretchers were left here - half no use as lost over open ground to LOOP TRENCH	
CATERPILLAR WOOD			4 hand-Stretcher left here - We then proceeded to CATERPILLAR TRENCH - is hollow by WOOD	
		11.30 AM	attack had begun - AID POST in Dug-out there. M.O's 16 Welsh, 10 SWB were there, here we dressed a large number of Cases - but fired fresh Nurses for evacuation, as troops were coming along trench all the while - 4 German Prisoners found. These cleaned out + Serious Cases put on Stretchers there, formed Bivouac in open with our own Walking-Part Shields to attend wounded, collected during this - Private Harry Andrews Rane (46212) of this unit, was wounded by a Shell	
		2.30 PM	Capt FFOULKES called Sectional Sergts together + said that a way must be found to evacuate wounded. Chance lay between open ground remained hand along which Cases were carried but which was to means for Stretcher. With Sergt King. 10 WSc, 5 Stretchers. I then proceeded to evacuate wounded over open ground. On right of the trench hand ( ) - I led Men along a Path, thro' the trenches, connected with CATERPILLAR TRENCH+ There was a great risk all the way up, the Men were very much exposed to the enemy who were best Snipers	

WAR DIARY or INTELLIGENCE SUMMARY

Army Form C. 2118.

Johnston Dawrd Lieut Col RAMC
OC 130 (St John) Fd Amb

Place	Date	Hour	Summary of Events and Information	Remarks and references to Appendices
MORLANCOURT — MINDEN POST — CATERPILLAR WOOD	7/7/16		Sergt Hopkins report (continued) badly snipped. — We carried twice but gilted together into CATERPILLAR TRENCH, we carried wounded up this for 300-400 yards. — then into the open ground again — from there to LOOP TRENCH — over the open again a TRIANGLE,) returned to the AID POST; again tried wounded until all Bry ords stretchers there were (rd we then again started to carry them over the open to LOOP TRENCH, in a hollow calibre down So Rating him at once a Shell Shuick L/Cpl WEST 45217 of this lund & still blew his head off — pagiside also Shuck WE JONES 48147 of this unit; Sergt Hill. At daylight we buried L/Cpl WEST (45217) in hollow at bottom of CATERPILLAR TRENCH. We put a Cross above his body. I rode his No. Rank Name & Unit of the same, will copying Pencil. His position is roughly 40 yards to the R. on the W of the TRENCH with the left of the ref—inforcements from 129 & 131 we Evacuated 11 cases at 6 A.M. — All/but We had, one cases of the difficulty of getting along hiroal to Evacuate these cases over the open. but amongst the 11/Squad got in the open Private HOUSTON (35231) of this unit, had shot by Sniper & W L/Sye, he was transd into 151 Field Dressing Station back in direction of AID POST, Escort by MO-16th Losbs, he was He Evacd the Stretchers to Carry him up the heads & we had our Stretcher above our hands on a Account of the Thinness of the Shellbran — this man got fripoid wose, & died soon after the Suburbs company.	

Army Form C. 2118.

WAR DIARY
or
INTELLIGENCE SUMMARY.
(Erase heading not required.)

John 2/Lt Daniel
Lawler Rawe
OC 130(?) John McAuley

Instructions regarding War Diaries and Intelligence Summaries are contained in F. S. Regs., Part II. and the Staff Manual respectively. Title pages will be prepared in manuscript.

Place	Date	Hour	Summary of Events and Information	Remarks and references to Appendices
MORLANCOURT	9/7/16		Sgt/Hopkins report cont. —	
MINDEN POST			We started carrying him up the trench — troops were now meeting up in big numbers in the trench —	
CATERPILLAR WOOD			we buried HOUSTON in shell hole on the S side of the trench, about this time a very severe bombardment was taking place, & we had a large number of cases to Dsr/Hakouse(?) let in	
			the trench we were in ?	J.L.H.D

Army Form C. 2118.

WAR DIARY
or
INTELLIGENCE SUMMARY.
(Erase heading not required.)

John N Bewsher W.E. RAMC
OC 136th (St John) Field Amb

Place	Date	Hour	Summary of Events and Information	Remarks and references to Appendices
MORLANCOURT	7/7/16		48217 L/Cpl Lost (W. James) Killed in action this day.	
			56231 Pte HOUSTON (W.) Killed in action this day	
			48212 William H wounded - Contusions Rt Chest - Shell, transferred to R82nd. Fractured Rib 9 & 10. Haemoptysis.	
			48147 Jones W.E. wounded, Shrapnel Wd. Rt Ear.	
			Cases from MAIN DRESSING STATION cleared to 36 CCS HEILLY.	
			The following 5 pre-reinforcements reported 106386 Pte WARN J.J. 27937 Pte WIX L, 80512 Pte WILLIAMS P. 80232 Pte WEBB, W.G. 80723 Pte WILSON S.Lt	
			These men sent up to OC 131st 16 arrest under L/Cpl ARNOLD 16 Same Army	
			Casualties admitted - from 6 AM - 12 Noon 29	
			12 Noon 9 PM 67	
			96	

Army Form C. 2118.

WAR DIARY
or
INTELLIGENCE SUMMARY.
(Erase heading not required.)

Place	Date	Hour	Summary of Events and Information	Remarks and references to Appendices
MORLANCOURT	8/7/16	9am	Capt FFOULKES reports - "relieved by 131 Fd Amb - one party of 130th returned w/comes under Capt JONES to MORLANCOURT other party went direct to CITADEL arriving at 5 PM"	
			Arrivals & Casualties at Advanced MORLANCOURT: 9PM 7/7/16 .15	
			6AM 8/7/16 .15	97
			6AM 8/7/16 to 12 Noon 8/7/16	16 } 119
			12 Noon 8/7/16 - 9 PM 8/7/16	6

Army Form C. 2118.

John S.H. Dawell
Lieut Ramc
OC 130th St. John Fd. Amb.

WAR DIARY
or
INTELLIGENCE SUMMARY.
(Erase heading not required.)

Place	Date	Hour	Summary of Events and Information	Remarks and references to Appendices
MORLANCOURT	9/7/16		Casualty Cammons 9PM 8/7/16 - to 6AM. 9/7/16. 34	
			6AM 9/7/16 - 12 Noon - 6 } 67	
			12 Noon - 9PM 9/7/16 27	
		9PM	Capt Anderson, Lieut Anderson, 7 Bucklen with 69 other ranks left MORANCOURT and proceeded to MINDEN POST, where Capt Foulkes Lieut Page from CITADEL with S. Other ranks reported at 10. PM - Capt Anderson reported to OC 131. and received instructions to collect wounded from 114th Brigade, who at 3. 50AM the following morning were making an attack on the front of MAMETZ WOOD, the rendezvous of 130th F.C. Amb. would be at SAPPER Corner - the Field Amb. to take up position there at 3 AM. It was also hoped in touch with OC Sowden Section who would have a Collecting Station here - from SAPPER CORNER an officer & bearer proceeded to the TRIANGLE, Lieut Page left at TRIANGLE	
	10/7/16		with 12. SBs to act as relay. Orders were received at 3. 40 AM from ADMS that 130th Field Ambulance, was to detail 1 MO + 10 bearers to report to 114th Bde HQ at POMMIERS REDOUBT, Lieut Buckler, detailed with these bearers. - Capt Anderson at the same hour (3. 40 am) detailed 1 NCO. 10 bearers, to report to Capt Roberts MO 10th Yorks LI	

Army Form C. 2118.

WAR DIARY
or
INTELLIGENCE SUMMARY.
(Erase heading not required.)

Place	Date	Hour	Summary of Events and Information	Remarks and references to Appendices
MORLANCOURT	10/7/16		Continued	
			M.O. 10' Welsh at AID.POST. Near BEETLE ALLEY, also Capt Ffoulkes with Lt Anderson ordered to go forward with 12 Squad S.B's [stretcher bearers], to get into touch with R.M.O's of the 13th, 14th & 15th Welsh, whose AID POSTS were likely to be in CATERPILLAR TRENCH. A relay of bearers took up a position, a little distance under cover, N of LOOP. After detailing these parties Capt Anderson returned to the TRIANGLE, on crossing Kene [?] Causeway, which had not passed the AID POSTS, were coming in. Kene. A message was received from N.C.O. in charge of bearers sent to 10 Welsh that the AID POSTS of R.M.Os 14' Welsh, 15 Welsh, were located near BEETLE ALLEY and reported that both these R.M.O's were in need of Extra bearers. Capt Anderson ordered bearers left as relay N of LOOP, to proceed with guides to M.O's 13-14 Welsh, 15 Welsh near BEETLE ALLEY. - Capt Anderson then sent the Reserve bearers at	
		4.45 AM	the TRIANGLE to Relay post N. of LOOP. - at 4.45 A.M. M.O 13' Welsh reported his AID POST at ...., and asked for Extra bearers, its position of this Aid post was notified to Capt Ffoulkes, as also was position of all other AID POSTS, which include Oxford Copse [?] to D.C. Bearers (Capt Ffoulkes to get immediately into touch.) Lieut Buckley of S.A.M. reported that he had opened AID POST close to POMMIERS REDOUBT. on account	

WAR DIARY
or
INTELLIGENCE SUMMARY.
(Erase heading not required.)

Army Form C. 2118.

John Stanley
Lieut Col RAMC
OC 130 (S. John) Fd Ambce

Place	Date	Hour	Summary of Events and Information	Remarks and references to Appendices
MORLANCOURT	10/7/16	5 AM	of the large number of wounded, which were passing the post, which had not come thro an AID POST. - Extra Bearers & Stretchers were immediately sent forward to them from the TRIANGLE, on account of the large number of casualties both Capt Foulkes & Lieut Anderson were assisting RMO's of the 10th, 13th & 15th Welsh to deal with their cases, & regulating the distribution of Bearers in that forward area.	
		6. AM	Capt Anderson found it necessary at this hour, to apply to O.C. 131 at MINDON POST A.D.S. for extra Bearers, as between 50 52 Stretcher Cases whom it was lying at TRIANGLE awaiting removal to A.D.S. His message appears to have been sent back to 130th at MORLANCOURT & thus at A.D.S. at MORLANCOURT at the time. The message was received by 130th ten left in absence, at MORLANCOURT by Capt A. Jones. R.A.M.C. who paraded seen men in the Headquarters and asked for Volunteers - Every man volunteered, including a large number of men who had been up. All the previous night drawing wounded at MORLANCOURT, 31 of these most Sgt were chosen, - & sent in Motor Ambulance lorries to MINDON POST, reported at MINDEN POST, & were then sent on to the TRIANGLE at 12.30 P.M. Capt Williams OC Sanitary Company, offered local & sent up "Six Bearers to work between the TRIANGLE	

Army Form C. 2118.

WAR DIARY
or
INTELLIGENCE SUMMARY.
(Erase heading not required.)

Instructions regarding War Diaries and Intelligence Summaries are contained in F.S. Regs., Part II. and the Staff Manual respectively. Title pages will be prepared in manuscript.

Place	Date	Hour	Summary of Events and Information	Remarks and references to Appendices
MORLANCOURT	10/7/16	1.PM	and SAPPER CORNER. —	
MINDON POST		2 PM	TRIANGLE, RAMC Officer of 142nd Field Amb: whose advanced bearer Post was also situated in a dug-out near the TRIANGLE, reported to Capt Anderson, and offered to send 3g. Stretcher and Conferred of Bearers. — These were employed to carry cases from TRIANGLE	
TRIANGLE.			to SAPPER CORNER. — and rendered Excellent Service, between 2PM – 5PM when they were withdrawn. —	
		3.30PM	20 ASC HT, of the 131st, 13 1/5th, 2nd Amb. reported at the TRIANGLE — and conveyed Stretcher cases between the points referred to. — These men worked until 8-9 P.M. and did Excellent work, advantage was taken of the lull referred to above to allow half (50) of the 130th Field SR's to rest for 3 hours.	
		4.30PM	Capt Ffoulkes + Lieut Anderson — after being on duty Since 3 A.M. repaired to the a.d posts of 10th, 13th, 14th + 15th + 19th Pioneers, reported at TRIANGLE, + relieved Capt Anderson + Lieut Page. — who moved back to SAPPER CORNER. hitherto Capt Anderson + 9 Page — then took duty at TRIANGLE from 6PM to 12 midnight. — and Capt Ffoulkes + Lieut Anderson rested at SAPPER-CORNER until 12 midnight, when they relieved Capt Anderson + Lt Page until 4 A.M. 11/7/16 + 6 A.M. 11/7/16.	

WAR DIARY
INTELLIGENCE SUMMARY
(Erase heading not required.)

Army Form C. 2118.

Place	Date	Hour	Summary of Events and Information	Remarks and references to Appendices
MORLANCOURT	1/7/16	4 AM	Capt Anderson reported to ADMS, "OC 13 F.", as men of 130th were (seeming strange) stranded, to see if other help	
MINDON POST			could be obtained, but none was available – The men of the Bat. were obliged to carry on	
SAPPER CORNER			which they did, until 5 PM.	
TRIANGLE		11 AM.	Information received at TRIANGLE, that all cases from AID POSTS of 14th Bat 16th Bat, had been cleared, and only	
			7 remained at AID POST of the 13th below. –	
		4 PM.	At AID POST No 50 stretcher cases reported at AID POST 19f (PIONEER) West – which covers Rel-	
			be cleared on account of heavy shelling – All other aid posts being clear	

Army Form C. 2118.

WAR DIARY
or
INTELLIGENCE SUMMARY.
(Erase heading not required.)

Instructions regarding War Diaries and Intelligence Summaries are contained in F.S. Regs., Part II. and the Staff Manual respectively. Title pages will be prepared in manuscript.

Place	Date	Hour	Summary of Events and Information	Remarks and references to Appendices
MORLANCOURT	10/7/16		Casualty Returns: 9 PM 9/7/16 to 6 AM 10/7/16 — 39	
			6 AM 10/7/16 to 12 Noon — 74	
			12 Noon to 9 PM 10/7/16 — 350	463
	10/7/16	6.30 am	At 6.30 am, I pass over to the A.D.S. at MINDEN POST, near the Post. Everything was quiet. A large number of wounded officers were brought over there, also about 15 - to 20 German wounded, including the Revd + Major —	
		8.0 am	with Major DAVIES 13th S.J. Tipperary, a large number of the most serious cases including Lt Roberts, 10th Welsh, Major Williams, 15th Welsh. Private Scudder + others — As I last night left 2 MO's at MORLANCOURT. A German with both shattered Pt Stalker. + others — As I last night left 2 MO's at MINDEN POST at 2.30 P.M. — Called one Sy Colm has been up all night I left MINDEN POST at 2.30 P.M. — Called at Divisional Dressing Station on my way. Sew Major Edward Ramo.	
			Capt Anderson reports that at 4.30 P.M., a runner reported, that 4.5 - 15.30 Stretcher Cases, in 15th Yorkshire ft. Dug-outs No 1 CATERPILLAR TRENCH were without Water, rations, + dressings. He are around the Dug bands, stated from Capt Wallace two (15th Yorks)	

Army Form C. 2118.

WAR DIARY
or
INTELLIGENCE SUMMARY.
(Erase heading not required.)

Instructions regarding War Diaries and Intelligence Summaries are contained in F. S. Regs., Part II. and the Staff Manual respectively. Title pages will be prepared in manuscript.

Place	Date	Hour	Summary of Events and Information	Remarks and references to Appendices
MORLANCOURT	11/7/16		Casualties. 9 PM 10/7/16 — 6 AM 11/7/16 270 6 AM 11/7/16 — 12 Noon 11/7/16 28 } 377 12 Noon 11/7/16 — 9 PM 11/7/16 79	

WAR DIARY
or
INTELLIGENCE SUMMARY.

Army Form C. 2118.

John Basil Lancelot Rowe
OC 130 (St John) Field Ambulance

Place	Date	Hour	Summary of Events and Information	Remarks and references to Appendices
MORLANCOURT	12/7/16	9 PM 11/7/16 – 6 AM 12/7/16 6 AM 12/7/16 – 9 AM 12/7/16	Casualties evacuated 129 ? 190 Total at MORLANCOURT – 1349 –	
			Main dressing Station taken over by 23rd Field Ambce (Lt Col Bourke) at 9 a.m. – orders received for this unit to proceed MERICOURT these were cancelled – orders received for transport to proceed by road under an officer. Capt Jones detailed. – Left MORLANCOURT at 4.30 pm marched to EDGE-HILL Station. Entrained 6.30 P.M. – both officers mgr. crowded in horse-boxes. – Crowded Stowed along and arrived at LONGPRE at 1.30 A.M.	
LONGPRE	13/7/16		after cup of coffee in YMCA marched up hill to BELLANCOURT, arrived 8 A.M. Capt Jones arrived with transport COISY (N of AMIENS) 2 A.M., left again 8 A.M.	
BELLANCOURT	13/7/16		arrived 8 A.M. – billeted in Grounds of CHATEAU. – Officers men slept until late afternoon absolutely worn out, after heavy stretcher work in MAMETZ wood followed by sleepless nights & long marches. Lieut. Hunter R.A.M.C. reported, to be temporary attached, pending opportunity to send to 129th Field Ambce	
BELLANCOURT	14/7/16		Transport (under Capt JONES.) arrived 1 A.M., orders received to proceed with the 114th Brigade to GORENFLOS, leaving starting point at 11.16 A.M.	

Army Form C. 2118.

WAR DIARY
or
INTELLIGENCE SUMMARY.
(Erase heading not required.)

John H David Lieut Col RAMC
OC 130 (S)fld Fld Amb
38 Div.

Place	Date	Hour	Summary of Events and Information	Remarks and references to Appendices
BELLANCOURT	14/7/16	(Continued)	While on March Congratulations by Brigadier 114th on work done by men of this Unit later on the hand written general Brigadier-General C.G. BLACKADER. D.S.O. ADC Commanding 38th (Welsh) Division to whom I was called out, instructs to state that it has been reported to him that the men of this Unit had done good work.	

Army Form C. 2118.

WAR DIARY
or
INTELLIGENCE SUMMARY.
(Erase heading not required.)

John W Doage
L/Cpl Rowe
OC 130(S) 3rd NSW Cent

Instructions regarding War Diaries and Intelligence Summaries are contained in F.S. Regs., Part II. and the Staff Manual respectively. Title pages will be prepared in manuscript.

Place	Date	Hour	Summary of Events and Information	Remarks and references to Appendices
LE PLUOY	15/7/16	6.15 AM	Horse transport left LE PLUOY, under Lieut. ELLIOTT, and moved, following ASC – 1st WELSH via RIBEAUCOURT, BERNAVILLE, CANDAS, BEAUVAL, TERRAMESNIL, SARTON and eventually reported THIEVRES at 10.15 P.M.	
		9.30 PM	The Unit Headquarter Section left in 3 motor lorries and with the 113th & 114th	
		2.0	Brigade arrived AUTHIE. No billets could be obtained. Three Lieutenant Billets obtained. THIEVRES. & School House used as orderly room.	
		9.0 PM	Capt. FFOULKES, Lieuts. ANDERSON, BUCKLEY & PAGE with 105 other ranks (Stretcher bearers & Nursing Section) reported from WARLOY – BAILLOY	

WAR DIARY
or
INTELLIGENCE SUMMARY
(Erase heading not required.)

Army Form C. 2118.

John E. Bowes Wentworth Paine
OC 130(St John) Field Amb
38th Div

Place	Date	Hour	Summary of Events and Information	Remarks and references to Appendices
THIEVRES	19/7/16		Dentist from 29th CCS GEZAINCOURT attended 7 D. Officers, 11 Other Ranks attended. Dispersal Returns to Duty.	
		10.30	Number of Cases treated 13.	
			ADMS visited Unit	
			Number of Cases of Scabies and other Contagious Skin Diseases admitted 15, 12 Nor 19.	JS HD
THIEVRES	20/7/16	12.10 am	Very urgent order for an ADWS picquet for one officer + 30 Other ranks from 130¹, 130/Am 131, 1-20/Am 129. 16 picquet OC 123rd Field Co RE at J16B.2 at 8 am. b be employed on hedge clipping.	
			Lieut ELLIOTT obtained for the Unit, paired with 50 men at 6 AM.	
		5.45 PM	Number of Cases admitted up to 12 noon 3	
		4 PM	Brigadier General C.G. Blackader D.S.O. ADC Commanding 38th (Welsh) Division into ADWS.	
			Visited the Field Ambulance	
			Number of Cases of {Scabies / Other Contagious Skin Diseases} admitted 6 up to Noon 1, Returns to Duty Nil	JS HD
THIEVRES	21/7/16		Visited SAILLY-DELL A.D.S. + baths	
			Bath arks of No 146a (Ind) Can India at SAILLY. Men of 130¹(So) 131, (30) 125, (20) under Lieut Elliott, now employed repairing roads near SAILLY. Cases admitted 20, Returns to Duty Nil	JS HD

Army Form C. 2118.

WAR DIARY
or
INTELLIGENCE SUMMARY.
(Erase heading not required.)

Instructions regarding War Diaries and Intelligence Summaries are contained in F.S. Regs., Part II. and the Staff Manual respectively. Title pages will be prepared in manuscript.

John H Passel
W/Gr R auro
oc 130th (S. Staffordshire Reul)

Place	Date	Hour	Summary of Events and Information	Remarks and references to Appendices
THIEVRES	22/7/16	am 7.45	Car sent for Dentist to 29 C.C.S. GEZAINCOURT. Dental cases treated as follows:- allowed 5 Officers 46 Other ranks = 51. To Bde, 5 Officers 45 Other ranks - To No 29 CCS 1 Other rank.	
			Corpl Clinton P. 4413, transferred to 131st S¹ P Amb² as from today 22/7/16 Pte Thomas WJ 48201 transferred to 113th M.G.C. to take Duties as from 22/7/16 Capt Howkes - posted to ADVANCED POST vice CAPT JONES recalled to HQ's.	
			A Ford Car A 14649. Its driving shaft of rear axle, broke near SAILLY-AU-BOIS on 21/7/16 and wheel was twisted into fiercist pieces by Shells as it crossed the lines, on account of Shaft bearing 2" from wheel, it was the fog - by act of Enemy Shrack by Shell material damage Done	
THIEVRES	23/7/16		Ford Car A. 14584 reported to DDMS viii Corp for Duty. Rifle Inspection - of ASC attached - Clothing Inspection. ASC	

Army Form C. 2118.

WAR DIARY
or
INTELLIGENCE SUMMARY.
(Erase heading not required.)

Arthur Prior? Lt Colonel
OC 1/30th S. John ????

Place	Date	Hour	Summary of Events and Information	Remarks and references to Appendices
THIEVRES LE PUM	16/7/16		Lieut D.C.M Pope S/Sgt Irish posted to 13th R.W.F. as Requested W.O. Took over from the 2nd Field Amb: 48 Division the following ADS. COLINCAMPS = K.25.c.2.8. — Lieut Burke personnel a chaplain + 8 other ranks 16 other ranks (3 officers of other ranks are attached to the ADS for relays.) ADS SAILLY. J. 16.8.2 Lieut Anderson personnel 1 Chaplain, 30 other ranks Bath SAILLY-DELL J 16.6.8.2 These are under the Same officers, — an N.C.O. 15 other ranks. under his command being specially detailed for these baths. These men looked after baths at LA COROUE. Advanced Post. EUSTON POST K.28 a 3.1. Capt Jones Posted with one Chaplain and 21 other ranks QM Thompson with Broken/?? proceeded.	

Army Form C. 2118.

WAR DIARY
or
INTELLIGENCE SUMMARY. 2/1 2/4 Divsnl. Lieut Col. Rowe

(Erase heading not required.)

Instructions regarding War Diaries and Intelligence Summaries are contained in F.S. Regs., Part II. and the Staff Manual respectively. Title pages will be prepared in manuscript.

Place	Date	Hour	Summary of Events and Information	Remarks and references to Appendices
THIEVRES	17/9/16	10 AM	Took over site occupied by 131st Field Ambce I.1.d.4.2.	
			Visited with Capt Anderson the two A.D.S's + advanced Post at EUSTON	
			The baths in charge of Lieut Anderson at SAILLY-DELL, found in full working order	
			arranged for them to be open from 8am–12 Noon – 1PM – 5 PM. Capable of bathing	
			100 men an hour; – these baths are shower baths, – also two 2 mc for Officers.	
			The A.D.S at Sailly is composed of Huts 3 in number, total 150 lying 50. Sitting = 200	
			at COLLINCAMPS. – 5 steel shelters built in Dug-outs, – which communicate with	
			one another, – these can hold 100 dying & 50 sitting = 150	
			At EUSTON POST. = 80 lying = also here are 5 steel shelter built in Dug outs.	
			MAIN DRESSING STATION, at THIEVRES can accommodate 100 dying 100 sitting.	
			Total Accommodation = 430 lying 200. sitting = 630	
			By Order of ADMS 48064 Staff Sergt L.W.Williams reported to DDMS. VIIIth Corps	
			for duty, accordingly dispatched off strength of this Unit (not 3rd D)	
			Order received to open Hospital for Scabies and other Contagious Skin	
			diseases, — a Barn at I.1.d.4.2 Ep. of Hamel for this purpose	
			Number bathed at SAILLY Dell. 56th Div. 85. 38th Div 415 & 15 Officers = 515 -	
			Visited at Main Dressing Station by A.D.M.S.	

Army Form C. 2118.

WAR DIARY
or
INTELLIGENCE SUMMARY.
(Erase heading not required.)

Instructions regarding War Diaries and Intelligence Summaries are contained in F. S. Regs., Part II. and the Staff Manual respectively. Title pages will be prepared in manuscript.

Place	Date	Hour	Summary of Events and Information	Remarks and references to Appendices
THIEVRES	12/7/16		Mobilization Scheme dissolved	
			One Officer proceeding home. Seconded to Veh. Motor School	

… Army Form C. 2118.

WAR DIARY
or
INTELLIGENCE SUMMARY.

John 2/1 Field Ambulance RAMC
OC 130 (Si) Field …

Place	Date	Hour	Summary of Events and Information	Remarks and references to Appendices
THIEVRES	24/7/16	9.30 am	Acting on orders from A.D.M.S. proceeded to MAILLY – MAILLET, for the purpose of taking over the Sugar Factory Advd Post at K33C.2.4 + Bearer Post at N34d.4.8, by arrangement with OC 36 F.Amb. - hence I proceeded the necessary examination & instruction - Hence proceeded to A.D.S at COLINCAMPS, with LIEUT BURKE along tracks from HEBUTERNE ROAD to R.E. Dump on ROAD – EUSTON – MAIN ST COLINCAMPS. Then proceeded along TROLLEY RAILWAY. In heavy parallel to the Road – running from to EUSTON – This line is in good order + can be used for conveyance of Stretcher Cases	
		11 AM	Arrived EUSTON POST – Inspected looks clean, kitchen was dug-out, very considerable improvement – a large amount of cleaning has been done, - walked to SUCRIE. The Crest of two Commukating Cellars capable of holding 20 7 12 lying Cases - Here are natural Cellars but not in present Shell part – The SUCRIE is equally shelled – there is a good supply of water – Now, returned EUSTON Capt Faulkes last that returned	
		1.40 PM	Returned COLINCAMPS – Lieut Burke – proceeded to RED HOUSE, the A.D.S of 36 F.Amb. - to go with him through CAPT. YOUNG's to see the Advd Post at K33C.2.4 + N34C.4.8 – Visited refreshments at A.D.M.S. office at COUIN – also 12" + 2" Field	

WAR DIARY
or
INTELLIGENCE SUMMARY.
(Erase heading not required.)

Army Form C. 2118.

John 2nd Baron [?]
OC 138 (S. John) Fd Amb[?]

Place	Date	Hour	Summary of Events and Information	Remarks and references to Appendices
THIEVRES	24/7/16		Applied for, & obtained Permission to withdraw 1 NCO, + 12 men of this unit, employed road mending, & hedge clipping - Master RE, to Lt Elliott in charge. - 16 proceed immediately to EUSTON POST, + report to OC in charge of Works - Staff Serg. Williams i/c this unit reported from leave from Dft - D.D.M.S's Office VIII Corps.	
THIEVRES	25/7/16 10.30 am		MAIN DRESSING STATION visited by A.D.M.S. + DAD.M.S. Lt + QM Thompson reported sick. Internal disarrangement of Rt Knee. Health Inspection held, at MAIN DRESSING Station + ADS's - reports received "all men in healthy condition."	
THIEVRES	26/7/16		Dentist attended from 29 CCS GEZAINCOURT QM + Hon Lt THOMPSON sent to 129th Field Amb[?] S/Kw Hospital - Admission to 12 NOON 11 - Discharges to July 9	

Army Form C. 2118.

WAR DIARY
or
INTELLIGENCE SUMMARY.   John H Davis Lieut Col. RAMC
(Erase heading not required.)

Instructions regarding War Diaries and Intelligence Summaries are contained in F. S. Regs., Part II. and the Staff Manual respectively. Title pages will be prepared in manuscript.

Place	Date	Hour	Summary of Events and Information	Remarks and references to Appendices
THIEVRES	27/7/16		D.D.M.S. VIII Corps. DADMS XIV Corps. visited Main DRESSING STATION Advance Park, 37th Field Ambce. 20 DW reported + was sent up to COLLINGAMPS to EUSTON POST. OC 61 Field Ambce. Do. Do. visited + looked over MAIN DRESSING STATION One NCO + 4 Pts left by him to attend follow. 37 MD	
THIEVRES	28/7/16		Advance Dressing Station at SAILLY-DELL handed over to 60th F.Ambce. 3 P.M. SAILLY BATHS hand to Sanitary Section 20th Divn 5. P.M. COLLIN GAMPS handed over to 61st & 20 Ambce 6 P.M. MAHONDRES EUSTON POST handed over to 62nd 20 Aug 12 NOON SUCRE POST handed over to 62nd 20 Aug 12 Noon STERLING ST. handed out to 62nd 20 Ambce 12 Noon also. RED COTTAGE as post. 1 Officer 38. men reported at Headquarters - after being allocated for non-mars wf + haded Clothing to 124 G.R.E. All Officers from AID POST - A.D.S.'s reported same nights. 37MD	

T2134. Wt. W708—776. 500000. 4/15. Sir J. C. & S.

WAR DIARY or INTELLIGENCE SUMMARY

Army Form C. 2118.

Place	Date	Hour	Summary of Events and Information	Remarks and references to Appendices
THIEVRES	29/7/16		A.D.M.S. sscel. RAMC order No. 15 also Bsgde. Operation Order No 40 114th Brigade ord. Orde. from A.D.M.S. 130th 2nd Aub. attached to 114th Brigade to work Horse + Motor Ambulances Details. to follow, west to point of entrainment and pick up men who fell out, also 1st/3rd Ambulance to Corps, men unable to march. 89 m.o.	
THIEVRES	30/7/16		OC left THIEVRES for AUTHIE 1½ PM and proceeding with Brigadier-General MARDEN, 114th Brigade, to ARQUES, a second Car Convoy carrying 2 NCO's (Staff-Clerk + Nursing Sergt.) 3 Privates with Medical + Surgical Panniers arrived 7.P.M. ARQUES. 1 officer NCO's, sick in lorries, and unable to travel, own collected, wheeled during night of 30-31st + silver watches of sent larger NCO to 1st/3rd Ambce. in morning of 31st. JEtD	
THIEVRES ARQUES	31/7/16		left under Capt Anderson — moved on by THIEVRES at 8.5 PM. arrived DOULLENS SOUTH STATION — Advance Party 15/new 2nd & name INTERPRETER FM Capt Jones RAMC depoted ARQUES 4.30 AM	
VOLKERINCKHOVE			reported ARQUES 11.45 9 hours Walkerincknove MOTOR CAR COVER with	

OC 13th S. Bn. S. Wales

Vol 9

Confidential

War Diary

of

130th (St John) Field Ambulance

From 1st August '16 – To – 31st August '16

Vol. 9

130 (S?) F.A.

Aug. 1916.

COMMITTEE FOR THE MEDICAL HISTORY OF THE WAR
Date −5 OCT. 1916

Army Form C. 2118.

WAR DIARY
or
INTELLIGENCE SUMMARY.
(Erase heading not required.)

John F. Davis, Lt Col. RAMC
OC 130th (St John) Fd Amb

Place	Date	Hour	Summary of Events and Information	Remarks and references to Appendices
VOLKERINCKHOVE	1/8/16	1:15 AM	Main body of Unit arrived under Capt Austen, were billeted in Barns, + over School House - late Canvas Camp. Pickets in Orchard Site, one section's Canvas used for Scabies rather infectious skin affection, + placed apart from canvas of other Unit Sections used for Scots by 114th Brigade.	
		(6.35 PM 31/7/16)	Lieut F.A. Austen RAMC J this Unit. Sent to act Temporary as M.O. 13th Welsh	
	1/8/16		Visits HQ 114th Brigade, + also had Reputed RAMC (Pigeon) since been sick.	
			Over 100 cases humble-number to fell out on march to base to Baluik on Somme by 3/7/16	
			DADMS visits Site;	
VOLKERINCKHOVE	2/8/16		In accordance with R.A.M.C. order No 19 1/8/16, B Section under Capt Austen + Lieut Elliott left at 5:30 am to relieve a part of Trans Amb. 4th Div. at Ambulance Site at HERZEELE and take over the Divisional Rest Station, also the Divisional Rest Station, for Officers, at WORMHOUDT. Capt A. Jones R.A.M.C. (attached) at 5:30 to proceed Meet OC Sanitary Section at ZEGGERS CAPPEL Bolles at 9:30. - also orders for 1 Corporal + 20 Men to report at 10 am at WORMHOUDT in accordance with Brigade orders. Lieut Burke RAMC. The Interpreter in Civil life + reports to Staff Capt at BOLLEZEELE at 9 AM and act as bicycling party.	

WAR DIARY
or
INTELLIGENCE SUMMARY.
(Erase heading not required.)

Army Form C. 2118.

John R. Parsons
Lt Col R.A.M.C.
OC. 136 (2/1 N.M) Field Amb

Place	Date	Hour	Summary of Events and Information	Remarks and references to Appendices
VOLKERINCKHOVE	3/8/16	5:30 AM	Paraded Res marching order, followed Hd Qtrs to starting point, formed part of 2nd Column. (Inspection of 12th Fd. Coy Am Column cancelled)	
			No. 4 of unit fell out on march.	
			Arrived WORMHOUDT, 10.30 a.m., - D.R.S for Officers + for Men Nos 50-900	
			At 9.30.5 Capt Ogston. (one Officer on leave & in S.S. lookout in D.R.S. Lines - B.C. Sections proceeded in Officer to main Railway Station "HERZEELE"	
Cl. 10 3.2 Sheet 27.			D.R.S Officers is a Chateau facing Square - with good Garden Grounds behind.	
			An Anteroom, Dining Room, Conservatory for patients, Contains 12 beds - this number can be increased. - Good Kitchen. -	
			D.R.S. (men) - C.106.7.2 (Sheet 27). Corrish Dwell laid out camp of 10 wooden huts - Capable of each holding 10 to 15 patients - When taken over a hut with 9 patients = 72.	
			Shelves of easels, 2 huts being used for a Dining Room, + reading room.	
			Good cooking arrangements. Ablutions for Personnel Officials - Bath Room for patients laid in Very large Garden, a number of bell huts also to hand out.	
			D.R.S. (annexe) at C.106.7.1. Consists of two school Rooms - 15 patients in each.	
			The Camp, Guarded to 15 a 20th Sealh, a Dispensary, a couple of bell tents and Courses	
			Shed, for Pack - Stores	

WAR DIARY
or
INTELLIGENCE SUMMARY.

Army Form C. 2118.

John S H Brogg Lieut Col RAMC
OC 130 (St John's) Field Amb
38th Div.

Place	Date	Hour	Summary of Events and Information	Remarks and references to Appendices
WORMHOUDT HERZEELE.	3/8/16		HERZEELE, to which Capt. Anderson proceeded, is 6½ miles from WORMHOUDT on the WORMHOUDT-POPERINGHE road. Eleven tents were taken over on this site, which with our own canvas, was used to form a "Skin Depot" – a wire fence was erected to separate these cases from rest of Camp. Four of flies of scaling tents used as a Bath Marquee, from which an system of drains were dug. 16 filter pits. – to cleanse water. 1-9-inc. it – a shallow soak for wash & hand water. Kitchens erected – Stay proof latrines for Officers, NCOs, men & personal races. also for (a) Patients in Hospital, (b) Patients in Skin Hospital – These are all made out of (6" boxes, with self absorbing U, covering double tins, with bywaters U – to preserve (c) brine. urinals. Screen of canvas, & fosses in sawdust, with a sprinkling of Chloride of lime. Our forces front. A New incinerator built. – San Latrines, – Itrek's Trinifects Sinks. Short-numbered slip. Harness from QM Stores, allocated to different departments. Visited by ADMS. DADMS	89 AMS

WAR DIARY
or
INTELLIGENCE SUMMARY.
(Erase heading not required.)

Army Form C. 2118.

135 G.H. Road, W. Col. Rawe.
O.C. 30th (3/70th) Feld Amb.

Place	Date	Hour	Summary of Events and Information	Remarks and references to Appendices
WORMHOUDT HERZEELE	4/7/16		Special Warnord. Day to Commander in Chief, read at Parade. Manur. Graveline – Two Interpreters. Left mid-day under HERZEELE, Day occupied with fatigues transporting in both Camps	J.R.
WORMHOUDT HERZEELE	5/7/16		A Number of temporary R. bell Camps, procured with arrangements made for erection of Their transfer at HERZEELE. New Latrines on Cater System in process of completion. – Temporary subdivisioning in Billets of Personnel at WORMHOUDT	J.R.
WORMHOUDT HERZEELE	6/7/16		Divisional Rest Station for Officers. Turn. Hospital at Herzeele visited by Surgeon General PORTIER. D.M.S. VIII Corps., Inspected A.S.C. Fatigues in flee.	J.R.
WORMHOUDT HERZEELE	7/7/16		Capt. D. R. Williams Rawe, reported, replaced on Strength. Julue verd arrived from St.) visited HERZEELE.	J.R.
WORMHOUDT HERZEELE	8/7/16		Visited HERZEELE – No Personnel, health Inspection – Nothing further bought	J.R.

WAR DIARY or INTELLIGENCE SUMMARY

Army Form C. 2118.

John Barron Gerrard
to 136(E.Soh.) Field Amb.

Place	Date	Hour	Summary of Events and Information	Remarks and references to Appendices
WORMHOUDT	9/8/16		Visited by A.D.M.S. — P.B., T.U. were inspected at Hogyele Inoculation performed. Personnel.	
HERZEELE	10/8/16		A.A. & Q.M.G 38th Div visited D.R.S's Performed double inoculation into Civilian child, 2½ years injury — visits Con. Culley lucho Longo near WORMHOUDT. — visited HERZEELE	8/17
	11/8/16		Nothing to note.	8/17
	12/8/16		Nothing to note. Health inspection, inoculation performed, trefoleer Rifles, N.C.O.	8/17
	13/8/16		H.M. The King motored this afternoon thro WORMHOUDT, en route HERZEELE.	8/17
	14/8/16		114th Brigade moved up towards Bego Welcomed to act as Sanitary officer TOWN MAJOR. Visited with TOWN MAJOR, Butchers Shops, Abattoir — large numbers of small Beasts	8/17

WAR DIARY
or
INTELLIGENCE SUMMARY

Army Form C. 2118.

[Signature] Lt Colonel
OC 136 (2/1st) Field Ambce

Place	Date	Hour	Summary of Events and Information	Remarks and references to Appendices
WORMHOUDT - HERZEELE	15/8/16		Sergt. Naruns sent to G.H.Q. Insp: Supply Col. Sergt. Sumption to ballon COUTHOVE. Sanitary/Groom Scheme sent to Town Majr. Wormhoudt. Scheme of work on Suggested winter improvements submitted about visites HERZEELE.	JSHD
WORMHOUDT HERZEELE	16/8/16		Attended Conference D.D.M.S. office 11 A.M. COUTHOVE. Inspected ballon COUTHOVE Laundry	JSHD
WORMHOUDT HERZEELE	17/8/16		C.R.S. Officers, D.R.S. Insp. + Fees Ambulance at HERZEELE Visited. D.D.M.S. VIII Corps. TETANUS: reported to H.D. Hose at HERZEELE. QM + Hon Lieut. THOMPSON. reported for duty	JSHD
WORMHOUDT HERZEELE	18/8/16		Visited HERZEELE; a large number of improvements completed at WORMHOUDT. New Incineration in process of Construction - Baths ??	JSHD

T2134. Wt. W708—776. 500000. 4/15. Sir J. C. & S.

Army Form C. 2118.

John Zh. Davies Lt Col
OC. 130th (St John) Field Amb

WAR DIARY
INTELLIGENCE SUMMARY.
(Erase heading not required.)

Instructions regarding War Diaries and Intelligence Summaries are contained in F. S. Regs., Part II. and the Staff Manual respectively. Title pages will be prepared in manuscript.

Place	Date	Hour	Summary of Events and Information	Remarks and references to Appendices
WORMHOUDT & HERZEELE	19/16/8		D.M.S. visits C.R.S. Offers. Orders received to send Advanced Party to take over Divisional Reg Station at PROVEN from 12th Field Amb & Brs YPRES. HERZEELE (Orders to send Advanced Party Cancelled)	JEND
WORMHOUDT & HERZEELE	20/16/8		R.A.M.C. ox, No 20 poses 82. Capt Williams Some of this unit posted for temporary duty at Divisional Hospital School. VOIRE RINCKHOVE. Lieut F A ANDERSON. R.A.M.C. — having completed over four Courses returned to England, under orders s/k the Strength of this Unit being as from to day. visited 12th Field Amb & PROVEN Open Cesses No 13 suffering from. The lebhrans destroyed by our T A D.Rs. - Crews buried in deep pit without Cease.	JEND

T2134. Wt. W708—776. 500000. 4/15. Sir J. C. & S.

WAR DIARY
or
INTELLIGENCE SUMMARY.
(Erase heading not required.)

Army Form C. 2118.

John 3rd Field U.G.E. Raine
be ROE. John Rose Paul

Instructions regarding War Diaries and Intelligence Summaries are contained in F. S. Regs., Part II. and the Staff Manual respectively. Title pages will be prepared in manuscript.

Place	Date	Hour	Summary of Events and Information	Remarks and references to Appendices
WORMHOUDT / HERZEELE	21/6/16		Lieut. R.A.G. ELLIOTT. R.A.M.C. of this unit proceeded to 19th (Pioneer) Welsh. Regt. to act as M.O. in place of Capt. Wallace, granted 7 days special leave. New latrines completed at C.R.S. Ypres	JSH
WORMHOUDT / HERZEELE	22/6/16		D.M.S. & A.D.M.S. visited C.R.S. Officers New Incinerator Completed.	JSH
WORMHOUDT / HERZEELE	23/6/16		Advance Party in charge of Capt Foulkes proceeded to PROVEN to take over from 12th Field Amb Co. Visited PROVEN. Thest. O.C. 12th Field Amb Co. Lines of HQt hostile Veterinary Section inspected.	JSH
WORMHOUDT / HERZEELE	24/6/16		Main body proceeded by road to PROVEN - leaving 1PM, arriving 5PM. relieving 12th Field Amb Co. The Site (F76.3.3. Sheet 27.) is comprised of Class rooms of a Convent School & Belgian Hut (mud & brushwood), & Marquee a surgery, Dressing Hut, Van Belt Dentist, & Capt Saulley accommodation	

Army Form C. 2118.

WAR DIARY
or
INTELLIGENCE SUMMARY.
(Erase heading not required.)

10/132 H. Davel War Raws
O.C. 131 S. Dec Fld Ambce

Place	Date	Hour	Summary of Events and Information	Remarks and references to Appendices
PROVEN	24/8/16		100 patients in the School, available for the Tal number in huts & canvas, — both of our canvas, a total of 250 to 300 ones be accommodated. The Camp was clean — but latrines are not fly proof, & number of should latrine requirements are required.	
WORMHOUDT			Capt Anderson, & Bearers (evacuated at Wormhoudt) at Charge of C.R.S. (Officers) and found, & 3 horse bearer as Billet bearer & hers D.R.S. — 3 hrsn left on Billet bearers also at Herzeele — 1 NCO (4) was left 15 Camyon-baths Rousbrug at Wormhoudt under Cpl Jorox. also 1 NCO : 4 men at Balk COUTHOVE.	JAD
PROVEN	25/8/16		Visited by A.D.M.S.	JAD

Army Form C. 2118.

WAR DIARY
or
INTELLIGENCE SUMMARY.
(Erase heading not required.)

John J. Barrel W.G.E, Rams
OC. R.S.(F) Dn, Iral Auf.

Instructions regarding War Diaries and Intelligence Summaries are contained in F. S. Regs., Part II. and the Staff Manual respectively. Title pages will be prepared in manuscript.

Place	Date	Hour	Summary of Events and Information	Remarks and references to Appendices
PROVEN	27/8/16		Inspected Sanitary arrangements, and arranged for improvements at COUTHOVE. also A.S.C. H.Q.G.; 333 Co.; the latter attained most unsatisfactory especially cook houses, latrines. Hospital visited by D.D.M.S. VIII Corps.	R.H.D
PROVEN	28/8/16		Nothing to report — visited WORMHOUDT.	2.2 hrs
PROVEN	29/8/16		Health Inspection.	P.M.
PROVEN	30/8/16		Inspected Sanitary Arrangements of 330 Co. A.S.C. – much needed improvements required in Cook-house, Officers, NCO's Mess, - latrines most unsatisfactory.	S.H.D
PROVEN	31/8/16		Lieut T. J. BUCKLEY R.A.M.C. of this unit, having completed 12 months contract, returned this day to England, his taken off the strength of this unit, as from today.	

John J. Barrel
W.G.E. Rams
OC 133(F) Dn, Ital Aug

Confidential

War Diary

of

130th (St John) Field Amb.

38th Div.

From 1st Septr '16 To 30th Septr '16

1401734

Sept 1916

Committee for the Medical History of the War — Date 30 OCT. 1916

A.D.M.S.
38th Div.

I beg to enclose War Diary of this Unit for the month of September, please.

[signature]
O.C.

Lieut.-Colonel,
R.A.M.C.
130TH (ST. JOHN) FIELD AMBULANCE
38TH (WELSH) DIVISION

130th (ST. JOHN)
FIELD AMBULANCE
38th (WELSH) DIVN.
No. 2685
Date 30.9.16

WAR DIARY
or
INTELLIGENCE SUMMARY.
(Erase heading not required.)

Army Form C. 2118.

JoR2 H Page 2
V Cor Rouen

Instructions regarding War Diaries and Intelligence Summaries are contained in F.S. Regs., Part II. and the Staff Manual respectively. Title pages will be prepared in manuscript.

Place	Date	Hour	Summary of Events and Information	Remarks and references to Appendices
PROVEN	1/9/16		Handed over C.R.S. (Officers) & D.R.S. (other ranks) at WORMHOUDT to 127th Amb. Visited & Supervised N. Camp (10' Coolies) Visited 46 C.C.S.	JRP
PROVEN	2/9/16		O.C. departed on special leave today	aud
PROVEN	3/9/16		Camp and hospital visited and inspected by A.D.M.S. In accordance with A.D.M.S. instructions details of this unit which were left at the bath and laundry WORMHOUDT were transferred to the laundry at COUTTHOVE.	aud
PROVEN	4/9/16		Lieut J.H. Bankes R.A.M.C. and Lieut Hughes C/Lt R.A.M.C. reported for duty with this unit. In accordance with instructions from A.D.M.S. Lieut R.A.E. Elliott R.A.M.C. took over charge of the 38th Divisional Laundry and Baths.	aud

Army Form C. 2118.

WAR DIARY
or
INTELLIGENCE SUMMARY.
(Erase heading not required.)

Instructions regarding War Diaries and Intelligence Summaries are contained in F. S. Regs., Part II. and the Staff Manual respectively. Title pages will be prepared in manuscript.

Place	Date	Hour	Summary of Events and Information	Remarks and references to Appendices
PROVEN	5/7/16		A.D.M.S. visited and inspected this field ambulance. Capt D.R. Williams R.A.M.C. returned for duty to this unit from the Divisional Rining School	
PROVEN	6/7/16		Visited and inspected the A.O.D. with regard to the sanitation of their lines etc.	
PROVEN	7/7/16		Visited and inspected lines, kitchens, latrines etc of the 122nd Brigade R.F.A. A & B Batteries	
PROVEN	8/7/16		Visited and inspected lines, kitchens, latrines etc of the 122nd Brigade R.F.A. C & D Batteries	
PROVEN	9/7/16		O.C. returned from special leave to-day.	
PROVEN	10/9/16		Nothing to note	
PROVEN	11/9/16		Visited Camps of 330th Co. 331st, 332nd, 333rd Companies A.S.C. & Supernumery Sunday Ammunition.	
PROVEN	12/9/16		Field Amb. Visited by G.O.C. 36th Div. & D.D.M.S. Visit to Camp 10th Welsh.	

WAR DIARY
or
INTELLIGENCE SUMMARY.

Army Form C. 2118.

No 2 Dn Basal
Lieut Col. R.O.McC
OC. 130th (St Johns) Field Amb 38th Divs

Place	Date	Hour	Summary of Events and Information	Remarks and references to Appendices
PROVEN.	12/9/16		Lt. D.C.M. PAGE. R.A.M.C. relinquishes duty as M.O. 13th R.W.F. and placed on the strength of this unit on & from this date. Capt. M. FFOULKES. R.A.M.C. of this unit, posted for temporary duty as M.O. to 119. R.F.A. Capt. D.R. WILLIAMS. R.A.M.C. of this unit. Posted as M.O. 14th Welsh. and is struck off strength of this unit. Capt. D.H. GRIFFITHS. R.A.M.C. M.O. 14th WELSH, posted to this unit, and taken on strength as from. 13.9.16. Capt. D.H. GRIFFITHS R.A.M.C. proceeded to 38th Divisional Sanitary Section and took over temporary duty as O.C. 77 Sanitary Section. Supervised the Sanitary arrangements in following Camps. 330th Coy ASC. 331st Coy. ASC. 332 Coy. ASC. 333rd Coy. ASC.	ROMcC JSHG
PROVEN.	14/9/16		No matters to report	JSHG

WAR DIARY
INTELLIGENCE SUMMARY.

Army Form C. 2118.

John Dasal
Lieut.Col. Raws
OC 135th(?) Fd Amb

Place	Date	Hour	Summary of Events and Information	Remarks and references to Appendices
PRONEN	15/9/16		Visited & Supervised the Sanitary arrangements in the Camp of the 49th Mobile Veterinary Section — This I found in good order — latrines well kept, cook house, with proper seats — cook-shelter, — ablution place for OR, fly proof latrines — Arrangements made for drinking water which is drawn from farm stone Pump (well) ordered to be regularly tested by the Bact Lab for drinking purposes while water to be chlorinated and in the meantime water to be chlorinated in jars, as this Section is not provided with water cart. JSMD	
PRONEN	16/9/16		This Field Ambulance, visited, in accordance with instructions of O.C. 3rd Div. by Officers & NCO's of 38th Divisional School — who reported under the OC Sanitary Section — There were visited huts — four — Latrines, Urinals, the whole of the Camp under charge of Infantry, 3 Senior Officers, — these shown the kitchen, all Sanitary Arrangements — Brunstralines incinerator, and full explanation — Incinerator, Ovens & Soakage JSMD	

WAR DIARY
INTELLIGENCE SUMMARY
Army Form C. 2118.

O.C. 130th (S.Mid.) Fd. Ambce

Place	Date	Hour	Summary of Events and Information	Remarks and references to Appendices
PROVEN.	16/9/16		Orderly wagon with bearers from A.D.M.S. – Capt. ANDERSON & lieutenant with 8 other ranks, proceeded to LORMHOUDT to take over VIII Corps Rest Station for Officers, pending the arrival of Fd. Amb. of the same name and had the 12th Fd. Ambce and also the arrival detachment of horses from D.R.S. WORMHOUDT. 7 Bis – also to post 2 Bilet Wardens at D.R.S. WORMHOUDT. 2 Other ranks were also posted at HERZEELE as billet wardens to hold site, taking over from the 11th Field Ambce and 2 other/ranks at Field Ambce site at WATOU, taking over from the 10th Fd. Ambce. detachments also released to post billet Wardens at the laundry/Baths at WORMHOUDT. The baths/laundry at ZEGGERS CAPEL, BOLLEZEELE DHO	
PROVEN	17/9/16		Received notification from A.D.M.S. as follows:- "O.C. 130th Fd Ambce – under authority granted by His Majesty the KING, the Corps Commander awards Military Medals to the following N.C.O.s + Men – The Corps Commander also wishes you to convey his congratulations to the/respective 130th Fd. Amb. 45124 Sergt. Thomas George HOPKINS. 48559 L/Cpl. Trevor John NICHOLAS. 48584 Private Wm Hy JONES. 48181 Pursue Wm Jno RIDGEWAY"	

WAR DIARY
or
INTELLIGENCE SUMMARY.

Army Form C. 2118.

(Erase heading not required.)

Place	Date	Hour	Summary of Events and Information	Remarks and references to Appendices
PROVEN	18/9/16		Unit paraded in Shelter Rd. at 9.30 A.M. — for presentation of military medals by the A.D.M.S. to Sergt Hopkins, L/Cpl Nicholas, Pte W.H. Jones, Pte W. Ritchie. A.D.M.S. congratulated unit, and issued ribbons to the recipients. Visited WORMHOUDT, (the Corps Rest Station for Officers), the D.R.S., also HERZEELE, WATOU.	
PROVEN	19/9/16		Nothing to report.	
PROVEN	20/9/16		Nothing to report. — Inspection of A.S.C. tin Drill to Riflers.	
PROVEN	21/9/16		Capt. GRIFFITH, R.A.M.C. of this Unit, who has been acting O.C. 77th Sanitary Section rejoined this unit. Visited 129th Field Amb Co. Lieut J.H. Bawkes R.A.M.C. — has rejoined 129th Field Amb & ceases to be attached this unit. Visited "Improved Sanitary Arrangements at Headquarters A.O.D — Cesspool, new boiler"	

WAR DIARY
or
INTELLIGENCE SUMMARY.

Army Form C. 2118.

O/C 130th (St John) Field Amb

Place	Date	Hour	Summary of Events and Information	Remarks and references to Appendices
PROVEN	21/9/16 (Cont)		Comfort near base of Office - present chaves no (? the Fry) - Latrine not satisfactory, (open trench) - D.A.D.O.S. will arrange for new site, with St. Prof. Latrines.	85 H2
PROVEN	22/9/16		Entering YPRES for purpose of advising huts - on 21/9/11 Dr J.D. EVANS A.S.C. 130 Divn at rest of the G.S. Wagon was slightly wounded in back, by H.E. Shell. - the Wagon damaged, and the team of 2 horses which were following reserves superficial cuts rearing in both hind legs of near horse, from the falling of debris -	85 H2
PROVEN	23/9/16		Nothing to report.	85 H2
PROVEN	24/9/16		In accordance with instructions from A.D.M.S. Capt GRIFFITH RAMC of this Unit took over temporary charge of No 77. Sanitary Section. Appointments:- Temp/Capt A. JONES, RAMC, (130th Field Amb) appointed D.A.D.M.S. 38th Welsh Div. vice Capt. S.J.A.H. WALSH. D.S.O, RAMC.(SR). - Vacated duties of S.R.G.S. Officer.	85 H2

WAR DIARY
or
INTELLIGENCE SUMMARY.
(Erase heading not required.)

Army Form C. 2118.

John H Davies
Lieut Col. RAMC
O.C. 130' (S. John) Field Ambce

Place	Date	Hour	Summary of Events and Information	Remarks and references to Appendices
PROVEN	25/9/16		HONOURS + REWARDS. - Routine Orders No 66. Dated 25/9/16 inter alia authority delegated by HIS MAJESTY THE KING. - The General Officer Commanding in Chief has awarded the following decorals: — 48076. Pte. T. ALLEN, 130' 3' Amb. MILITARY MEDAL. to heroic Act on Night of 23/24 July (unit parade) 3.30 P.M. when A.D.M.S. pinned ribbon on & personally ADMS congratulated him on behalf of Corps Commander, Div Commander + himself.	82 MD
PROVEN	26/9/16		Visited. No 10 CCS, Inspected & examined Case of Well Broard (Pte W Andrew) under care of Capt. Stokes RAMC. Capt. Ryle RAMC. No events to note	82 MD
PROVEN	27/9/16			82 MD
PROVEN	28/9/16		Visited lines of Lancashire Divisions.	82 MD
PROVEN	29/9/16		Visited by acting A.D.M.S + D.A.D.M.S. Inspected A.S.C. 3rd Div crew	83 MD
PROVEN	30/9/16		No events to note	

John H Davies Lt Col RAMC
O.C. 130TH (ST. JOHN) FIELD AMBULANCE,
38TH (WELSH) DIVISION

Confidential.

War Diary of

130th (St. John) Field Ambulance.

38th (Welsh) Division.

From October 1st 1916 to October 31st 1916.

COMMITTEE FOR THE MEDICAL HISTORY OF THE WAR
Date −9 DEC. 1915

WAR DIARY
or
INTELLIGENCE SUMMARY.

Army Form C. 2118.

October 1916.

Jo... Lieut Col Rawe
S.C. 136 (S) (2nd?) Field Ambulance

Place	Date	Hour	Summary of Events and Information	Remarks and references to Appendices
PROVEN.	1/10/16		Lieut. KNAPP attached 19t Pioneer (Welsh) Regt. reported to ... Batt. Laundry vice Lieut ELLIOTT. R.A.M.C. of this Unit rifles. proceeded to A.S.C. horse transport, attached to this Unit. 92 HD	
PROVEN	2/10/16		Nothing to report.	
PROVEN.	3/10/16		Inspected N. Camp 10th Welsh. - visited Knehaus Theatre Company Divisional, Capt. Foulkes Rawe of this Unit proceeded to Corps Rest Station for 8 days. Capt Anderson Rawe. Pickets/leave from 4/10/16.	
PROVEN.	4/10/16		Nothing to report. - received FURBER Wheeled Stretcher from 10t Welsh Regiment.	92 HD
PROVEN	5/10/16		Lecture to Unit by Capt Foulkes Rawe on Box Respirator drill. Visited HQ A.S.C	92 HD

Army Form C. 2118.

WAR DIARY
or
INTELLIGENCE SUMMARY.
(Erase heading not required.)

J.O.P. 52nd Div R.A.M.C. [illegible]
OC 135 Field Amb

Instructions regarding War Diaries and Intelligence Summaries are contained in F. S. Regs., Part II. and the Staff Manual respectively. Title pages will be prepared in manuscript.

Place	Date	Hour	Summary of Events and Information	Remarks and references to Appendices
PROVEN	6/10/16		Inspected Baths Laundry at COUTHOVE. JOP	
PROVEN	7/10/16		LIEUT MYLES. COLT. RAMC of 1st Lincs proceeded to relieve M.O. 161st RF and take over Herreele Charge by that Unit. JOP	
PROVEN	8/10/16		Visited + inspected C.R.S (Officers) WORMHOUDT. also Sté held at HERZEELE. JOP	
PROVEN	9/10/16		Posted N.C.O. nursing as Billet Wardens at WATOU JOP	
PROVEN	10/10/16		Inspected following Coys. 330 Coy ASC, 331 Coy ASC. JOP	
PROVEN	11/10/16		Lieut R.G. ELLIOTT RAMC of 1st Lincs Lunt, posted temporarily as MO 19 W Yorks vice BURKE RAMC reported from Base. JOP	
PROVEN	12/10/16		A.D.M.S. 3rd Div inspected D.R.S. Poperinghe, with ADMS under 46 C.C.S.	

Army Form C. 2118.

WAR DIARY
or
INTELLIGENCE SUMMARY.
(Erase heading not required.)

John Passmore Hewitt
OC 130 (SI) Field Ambulance

Place	Date	Hour	Summary of Events and Information	Remarks and references to Appendices
PROVEN	13/10/16		A.D.M.S. 38st Bns. visited. D.R.S. "Field Amb"	
PROVEN	14/10/16		D.D.M.S. VIII Corps visited & inspected D.R.S., Field Ambulance. Inspection by myself of R.T.O. Camp, Railhead. - much needed Sanitary reform required; Verbal instructions given for grease trap, flytrap latrines, ablution benches, soak pit, [?] burning of press movements, - removal of loose manure.	JPH JPH JPH
PROVEN	15/10/16		Capt A.W. ANDERSON. R.A.M.C. of this Unit, reported from base, took over charge of ASC Corp Rear Park to officer Visited A.S.C. Camp.	JPH
PROVEN	16/10/16		Lieut. T. BORNE R.A.M.C. of this Unit took over lieutenant vice Capt McMILLAN, R.A.M.C. who proceeded to base. Capt. FFOULKES R.A.M.C. reported at HQ of this Unit, after handing over Charge of Corps Rest Station to Officers i/c Capt. ANDERSON.	JPH
PROVEN	17/10/16		Attended Corps School, for lecture & demonstration	JPH

WAR DIARY
or
INTELLIGENCE SUMMARY

Army Form C. 2118.

John St. Pascal Visit Ct. Rawls
No. 130th (St Johns Ford Amb)

Place	Date	Hour	Summary of Events and Information	Remarks and references to Appendices
PROVEN	18/10/16		Inspected 158 SIEGE BATTY, M.T. A.S.C. Stationed PROVEN. (Brechurst of 68 man) also Camp of R.T.O. PROVEN.	82 HZ
PROVEN	19/10/16		Capt. M. FFOULKES, R.A.M.C. of this Unit proceeded on leave	82 HZ
PROVEN	20/10/16		Lieut General Sir AYLMER HUNTER-WESTON, K.C.B. D.S.O. M.P. Commanding VIII Corps, visited and inspected Field Ambulance Hospital, Divisional Rest-Station – accompanied by the D.D.M.S. VIII Corps and A.D.M.S. 38th Div. the following were the points raised during the inspection. Baths – Source of water, if pond is in anyway contaminated by sewage? The method of laying the water Pipe in the pond, in such a manner that it is not sucked up the suction Pipe – The Pipe should have a rose or similar in part sucked up the suction Pipe – The Pipe should have a rose or strainer in (suspended) in a submerged, perforated barrel. Shower, and be suspended in a submerged, perforated barrel. Means of Baths Room, necessity for additional forms or trestles in the undressing room, with pegs above, for hanging up all parade clothes – The effluent water from the baths, method of dealing with same and place of final discharge.	

WAR DIARY or INTELLIGENCE SUMMARY

Army Form C. 2118.

John Rawl
Lt Col Rawl
OC 136th S[iege] Bn [?]

Place	Date	Hour	Summary of Events and Information	Remarks and references to Appendices
PROVEN	20/10/16		The C of O Commander's instructions – notes 57 – (continued) Drains should not be dug in sections, but in the entire length. To ensure uniform progress. Latrines. The importance of having more space in the front of seats. The character of the seat to be such that it does not come in contact with the penis. The top of bucket or double tin to fit close under the seat, to prevent the escape of urine above the bucket. Care to see that dust door at back of latrine should remain flyproof. Refuse. Drums in use to dry refuse should be provided with covers, thus preventing some fly-frost, and preventing dust from being blown out of same. Physical training of Patrols. The real importance of maintaining the keenness of patrols while in the real station. All men covered by M.O.'s as fit to attend Physical Drill (Müller) to do so in addition to usual march.	

WAR DIARY
or
INTELLIGENCE SUMMARY.

Army Form C. 2118.

(Erase heading not required.)

John H Panel Lieut Col R.A.M.C
OC 130th (St John) Field Ambce

Place	Date	Hour	Summary of Events and Information	Remarks and references to Appendices
Proven	20/10/16		The Corps Commanders Instruction — Notes of — Continued. Importance of having Patients respirators, Gas Helmets Symmetrically arranged in wards, about their Beds — Water Supply — Importance of having water supply from its source until it reaches the patients.	PSMO
PROVEN	21/10/16		No Sick Parade	DADMS
PROVEN	22/10/16		Visited 38t Divisional Train Camp	DSMO
PROVEN	23/10/16		Lieut Page of the unit, proceeded to report for instruction to the Chemical Advisor at OXALEARE. Examination for higher rate of Corps Pay of Clarke, Cooke, and Nursing orderlies of this unit, by the D.A.D.M.S	38 HO
PROVEN	24/10/16		Temp hand J. D. PEARSON, R.A.M.C. reported for Duty. had instructing this unit.	SSAD

Army Form C. 2118.

WAR DIARY
or
INTELLIGENCE SUMMARY.
(Erase heading not required.)

JOURDAIN Lieut Col. RAMC
DC 130-132nd Field Ambulance

Place	Date	Hour	Summary of Events and Information	Remarks and references to Appendices
PROVEN	25/10/16		Visit by A.D.M.S. D.A.D.M.S. 38th Div.	Initial
PROVEN	26/10/16		Lieut. D.C.M. PAGE. RAMC of this Unit, reported from Army Gas School at OXALEARE	2AW
PROVEN	27/10/16		No event to report.	3AW
PROVEN	28/10/16		Inspected, arrangements for bursting of Thermometers P.T.O. Proven.	3AW
PROVEN	29/10/16		Lieut. RAG.ELLIOTT. RAMC reported sick 28/10/16. This day proceeded to 10 CCS and later the strength of this Unit. Lecture (Gas) by Lieut. D.C.M. PAGE. RAMC of this Unit. Inspected H.T. A.S.C. riders etc.	3AW
PROVEN	30/10/16		CAPT. M. FFOULKES RAMC & Lieut Hunt, reported from Bars Gas lecture by Lieut DCM PAGE RAMC.	
PROVEN	31/10/16		No event to report.	JOURDAIN Lieut Col. RAMC DC 130H.S.FA Fieldambulance

2353 Wt. W2544/1454 700,000 5/15 D.D.&L. A.D.S.S. Forms/C. 2118.

Confidential.

War Diary

of

130th (St. John) Field Ambulance

38th (Welsh) Division.

From November 1st 1916 to November 30/1916.

Army Form C. 2118.

J.O? H Rassal
L/Cpl Rawe
OC 130 (St John) Fd Amb'ce
38th Division

WAR DIARY
or
INTELLIGENCE SUMMARY.
(Erase heading not required.)

Instructions regarding War Diaries and Intelligence Summaries are contained in F.S. Regs., Part II. and the Staff Manual respectively. Title pages will be prepared in manuscript.

Place	Date	Hour	Summary of Events and Information	Remarks and references to Appendices
PROVEN	1/11/16		Lieut. Pope RAMC, gave lecture on "Gas Poisoning in Warfare." "Gas Attacks", with description of various forms of Gas Attacks, and the mask to be used, in the past & present to combat these attacks. Capt Burke Rawe, of this Unit returned to duty from 38th Div Train.	? R.H.R
PROVEN	2/11/16		Above lecture repeated, to those who by the limit, attached, unable to attend previous lecture. Lieut. Pope Rawe approved "Gas Officer" to this Unit.	R.H.R.
PROVEN	3/11/16		Practical Demonstration in Gassing – R/V Pope – Every Respirator tested in Chamber, + Respirators changed in the Gas Chamber, for P.H. Helmets. Lieut. - A.D.M.S. visited A.S.C lines.	R.H.R
PROVEN	4/11/16		Visited + Inspected Capt. Rest Station for Officers, + D.R.S. Site at WORMHOUDT, also Site at HERZEELE.	82nd
PROVEN	5/11/16		Lieut. M. COLT. RAMC to attached to 16th Batt R.W.F. vShule of Shenyts of Must'd or from 7/11 – 8/11/16	7/11 – 8/11/16

2353 Wt. W3544/1454 700,000 5/15 D.D.&L. A.D.S.S./Forms/C. 2118.

Army Form C. 2118.

WAR DIARY
or
INTELLIGENCE SUMMARY.
(Erase heading not required.)

J.O.B. "A Darrel" War Diary
of 135[?]/30th Fco Ambce

Instructions regarding War Diaries and Intelligence Summaries are contained in F. S. Regs., Part II and the Staff Manual respectively. Title pages will be prepared in manuscript.

Place	Date	Hour	Summary of Events and Information	Remarks and references to Appendices
PROVEN	6/7/16		Inspection of Rifles. K.S.C. attached.	J3#D
PROVEN	7/7/16		No Sick to Scouts.	J3#D
PROVEN	8/7/16	5:30 pm	Re Rising horse Fallows in Strength, Lt D.C.M. PAGE R.A.M.C. posted for temp. duty with 14th R.W.F. — Visited site at WATOU. Night Drill with Respirators	J.E.H.O.
PROVEN	9/7/16		Capt. B. WOODHOUSE of 1st e hurt, posted for temporary duty, to 1st 13th WELSH. Visited Camp of 10th WELSH.	J3#D
PROVEN	10/7/16	5:30 pm	Capt. M. FFOULKES, R.A.M.C. of 1st e hurt, posted for temporary duty, to 10th WELSH. Respirator Drill —	J3#D
PROVEN	11/7/16		Lt. D.C.M. PAGE. R.A.M.C. reported from duty with 14th R.W.F.	J3#D

WAR DIARY
INTELLIGENCE SUMMARY

John Duval. V Gen. Rawg
1st and 2nd Army

Army Form C. 2118.

Place	Date	Hour	Summary of Events and Information	Remarks and references to Appendices
PROVEN.	12/11/16	P.M. 12.15	D.M.S. 2nd Army (General PORTER.) with D.D.M.S. VIIIth Corps visited Field Ambulance, D.R.S. and expressed satisfaction, with the arrangements for the care of patients, and work done by the men of the D.R.S Ambulance. Also with the kitchens + feeding arrangements.	
		P.M. 4.15	A.D.M.S. D.A.D.M.S. 2nd Div. visited and inspected Rations of Personnel, DRS. Inspection lost this day, of "Fur Coats" of Personnel. Inspection of Rifles A.S.C (HT) Clothing Inspection, A.S.O (HT). (ENT)	
PROVEN	13/11/16		The Officer in Charge of Corps Rest Station WORMHOUDT, reports that this Station and the Site of the D.R.S. at WORMHOUDT, was visited by the D.M.S. 2nd Army + D.M.S. VIIIth Corps. In Camp 10th Welsh, The Baths COUTHOVE, and the Camp of the 177 Mining Company visited and inspected by me.	
PROVEN	14/11/16		Visits WATOU by Major Jaquet of DDMS. — inspected Sanitary + Bathing arrangements of 38th Ammunition Sub Park. 150 all ranks with + 60	

WAR DIARY
INTELLIGENCE SUMMARY.
(Erase heading not required.)

Army Form C. 2118.

J.O.Q. & Divis'l
V/Col. Rawe
OC 130th Field Amb. Ce.

Place	Date	Hour	Summary of Events and Information	Remarks and references to Appendices
PROVEN	14/11/16		(Cont.) into 60 other ranks attached for rationing, composed of (5) Auxiliary Bus Coys: 30, Signals 9, R.A.M.C. 2, + details of R.E. making Hose standpipe on WATOU - POPERINGHE ROAD. The sanitary Kitchens, Bureaus, Billets, Baths, + latrines of the Ammunition Park are satisfactory. — Washing in men by own arrangements is satisfactory. — Ventilation is satisfactory. — few Sgts. sent by Motor Lorry, or Motor S.W. Car. Evacuation to Prover. — Lecture to Nursing Sergts. + Orderlies on "Infectious Contagious Diseases. Care of 9 hrs	9hrs
PROVEN	15/11/16	PM 6.30	Visited + inspected Camp of R.T.O Proven. Gas Helmet + Respirator Drill.	9 hrs
PROVEN	16/11/16		No Parade to report. (5.30 P.M.) Gas Helmet + Respirator Drill	9 hrs
PROVEN	17/11/16	PM 5.30	A.D.M.S. visited, and inspected Field Ambulance + B.R.S. — and inspected T.U. men — Lecture Lecture by Lt. PEARSON R.A.M.C to Tent Subdivisions of the Ambulance on "Infectious Diseases"	9 hrs

WAR DIARY
INTELLIGENCE SUMMARY

Army Form C. 2118.

John Z. Barrett
Lt. Col. R.A.M.C.
O.C. 130th (St. John) Field Ambulance

Place	Date	Hour	Summary of Events and Information	Remarks and references to Appendices
PROVEN	19/11/16		Lieut. D.C.M. PAGE R.A.M.C. proceeded to England, on expiration of his leave, and is taken off strength of this unit. The Ambulance site at WATOU handed over to 132nd Field Amb. & billets handed/quarters to site at HERZEELE handed over to 133 Field Amb. 39th Division.	JZHB
PROVEN	20/11/16		Corps Rest Station WORMHOUDT. handed over to 134th Fd. Amb. 39th Div. and also the site of D.R.S. WORMHOUDT. Capt. Anderson. with Personnel on duty at C.R.S. + D.R.S., reported at Headquarters. Visited detached party of this unit (1 N.C.O. + 24 other ranks) at Canal Bank, for purpose of inspecting their dug-outs, health inspection + pay. Visited drying room, POPERINGHE, inspected + paid detachment of unit employed there. — 5.30 P.M. Gas Helmet Drill —	JSHD TSHD JSHD
PROVEN	21/11/16	5.30 PM	Lecture on "Fever Nursing" by J.F. PEARSON. R.A.M.C. to Tent Subdivisions of this Ambulance	JSHD

Army Form C. 2118.

WAR DIARY
or
INTELLIGENCE SUMMARY.

(Erase heading not required.)

John H Prosser
L/Col. R.A.M.C.
O.C. 130 (St. John) Fd. Amb.

Place	Date	Hour	Summary of Events and Information	Remarks and references to Appendices
PROVEN	22/11/16	P.M. 5.30	No sent to report. Left as Helmet Drill.	JHP
PROVEN	23/11/16		Visited + inspected new camp sites of 331st - 332nd Co's. A.S.C.	JHP
PROVEN	24/11/16		Capt. WOODHOUSE, reported from duty with the 13th WELSH. Lt. QMr. THOMPSON proceeded on leave 24/11/16 to 4/12/16	JHP
PROVEN	25/11/16		D.D.M.S. VIII Corps visits this Office, in reference to arrangement in force, in this Unit, for discharge to duty Sick men of the 38th Div.	JHP
PROVEN	26/11/16		Lieut. PEARSON. R.A.M.C posted for duty with 10th WELSH, as M.O. and taken off strength of this Unit. — Visited + inspected R.A.M.C. detachs., at MACHINE GUN FARM (1 NCO + 24 other ranks of this Unit) — inspected billets — sanitary arrangements, water supply, cooking arrangements, — Clothing, kit, rifles A.S.C. inspection. A.S.C. attached.	JHP
PROVEN	27/11/16		Capt. M. FFOULKES. R.A.M.C. reported from duty with the 10th WELSH Rgt. Proceeded for Helmet Drill. Visited 3rd Bn Laundry, — inspected camp, billets, kitchen, latrines &c.	JHP

2353 Wt. W2544/1454 700,000 5/15 D.D.&L. A.D.S.S./Forms/C. 2118.

WAR DIARY
or
INTELLIGENCE SUMMARY.

Army Form C. 2118.

John H. Davies Lt.Col. R.A.M.C.
O.C. 130 (S.) Bde. Field Amb.

Place	Date	Hour	Summary of Events and Information	Remarks and references to Appendices
PROVEN.	28/11/16		Capt. FFOULKES, R.A.M.C. proceeded to ENGLAND, at the expiration of his Contract, and is this day struck off, the strength of this Unit. Full "marching order" inspection held of men of this Unit.	JHD
PROVEN	29/11/16		Capt. A.W. ANDERSON. R.A.M.C. of this Unit, proceeded to ENGLAND, at the expiration of his Contract, and is this day struck off, the strength of this Unit. This Officer, arrived in joining this Unit, and joined on its Formation in December 1914. - Apart from his devoted duty, he has at all times, both in the training, and administration rendered conspicuous Service.	JHD
PROVEN	30/11/16		Nothing to record	JHD John H. Davies Lt.Col. R.A.M.C. O.C. 130 (S.) Field Ambulance 38th (Welsh) Division

CONFIDENTIAL

WAR DIARY

OF

130ᵀᴴ (Sᵀ JOHN) FIELD AMBULANCE

Vol 13

DEC 1ˢᵗ 1916   TO   DEC 31ˢᵗ 1916

COMMITTEE FOR THE
MEDICAL HISTORY OF THE WAR
Date 31 JAN. 1917

Army Form C. 2118.

WAR DIARY
or
INTELLIGENCE SUMMARY.

(Erase heading not required.)

John Darrell Lr
OC 130th Fd Amb

Instructions regarding War Diaries and Intelligence
Summaries are contained in F. S. Regs., Part II.
and the Staff Manual respectively. Title pages
will be prepared in manuscript.

Place	Date	Hour	Summary of Events and Information	Remarks and references to Appendices
PROVEN	1/12/16		A.D.M.S. visited trioludes & examined men recommended as T.U.	(Sgd)
PROVEN	2/12/16		Visited Laundry, COUTHOUVE, Drying rooms POPERINGHE, detachment of men at Kis Huis, employed at CANAL BANK, for purpose of inspection Pay.	(Sgd)
PROVEN	3/12/16		Visited suspected N Camp - 10th Welsh - Capt J. BURKE R.A.M.C. reports to OC. 13th R.W.F. for temporary duty.	(Sgd)
PROVEN	4/12/16		Inspection Rifles, Kit, Clothing, ASC (MT) attached.	(Sgd)
PROVEN	5/12/16		Capt. BURKE. R.A.M.C. reported from duty with 13th R.W.F. Capt. RIDDELL (H.Y.) R.A.M.C. Capt. HONEY. R.A.M.C. Lt. T.D RENNICK R.A.M.C. Lieut T. ROBERTSON R.A.M.C. reported for duty, & placed on Strength of this Field Ambulance from this date	(Sgd)
PROVEN	6/12/16		Capt. W.B. HONEY R.A.M.C. posted for duty with 14th R.W.F. this day struck off strength	(Sgd)

Army Form C. 2118.

WAR DIARY
or
INTELLIGENCE SUMMARY.

(Erase heading not required.)

John Saval W.S.
OC 133 Fd. John Fd Aud

Instructions regarding War Diaries and Intelligence Summaries are contained in F.S. Regs., Part II. and the Staff Manual respectively. Title pages will be prepared in manuscript.

Place	Date	Hour	Summary of Events and Information	Remarks and references to Appendices
PROVEN	7/12/16		Hon/Lt.Q.M. P.S.THOMPSON. reported from leave.	ADMS
PROVEN	8/12/16		Nil. Report to report	ADMS
PROVEN	9/12/16		Nothing to report.	ADMS
PROVEN	10/12/16		Inspection, Rifles, A.S.C. attached. O.C. 132 Field Ambulance visited site PROVEN, in reference to taking over.	ADMS
PROVEN	11/12/16		D.D.M.S. 2nd Army visited site of 133 Field Ambulance, with acting ADMS in reference, to taking over, and the possibility of converting site for use as D.R.S.	ADMS
PROVEN	12/12/16		Capt. D.H. GRIFFITHS. R.A.M.C. of this Unit, proceeded to England, on termination of his contract, and is this day, Struck off Strength of this Unit. One Officer, and 10 other ranks, proceeded, as Advance Party to HERZEELE. Advance Party from 132 Fd Amb. reported at PROVEN. A.D.M.S. 39 Div visited PROVEN.	ADMS

WAR DIARY or INTELLIGENCE SUMMARY

Army Form C. 2118.

John A Rowe Lt Col RAMC
OC 130(1/3 S.M.) Field Amb Ste

Place	Date	Hour	Summary of Events and Information	Remarks and references to Appendices
PROVEN	13/12/16	8.15	52 Men discharged to Duty from DRS by 4 M.A.C.	
		8.30	68 Men transferred to 131st DRS WORMHOUDT by 4 M.A.C.	
		9.00	Our Transport under Capt RIDDELL proceeded by road.	
		9.30	Und Subunes under Capt A. WOODHOUSE.	
		12 Noon	Handed over & followed necessary records - from Officer in Charge 132 Fd Amb. Sie HERZEELE, and little or nothing whatever little to take over on this Sie HERZEELE, and little or nothing had been done, since a section of this Und were stationed here in August/September 1916.	JARawe
HERZEELE	14/12/16		DADMS VIII Corps visited Ste	JARawe
HERZEELE	15/12/16		Acting ADMS 38th Divn - Lees Conference with OC 136 & OC 129th officers in charge 131st DRS and forward. Lieut RENWICK RAMC Lieut ROBERTSON RAMC officers und reported from Course of instruction on sanitation at HAZEBROUCK.	JARawe

WAR DIARY or INTELLIGENCE SUMMARY

Army Form C. 2118.

O.C. 130th (St John) Field Amb.

Place	Date	Hour	Summary of Events and Information	Remarks and references to Appendices
HERZEELE	17/12/16		No event to note	JSMD
HERZEELE	18/12/16		Capt. LORNIE. R.A.M.C. of this unit, with Lt. PEARSON R.A.M.C. N.O. 16th WELSH (Proceeded) to Sanitary School of Instruction HAZEBROUCK	JSMD
HERZEELE	19/12/16		D.D.M.S. VIII Corps visited Ambulance	JSMD
HERZEELE	20/12/16		No event to report; 2. H.D. drawn this day	JSMD
HERZEELE	21/12/16		No event to report	JSMD
HERZEELE	22/12/16		No event to report	JSMD
HERZEELE	23/12/16		Capt. LORNIE R.A.M.C. of this unit, reports from Sanitary School of Instruction HAZEBROUCK	JSMD
HERZEELE	24/12/16		No event to report	JSMD

WAR DIARY
INTELLIGENCE SUMMARY

Army Form C. 2118.

Place	Date	Hour	Summary of Events and Information	Remarks and references to Appendices
HERZEELE	25/12/16		Christmas Day. - C.K. 116 & exception of men employed at the Baths COUTHOVE, drying huts K.a.f. No COUTHOVE, the drying rooms POPERINGE, one NCO attaches to baths at BOLLEZEELE, the men of the unit spent the day together, the Officers, N.CO, & men of each section, dining together. In Hospital, every comfort was & no mass for the patients, 38 in number, most of whom were hurt of war fever.	82HD
HERZEELE	26/12/16	10 AM	C section under Capt. RIDDELL. RAMC, Lt. ROBERTSON. RAMC proceeded by motor lorries to HOULLE to open up a hospital strength 2 Officers & 69 other ranks, (RAMC. St. HTASC 9, MTASC 2	82HD
		9	& Transport of above, under Sergt. proceeded by road —	82HD
HERZEELE	27/12/16		Acting A.D.M.S. visited Field-Ambulance.	82HD
HERZEELE	28/12/16		visited detached section C. at HOULLE —	82HD

Army Form C. 2118.

WAR DIARY
or
INTELLIGENCE SUMMARY.

(Erase heading not required.)

Place	Date	Hour	Summary of Events and Information	Remarks and references to Appendices
HERZEELE	29/12/16		Visited 46 C.C.S.	
HERZEELE	30/12/16		Capt. WATSON H.C. reported 29/12/16 + returned to his unit	
HERZEELE	31/12/16		Nothing to report this day	

John N Daniel
Lt Col
OC 136 (1st/1st) Fd Amb

CONFIDENTIAL.

WAR DIARY

of

130th. (St. John) Field Ambulance.

From   January 1st.   1917.

To   January 31st.   1917.

Army Form C. 2118.

WAR DIARY
or
INTELLIGENCE SUMMARY.

(Erase heading not required.)

Maj. A Davies M.G. Rand O.C. 130 (St. John) Field Amb.

Instructions regarding War Diaries and Intelligence Summaries are contained in F.S. Regs., Part II and the Staff Manual respectively. Title pages will be prepared in manuscript.

Place	Date	Hour	Summary of Events and Information	Remarks and references to Appendices
HERZEELE	1/7/17		Inspection + Drill in Respirators Gas Helmets. Works HOULLE into acting A.D.M.S. Transport section attached for duty at hospital Duty there.	JAD
HERZEELE	2/7/17		Nothing to report	
HERZEELE	3/7/17		Acting A.D.M.S. visited Field Amb. - 16 stretchers T.U. or P.B. men.	JAD
HERZEELE	4/7/17		Nothing to report	JAD
HERZEELE	5/7/17		Instructions received to take over baths HERZEELE. These are provided with 15 m. sprays +	JAD
HERZEELE	6/7/17		capable of bathing 60 men per hour. Nothing to report	JAD
HERZEELE	7/7/17		Inspection A.S.C. rifles. Capt WATSON. R.A.M.C. posted to 13 W.L.I. Lieut Kaufman as R.M.O.	JAD
HERZEELE	8/7/17		Gas helmet Inspection, - Inspection of A.S.C. Rifles	JAD

2353 Wt. W2544/1454 700,000 5/15 D.D.&L. A.D.S.S./Forms/C. 2118.

Army Form C. 2118.

WAR DIARY
or
INTELLIGENCE SUMMARY.
(Erase heading not required.)

JOHN PARSELL/Lce. Rawl
OC. 130th (S.) Hy. Field Ambce.

Place	Date	Hour	Summary of Events and Information	Remarks and references to Appendices
HERZEELE	9/7/17		Detached N.C.O. & men 1st Div. Baths, Div. Dressing Room, returned to hand.	JGHD
HERZEELE	10/7/17		Acting A.D.M.S. visited Field Ambulance	JGHD
HERZEELE	11/7/17		No event to report	JGHD
HERZEELE	12/7/17		A.D.M.S. visited Field Ambulance. — Capt. WOODHOUSE RAMC with 10 other Ranks proceeded to CANAL BANK for the purpose of taking over from the 134th Field Ambce 39' Division the A.D.S. Advanced Dressing Station at SUSSEX FARM C.19.c.2.6., & at ESSEX FARM C.19.a.4.4. together with all Posts and one Reserve Dressing Station	JGHD RAMC OSC. No.26 dated 11/1/17 attached
HERZEELE	13/7/17		Advanced Party consisting of one Officer, and 10 other ranks proceeded to take over the Ambulance site at A.23.c.2.9. from 134. Field Ambce. 39' Div. 1 Officer and 20 other ranks of the 129 Field Ambce attached for duty to the 130th Field proceeded to CANAL BANK and relieve with party already posted there, the 134th Field Ambce in accordance with. ADMS RAMC order No 26.	JGHD

2353 Wt. W2544/1454 700,000 5/15 D. D. & L. A.D.S.S./Forms/C 2118.

Army Form C. 2118.

WAR DIARY
or
INTELLIGENCE SUMMARY.
(Erase heading not required.)

John H. Basset. L/Cpl. RAMC
OO 130(2/1st) Field Ambce

Place	Date	Hour	Summary of Events and Information	Remarks and references to Appendices
HERZEELE	14/7/17	A.M. 7.30	Transport proceeded to new Station, arriving 1.30 P.M	
		8.30	Patients transferred in our Cars, in two Cars from 4 M.A.C. temporarily attached for duty	
		9	Main body proceeded by Motor lorries to new Site at A.23.c.2.9.	
		12.30	Handed over field Ambulance Site at HERZEELE to 2/1 WESSEX Field Ambce of the 55th Div.	(98 H2)
ESSEX FARM & SUSSEX FARM and Main Dressing Station at A.23.c.2.9	15/7/17		Visited A.D.S. at ESSEX & SUSSEX FARM. - Arranged for cleaning, and further improvements there.	98 H2
A.23.c.2.9	16/7/17		Occupied in watering pathway, to Horse Standing at Main Dressing Station	98 H2
A.23.c.2.9	17/7/17		Capt. WATSON. R.A.M.C. Reported from 13th H.F./Ab.	98 H2
A.23.c.2.9	18/7/17		A.D.M.S. visited & inspected A.D.S.	98 H2

Army Form C. 2118.

WAR DIARY
or
INTELLIGENCE SUMMARY.
(Erase heading not required.)

J.C.D. McDavid
O.C. 130th Div. San. [Coy?]

Place	Date	Hour	Summary of Events and Information	Remarks and references to Appendices
A.23.C.2.9	19/1/17		Detailed 2 Corporals to attend School at Santelette. Visited 17 C.C.S.	J.C.D.
A.23.C.2.9	20/1/17		Capt. WATSON R.A.M.C. proceeded C. Section detached at EPERLECQUES to relieve Lt. Renwick R.A.M.C. proceeded on duty	J.C.D.
A.23.C.2.9	21/1/17		Lieut. RENWICK R.A.M.C. proceeded 16th R.W.F. which Bn. changed billets and is to relieve Lieut. COLT. R.A.M.C. attached placed on Sick list.	J.C.D.
A.13.C.2.9	22/1/17		Proceeded on leave — handed over to Major J.C. DAVIES R.A.M.C. of 1st/3rd S. Midland Amb. 131st F.A. looks temporarily 15 Command of 130th Field Ambce. 22nd	J.C.D.
A.23.e.2.9	23/1/17		A.D.M.S. 38th Division visited the unit, inspected the wards, made enquiries as to numbers of cases of Trench Foot reported. Stayed to Lunch. Inspected a Epi Hut as many officers as possible would attend read army medical meeting at BAILLEUL on Friday 26/1/17.	J.C.D.
A.23.e.2.9	24/1/17		D.D.M.S. VIII Corps, Col Girvard visited field ambulance and examined 7 cases of Trench Foot.	J.C.D.

Army Form C. 2118.

WAR DIARY
or
INTELLIGENCE SUMMARY.
(Erase heading not required.)

Instructions regarding War Diaries and Intelligence Summaries are contained in F.S. Regs., Part II. and the Staff Manual respectively. Title pages will be prepared in manuscript.

Place	Date	Hour	Summary of Events and Information	Remarks and references to Appendices
A 23. C.2.d.	24/11/17		Visited Field Cashier, & Obtain pay for Unit.	JPD.
"	25/11/17		Visited EPERLECQUES. 2 by O. Pickerin.	JPD.
	26/11/17		DDMS + ADDMS visit Corps, visited field Ambulance, examined all patients suffering from Trench foot & found trapped from Trench foot, destroyed by fire this morning. Attended medical meeting II army at BAILLEUL. SN Purry RAMC 131st Field Ambulance, a Board of Enquiry convened by Captain Evans, and Lieut Coll RAMC 130st Field Ambulance sat this morning to make enquiries into the circumstances under which the Hut was destroyed & assess the damages caused.	JPD.
	27/11/17		Attended Conference of O.C. Units at ADMS Office B Pritte at 3 p.m.	JPD.
	28/11/17		Visited ADS's, arranged for "Emergency Supply" of Rations, Firewood, and Medical Comforts borne home Captain Evans forwarded for duty of ESSEX FARM.	JPD.
	29/11/17		Made a minute investigation as to the supply of coal & wood for heating the patients quarters & found that the supply was totally inadequate.	JPD.
	30/11/17		ADMS visited unit. Acting upon his visited indoor visited ROUSSEL Fm. and enquired as to the accommodation for sick & wounded in the event of ESSEX and SUSSEX Fm. becoming untenable. Visited ELVERDINGHE CHATEAU and obtained instead with room for emergency and	JPD.

WAR DIARY
or
INTELLIGENCE SUMMARY.

Army Form C. 2118.

Place	Date	Hour	Summary of Events and Information	Remarks and references to Appendices
	31/1/17.		Medical comforts debited Lieut Major 6th RAMC to take medical charge of 16 NZR. Visited ROUSSELL T^m and ELVERDINGHE CHATEAU & completed arrangement. Received from ADMS list of articles to be stored at ELVERDINGHE CHATEAU.	108.

J O'Farrell Major RAMC

Confidential.

War Diary

of the

130th (St John) Field Ambulance.

38th (Welsh) Division.

From February 1st to February 28th.

1917.

Army Form C. 2118.

WAR DIARY
or
INTELLIGENCE SUMMARY.
(Erase heading not required.)

John Shaw David McFarland
OC 130th Field Amb.
J.C. DAVIES. Maps RAMC 131 Fd Amb
(Acting OC - 16/1/2/17)

Place	Date	Hour	Summary of Events and Information	Remarks and references to Appendices
A 23. c 2 9	1/2/17.		Visited ELVERDINGHE CHATEAU and completed arrangements for storage of Emergency Equipment. Lieut Myles Lat. R.A.M.C. returned to Field Ambulance from 16"Nrbol, being replaced by Capt. Hamilton R.A.M.C. Ants - one craft shell fell through roof of N°1 hut, intended for emergency dressing and medical stores for ADS's on Canal Bank.	JCD
	2/2/17.		Col. J.J. Morgan ADMS 38' (Welsh) Division visited the unit, addressed all the officers & men, informing them of his appointment DDMS. Cavalry Corps. Captain Hawthorne, and Lieut Myles Lat. R.A.M.C. attended a meeting of the medical society of the 2nd Army, where a paper was read on "Trench Foot".	JCD
	3/2/17		Received instructions from ADMS to find one to HAZEBROUCK to meet Col. Gill the new ADMS 38' Division. He did not turn up.	JCD
	4/2/17		Received fresh orders from ADMS regarding the action to be taken in case of an advance or retirement.	JCD
	5/2/17.		In accordance with ADMS circular memo. 38 DM/566. 30.1.17 Visited all Regimental Aid Posts fixed by the ADS's.	JCD
	6/2/17		Anti Air Craft Shell once cafo fell in B ward. Saw ADMS re shortage of fuel.	JCD

Army Form C. 2118.

WAR DIARY
or
INTELLIGENCE SUMMARY.
(Erase heading not required.)

John Sam Davies W.Col
O.C. 130 (St John) Fd Amb

Instructions regarding War Diaries and Intelligence Summaries are contained in F.S. Regs., Part II. and the Staff Manual respectively. Title pages will be prepared in manuscript.

Place	Date	Hour	Summary of Events and Information	Remarks and references to Appendices
A 23 c.2.9	4/7/17		Lieut Myles Cutts attended "Preliminary Inquiry" at HERTZEELE into a charge of drunkenness against a man of the 39th Bn. S.C.	
			Reported from leave 6/7/17. - 1502 overs from Major J.C. Davies. Acting OC 7/7/17	
			A.D.M.S. 39th Div. D.A.D.M.S. visited Station	82 AD
A 23 C.2.9	8/7/17		No special report.	82 HD
A 23 C.2.9	9/7/17		To COUTHOVE to draw 7,500 ft. for Bay - Attended 2nd Army Medical Society - 3 Canadian CCS. Words of Course by Major W.A. GARDNER C.A.M.C.	82 HD
A 23 C.2.9	10/7/17		Visited ESSEX FARM, and SUSSEX FARM ADS's., Rewards for service in field CROIX DE GUERRE awarded to 45916 L/Cpl. GWILYM IVOR REES 130th Field Amb	82 AD
A 23 C 2.9	11/7/17		No special report. Divine Service. 6. P.M.	82 AD
A 23 C.2.9	12/7/17		A.D.M.S. visited Main Dressing Station	82 AD

2353 Wt. W2544/1454 700,000 5/15 D.D.& L. A.D.S.S./Forms/C. 2118.

Army Form C. 2118.

WAR DIARY
or
INTELLIGENCE SUMMARY.
(Erase heading not required.)

John 2h Barnes
Lt Col RAMC

Place	Date	Hour	Summary of Events and Information	Remarks and references to Appendices
A23 C.2.9.	13/2/17		No Events to report.	JSHD
A23 C.2.9	14/2/17.		Conference at A.D.M.S. Office.	JSHD
A23 C.2.9	15/2/17		With A.D.M.S. 38th Div. Visited & Inspected C. Section of this Unit at EPERLECQUES found Hospital run by this Section, well equipped in good order, Inspected billets and Personnel, Sanitary Arrangements, horse lines, Wagon lines, — D.D.M.S. VIII Corps Visited Main Station 130th F Amb. Visits D.M.S. 2nd Army at - HAZEBROUCK, and was notified that the Section (C) would shortly be released.	JSHD
A23 C.2.9	16/2/17		Visited Camp of 11th S.W.B. Capt. WOODHOUSE, R.A.M.C. of this Unit relieved Lt. PEASON, R.A.M.C. took over temporary Charge of 10th WELSH Lt. PEARSON R.A.M.C.	JSHD
A23 C.2.9	17/2/17		Lt. PEARSON R.A.M.C. reported to M.O. 11 S.W.B. for instruction in duties as R.M.O	JSHD

WAR DIARY
or
INTELLIGENCE SUMMARY.

Army Form C. 2118.

John H Dawes
OC 136th (S) Field Amb

Place	Date	Hour	Summary of Events and Information	Remarks and references to Appendices
A23c2.9	17/7/17	5-7 P.M.	Visited A.D.S. Essex Farm & Sussex Farm, with D.A.D.M.S. - made Arrangements for evacuation of wounded into G.O.C 113 & 113½ in the area of 14th R.W & Saw M.O. 14th R.W & and Officer in Charge of A.D.S, and Aid Posts of 15th R.W at Main Dressing Station. Arranged that 30 beds in ward A here vacated for reception of wounds - all convalescent patients invalided to Mons's Dressing Hall. D.A.D.M.S. arranged to stand-by at A.D.S. that arrangements with 4 M.A.C. for Cars to remain night at Main Dressing Station	15 R.W.D 113 B½ 15 R.W.D 8 R.W.D 8 H.D 8 H.D
A23 c2.9	18/7/17		Between 35. 40 wounded admitted, incl early morning, largely (not 14 R.W.D.) in afternoon to No 46 C.C.S	8 H.D 8 H.D
A23 C2.9	19/7/17		No event to record	8 H.D
A 23 C2.9	30/7/17	2.30 PM	Conference at A.D.M.S. Office	8 H.D

WAR DIARY
or
INTELLIGENCE SUMMARY.
(Erase heading not required.)

Army Form C. 2118.

[Signatures at top right:]
John D. Duval
J/Col R.A.M.C.
O.C. 130th St Johns Field Amb

Place	Date	Hour	Summary of Events and Information	Remarks and references to Appendices
A.23.C.2.9	21/2/17		Conference at A.D.M.S' Office.	JNZ
A.23.C.2.9	22/2/17		Capt J. BURKE R.A.M.C. reported from Base, detailed between Follestone + Boulogne. Visited A.D.S.'s, Shafeits.	JNZ
A.23.C.2.9	23/2/17		A.D.M.S visits Main Dressing Station.	JNZ
A.23.C.2.9	24/2/17		Men paid. Visited A.D.S, Inspected all Posts at Canal Bank.	JNZ
A.23.C.2.9	25/2/17	5.19 am	Wire received from Officer in Charge of A.D.S. at Canal Bank "Many have been wounded expected" & the Motor Cars sent to A.D.S. — 150 (first wounded) from the Raid by the Enemy, arrived at A.D.S. between 5.30 to 6 am. The Earliest arrived at Main Dressing Station at 6 am. In all, in quick succession 27 Cases were admitted, from following units 19th WELSH 14 , 14 L. R.W.F. 10 , 16 R.W.F. 2 , 113 M.G.C. 1 , 19 R.W.F. 1(one) at R.D.S. Character of Cases — one Death in man of 19 R.W.F (Surname of Case, 1 Six Moderate Serve + the remainder of Slightly Disposed of Cases as Mullen H60 UBO Pvy Serve, Six Moderate	JNZ

2353 Wt. W2544/1454 700,000 5/15 D.D.&L. A.D.S.S/Forms/C. 2118.

Army Form C. 2118.

WAR DIARY
or
INTELLIGENCE SUMMARY.
(Erase heading not required.)

JOHSH Davod
W.G.Raine OC 130 of July Trans On

Place	Date	Hour	Summary of Events and Information	Remarks and references to Appendices
A23C2.9	25/3/17		Lieut Robertson Raine with 31 other ranks, reported from 7ck. at EPERLECQUES. Visited 14 M.A.C. Examined 14 Candidates for S.1.B.D. Voucher	
A23C2.9	26/3/17		Capt WATSON, R.A.M.C. in charge of Transport, +17 other ranks reported from EPERLECQUES. 129th Men from A.D.S. returned to their Unit. Visited Transport lines of 13" R.W.F. - one Private proceeded to DDMS	
A23C2.9	27/3/17		Capt. WATSON, R.A.M.C proceeded to HAZEBROUCK for course in Sanitary Science. Org NCO + 2 other ranks posted to Baths at A.30. Visited Incinerator Baths at A.30, Cook house + Billets for the Baths Personnel.	
A23C2.9	28/3/17		Conference at A.D.M.S. Office	

JOHSH Davod WGRaine
OC 130 of July Eng

Confidential

War Diary

of

130th (St John) Field Ambulance

38th (Welsh) Division

From March 1st 1917

to March 31st 1917

WAR DIARY or INTELLIGENCE SUMMARY

Army Form C. 2118.

John H. Davies
Lt Col R.A.M.C.
O.C. 130' (St John) Fld Amb[?]

Place	Date	Hour	Summary of Events and Information	Remarks and references to Appendices
A 23 C 2.9	1/3/17		Visited A.D.S's. ESSEX, SUSSEX FARMS, - these and Post worked also by A.D.M.S. Capt. BURNE W/WINNER [?] - 9 pm.	
A 23 C 2.9	2/3/17		Capt. BURNE, Capt. LORNIE of this Unit, attended lecture at 10 C.C.S. of whom paper read by Capt. J.A. RYLE on "Some notes on the treatment of Casualties, due to Asphyx. Gas".	
A 23 C 2.9	3/3/17		Capt. WATSON. Officers [?] Unit, reported from School of Sanitation All Officers, NCO's, Nurs-., with Communal and Patients, has their respirators tested in Chamber with lacrymal Gas.	
A 23 C 2.9	4/3/17		Lt. PEARSON. R.A.M.C. of this Unit, proceeded to 13th WELSH to Temporary relieve Lt. REYNOLDS. Capt. WATSON. R.A.M.C. to 14 R.W.F. to relieve (temp) Capt. HONEY R.A.M.C. Unit visited by Gen. MARDEN. C.M.G. acting G.O.C. †A.A. Q.M.G. [?]	

Army Form C. 2118.

WAR DIARY
or
INTELLIGENCE SUMMARY.
(Erase heading not required.)

John Raad
WAIKANE
OC 130 (S.198m) Field Amb

Place	Date	Hour	Summary of Events and Information	Remarks and references to Appendices
A23 C29 5/2/17	5/2/17	3 PM	In accordance with A.D.M.S. orders, a Medical board assembled at this Field Ambulance, this day, for the purpose of examining 13 P.B. details. – President, Lieut. T.E.H. DAVIES. R.A.M.C. Members Capt. A. JONES R.A.M.C. D.A.D.M.S. 36th Bde., Capt. T. BURKE R.A.M.C. 130th S.W. Borders. The Condition of the 13th P.B. men, was found in each case, unchanged. The Proceedings of the Board, in triplicate were forwarded to the A.D.M.S. 49 Div.	
A23 C29 6/2/17	6/2/17		Lt. PEARSON. R.A.M.C. proceeded on special trans. with O.C. 131st Field Ambulance (acting A.D.M.S.) the Doctors visited Regimental Aid Posts at BELLE ALLIANCE, also worked line, at the WILLOWS. arrangement made, with R.E.'s to erect Regimental Aid Post, at the WILLOWS. the work to be done by R.A.M.C. Personnel working in 4 hour shifts from 6 a.m. to 6 P.M. & additional R.A.M.C. proceeded to A.D.S. ESSEX FARM arrangements made to relieve 16 (INCESTOR) men of the 129th Field Amb used with the construction of the Aid Post.	

2353 Wt. W2544/1454 700,000 5/15 D.D.&L. A.D.S.S./Forms/C. 2118.

WAR DIARY
or
INTELLIGENCE SUMMARY.

Army Form C. 2118.

JOAB 21st Army
J.W.E.V. Rawe OC 136 Fld Amb

Place	Date	Hour	Summary of Events and Information	Remarks and references to Appendices
A 28 C 2.9	6/2/17		(Continued) Acting A.D.M.S. visited (31st Lan Amb) whose cases for P.B. & T.V. were sent by us.	
A 23 C 2.9	7/2/17		With Acting A.D.M.S. + A.D.M.S. visited Aid Posts at LANCASTER FM, inspected all trolley lines & left of line laid by this division. D.D.M.S. VIII Corps visited Main Dressing Station	
A 23 C 2.9	8/2/17		All Stores inspected by Officer of 151 R.E. Special approval for this July.	
A 23 C 2.9	9/2/17		Lieut ROBERTSON. R.A.M.C. of this unit, took over temporary charge as M.O. 13 RWF in place of Capt. HADLEY. R.A.M.C. proceeded on Special leave. Lt. BANKES. R.A.M.C. relieved Lt. ROBERTSON in the duties of Sanitary Officer Canal Bank. Incorporation at Baths laundry at A. 30 inspection by M.O. of this unit, + Refreshments, + P.H. Helmets tested	

WAR DIARY or INTELLIGENCE SUMMARY

Army Form C. 2118.

John H. Barnes Lt Col RAMC
OC. 136th (St John) Field Amb.

Place	Date	Hour	Summary of Events and Information	Remarks and references to Appendices
A23C29	10/3/17		Acting A.D.M.S. visited main Dressing Station. Capt. WATSON RAMC attached temporary to A.D.S. to relieve Lt. ROBERTSON RAMC attached temporary to 13. R.W.F.	82MD
A23C29	11/3/17		Visited Bath - A.30, ED Camp.	82MD
		10.45	Capt. WOODHOUSE R.A.M.C. of this unit, attached to 10th WELSH, reported sick temporary detained. - M.O. from 129th Fd Amb sent to act as temp M.O. 10th Welsh. Fire occurred in Armstrong hut, occupied by Capt. Burke, R&M.C. of this unit. Alarm given unnecessarily by Police Picket. - Fire Picket called out, and fire extinguished at about 11 P.M. - Canvas of Ant. Grahoves, also Officers Kit, Remainder of hut not seriously damaged. - Probable cause spark from chimney of stove setting fire to roof.	82MD
A23C29	12/3/17		Capt. LORNIE RAMC to A.D.S. to relieve Lt. COLT. RAMC who returned to headquarters.	82MD
A23C29	13/3/17		Court of Inquiry held at this Field Ambce as to cause of fire, - President Lt. Col. W.B. EDWARDS 129th Field Ambce Enquiry of Court forwarded A.D.M.S. - Visited A.D.S, + held inquiry into complaint, re. SUSSEX FARM	82MD

Army Form C. 2118.

WAR DIARY
or
INTELLIGENCE SUMMARY.
(Erase heading not required.)

John Stewart
Major RAMC
OC 130th (St John) Field Amb.

Place	Date	Hour	Summary of Events and Information	Remarks and references to Appendices
A.23.c.3.9	14/3/17		No event to report. Visited A.D.S.	JS MO
A.23.c.2.9	15/3/17		Received orders of G.S. 4584	JS MO
A.23.c.2.9	16/3/17		Received A.D.M.S. routine orders 248 - 251. Dated 15/3/17. Capt. LORNIE. R.A.M.C + Lt COLT R.A.M.C. attended books at 50 C.C.S. HALTBROUCK.	JS MO
A.23.c.2.9	17/3/17		No event to report.	JS MO
A.23.c.2.9	18/3/17		Lt. PEARSON R.A.M.C. reported from base	JS MO
A.23.c.2.9	19/3/17		Visited A.D.S Essex Farm. - Lt. Robertson R.A.M.C. took over temporary charge 15 West vice Capt. SODEN R.A.M.C. evacuated to Hospital. Lt. PEARSON R.A.M.C. to A.D.S	JS MO

WAR DIARY or INTELLIGENCE SUMMARY

Army Form C. 2118.

[Heading handwritten: A/DDMS 19th Corps? / O.C. 130 (S)Fd.Amb? Fd. Amb]

(Erase heading not required.)

Place	Date	Hour	Summary of Events and Information	Remarks and references to Appendices
A.23.C.2.9	20/5/17		Capt. WOODHOUSE R.A.M.C. returned to duty with 10th WELSH, Equipment Inspected	JSHD
A.23.C.2.9	21/5/17		Mess Tin Inspection. Rifle Inspection.	JSHD
A.23.C.2.9	22/3/17	10.30 am	Brigadier General B. ATKINSON, D.A.Q.M.G. VIII Corps, Inspected Fd. Ambce. with Lt. Colonel H.M PRYCE-JONES AA & QMG 38th Division & proposed Evacuation with worksome, Ambulance roster & MT Camp Erection & Powers, Horses &c. Visited A.D.S's ESSEX - SUSSEX FARM, and R.A. Posts on Canal Bank. a number of Casualties evacuated from 10th Welsh, 22 Evacuated to 46 C.C.S	JSHD
A.23.C.2.9	23/3/17		Inspection of Saddlery. Discd. Ramc, MTASC. +HTASC, inspection of Road Gals	JSHD
A.23.C.2.9	24/3/17		Inspection of Shoes - all Ramc, MTASC. +HTASC, — Main Evacuating Station Inspected. A.D.M.S.	JSHD
A.23.C.2.9	25/3/17		Trucks 46 C.C.S. take D.R.S. 38th Bn. — Brow Pan —	JSHD

Army Form C. 2118.

WAR DIARY
or
INTELLIGENCE SUMMARY.
(Erase heading not required.)

[Signature] for Rame
OC (130) St. John Stan Ambce

Place	Date	Hour	Summary of Events and Information	Remarks and references to Appendices
A23C2.9	26/3/17		Visited A.D.S.'s ESSEX, SUSSEX Fus. & Ardfort in Canal Bank.	
A23C2.9	27/3/17		No. Sent to report.	
A23C2.9	28/3/17		D.D.M.S. VIII Corps. Visited HdQrs Aubers Site	
A23C2.9	29/3/17		Sergt. Price, & Sergt. Rump sent to 2nd Army Gas School OXALEARE.	
A23C2.9	30/3/17		D.M.S. 2nd Army accompanied by D.D.M.S. DADMS VIII Corps ADMS DADMS Sgt. Division, Visited inspected the Main Dressing Station of this Stan Ambce The D.M.S. at conclusion of his inspection expressed his satisfaction. He agrees that the site was suitable for the erection of additional accommodation.	
A23C2.9	31/3/17		No sent to report.	

[Signature] for Rame
OC 130 (St. John) Stan Ambce

Confidential

Vol 17

War Diary

of

130th (St John) Field Amb.

COMMITTEE FOR THE
MEDICAL HISTORY OF THE WAR
Date 6 JUN. 1917

From 1st April 17 To 30th April 17

WAR DIARY or INTELLIGENCE SUMMARY

Army Form C. 2118.

OC. B.S.(?) John 123rd Amb

Place	Date	Hour	Summary of Events and Information	Remarks and references to Appendices
A.23.C.2.9	1/4/17		Main Bearing Station visited 31/3/17 (after bar from for march last Sun seater) by G.O.C. 3th Div, AA.& QMG. Sgt. - O/C Expressed satisfaction with condition of Ambulance. Water 46 C.C.S.	JER
A.23.C.2.9	2/4/17		Rfle Inspection. A.S.C. Kit inspection A.S.C.	JER
A.23.C.2.9	3/4/17		Lecture on Flies & Their prevention by Capt. Lowie. Rawe, MT.ASC, & NTASC. Main Dressing Station. Weekly Inspection of Latrines, 2nd Army.	JER
A.23.C.2.9	4/4/17		A.D.M.S. Visited A.D.S's + Aid Posts at Canal Bank.	JER
A.23.C.2.9	5/4/17		Visited and inspected 122 Bde. R.F.A. at REIGERSBURG. CHATEAU and TROIS TOURS mess arrangements for early improvement of Kitchen, Ablution Places & Sanitary Conditions at these Sites - looked NCO Privates to carry out such improvements. Special Parade of lieut attached, inspection & drills, & Reparatoin. F.H. Aelwels.	JER

WAR DIARY
INTELLIGENCE SUMMARY

Army Form C. 2118.

John Evans
W.Col RAMC OC 156th John FieldAmb

Place	Date	Hour	Summary of Events and Information	Remarks and references to Appendices
A23C3.9	6/4/17		Attended Medical Society meeting at 17 C.C.S. - papers read by Capt. DC TAYLOR, M.C. on Gunshot wounds of the large Intestine, & Capt. L. DICKSON, J.M. later, on Strength of these lines, masterly an instructive.	J/NR
A23C3.9	7/4/17		Capt. WAC	
A23C2.9	7/4/17		Capt. WOODHOUSE. R.A.M.C. taken off strength & posted to 10th W'sh Lt. ROBERTSON R.A.M.C. taken off Strength & posted to 15th W'sh O.C. 3rd Divisional Train visited Mules & Horses Visited A.D.S's ESSEX, SUSSEX FR's also REIGERSBURG CHATEAU, inspected work done by R.A.M.C of this line.	J/NR
A23C2.9	8/4/17		Attended Conference at A.D.M.S's Office. Capt. MELHUISH/7th R.A.M.C. reported taken on Strength, on transfer 8/4/17.	J/NR
A23 C2.9	9/4/17		No Signal to report	J/NR
A23C2.9	10/4/17		Lt. D.A.D.M.S. 38th Div. Med. Dr. HUTCHINSON (A.D.M.S.) in 1st American Conv Gen	J/NR

Army Form C. 2118.

WAR DIARY
or
INTELLIGENCE SUMMARY.

(Erase heading not required.)

Instructions regarding War Diaries and Intelligence Summaries are contained in F. S. Regs., Part II and the Staff Manual respectively. Title pages will be prepared in manuscript.

Place	Date	Hour	Summary of Events and Information	Remarks and references to Appendices
A.23.c.2.9	19/4/17		Continued. — Capt. COPELAND. D.S.O. 2nd Army. —	
		3.30	Attended Conference of D.D.M.S., A.D.M.S's, O.C's. Field Ambce At 35 Divisional Rest Station 1b. South Lane. Field Ambce. The D.D.M.S. drew attention to: — (1) the importance of (1) Gas Helmet Drill (2) O.C's ?? Ambulances keeping in constant touch with R.M.O. + Emergency R.M.O to visit their Cases in Field Ambces + keeping up their interest in them from them. (3) the possibility of better diagnosis in Field Ambces of Cases sent in as P.U.O. — the records of Such, the Classification of Such. Its also brought to the importance of scrutiny + checking B.R.C.S loan. — the drawing of Sufficients from Artillerous Places + better — After Conference inspected the post Station — which has had a very useful + simple Construction incinerator, in which waste heat is utilized in making a very Efficient Drying room. Several other points which have been allocated 2nd Army School of Musketry proposals at Headquarters looking by Capt. LORNIE RAMC on leave (Standoff being)	

John Sir Pownal
J.C.A Pownal

2353 Wt. W2544/1454 700,000 5/15 D.D.&L. A.D.S.S./Forms/C. 2118.

WAR DIARY

INTELLIGENCE SUMMARY

Army Form C. 2118.

John Daniel McRae
O.C. 130 (St John) Fd Ambce

Place	Date	Hour	Summary of Events and Information	Remarks and references to Appendices
A23 C 2.9	11/4/17	6.30 AM	Left HQ of the Fd Ambce with North O.D.M.S. — Radius, inspected area where Canal Bank for the purpose of Salving Site, where wounded (lying) cases to brought to trolley and trams, and posts loaded in Motor Ambulances. The point Selected was B 23 A 9.9 near cross roads. Arrangements are made to LOADING POST putting the Station in proper repair, viz - Sand-bagging, draining, putting a buried layer, + ½ an Elephant in front —. Inspected Trolley Line, to save from Canal Bank, work R.A.P. Posts on Canal, ESSEX, SUSSEX. A.D.S.'s visited and inspected work done by the head at REIGERSBURG CH[AT] B23 A 9.9 - recon[noite]red, approaches, B40 gates. Drill in Box Respirators - Lecture on Saving.	BMcR
A23 C 2.9	12/4/17	5.30 AM	A.D.M.S. DADMS visited this Ambulance, outlined up to A.D.S. for the night	BMcR
A23 C 2.9	13/4/17			
A23 C 2.9	14/4/17	10.16 AM	Tac. Gas alarm received 10.16am by Telephone, at the same time a Short-bus Horn, and other alarms in adjacent camps were heard. Immediate Scentries at this Camp, Sounded Alarm, and within 10 or 15 seconds, Men Officer, NCO, Man of the Unit, + attaches + Patients, had their Gas Respirators on, with the exception of two

2353 Wt. W2544/1454 700,000 5/15 D. D. & L. A.D.S.S. Forms/C. 2118.

Army Form C. 2118.

WAR DIARY
or
INTELLIGENCE SUMMARY
(Erase heading not required.)

Jo L.G. McGrane
OC. 130' (S.John) Field Amb.

Place	Date	Hour	Summary of Events and Information	Remarks and references to Appendices
A23C29	14/4/17	10.16 am	(Continued) two patients in hospital, who were suffering from less T scalp wounds, and who had been instructed by the M.O. in Charge, to put on their P.H. Helmets, when the alarm was given. Three cases of Bronchitis in hospital, were found to be able to wear their Respirators without difficulty. Two base wounded patients, gas casualties, on Stretchers, also got on their Respirators in this time. Even going has a great — The alarm were heard throughout the Camps. Skeleton 116 Horse lines were visited + inspected by an Officer, already detailed for that Duty, on his arrival. He found Bn/man, working with his Respirator properly fitted, and even horses has a nose bag on, filled with wet hay. The S.M. of A.S.C. reported that every man, has his respirator on in 1/2 seconds. All Officers + N.C.O. Continued to carry out, their duties, and were able to give the necessary orders during the 16 minutes. Box Respirators were worn, by a pre-arranged order, no Respirators were removed, until the OC gave a long whistle, at the end of 16 minutes after the alarm — The hooters were replaced some	

WAR DIARY
INTELLIGENCE SUMMARY

Army Form C. 2118.

John A Rowe? Lt Col RAMC
OC 130 (?) (late) Field Amb?

Place	Date	Hour	Summary of Events and Information	Remarks and references to Appendices
A23C2.9	14/4/17	AM 10.16	(Continued) "Tear Gas Glasses" replaced. Same in cases & worn in Albert Portion. The smoke labels were written up to date. The number of patients at the hospital area 1 Officer & 72 Other Ranks.	JG N.T.
		2 PM	Visited & inspected Sanitary Cookhouses, Latrines + Billets of 11th M.G.C.	JG N.T.
A23C2.9	15/4/17		Received R.A.M.C. order No 28 15/4/17. Visited A.D.S. SUSSEX, ESSEX F.M., and arranged for the handing over of the A.D.S. at ESSEX F.M. to a party from a Field Ambulance of the 39th Division on the 16/4/17. Visited F Camp. - Road Construction Co. (Capt. Dooley?) and arranged for the water-supply Trav - who appear to be absolutely ignorant of such rules, to report at the Dressing Station for instruction. Water Carts to instruction. OC 133 9th Aus. 39 Div. as J.S. this Camp.	JG N.T.
A23C2.9	16/4/17		ESSEX Fm A.D.S. handed over to 133 Field Amb	JG N.T.

WAR DIARY
or
INTELLIGENCE SUMMARY

Army Form C. 2118.

John B R Dwyer
Lt Col
OC 1/6th (?) Bn Seaforth

Place	Date	Hour	Summary of Events and Information	Remarks and references to Appendices
	17/4/17	12 noon	DDMS with "Lord Evelyn CECIL" visits. Mr Drewry Palison [?] made a short inspection. Interviewed a number of wounded.	
		3.30	Meeting of ADMS's OC Field Ambce DADMS of 3rd, 39th, 55th Divisions at Hqs 51st Ambce. DDMS brought forward several points that he wished to draw attention to — (1) Inclined to declare stunned by RWO — If rifle used as Splint? Co-Rds Spt Bns used? — Stokes are one Perfection. 25th [?] have patients sent down with the Greatcoats put up — on account of the fact that evidence rather puts on Sh Butn to increase the Shock. Always present through loss of Blood. If they become Kld Clothes can be left on. A rifle or Kerbg used as Splint is grating. Our horses at the spot, and put on a dressing, and army ground drags fetlow egg.	

WAR DIARY or INTELLIGENCE SUMMARY

Army Form C. 2118.

[Heading] 2/4th Battn. Welsh Regt. 53rd (Welsh) Div. (indistinct)

Place	Date	Hour	Summary of Events and Information	Remarks and references to Appendices
A22C29	17/4/17		(2) The importance of frequent inspection of Iron rations, Blankets, Haversack clothing etc. (3) The importance of watching water supply — present supplies scanty & (reports) pure and from deep wells — No research for small quantity of HSSO4 in pumps. (4) Each Field Ambulance Store has a reserve of 5000 dressings. (Other H.Q Stores i.e. Shell dressings) over & above equipment dressings, & other members of the working visited inspected this Ambulance.	
		PM 5.30	Until less in to (indistinct) by the ADMS, who after, presented the Ribbon of the Cour-St-Somme. to L/Corp. REES. (48176. GWILYM. IVOR. 1. to Services he on 10/7/16 & 11/7/16, in daylight, volunteered, with another man, and carried water, rations and dressings to a dug out which was isolated, and under heavy shell fire, where between 40–50 wounded were collected by Capt. WALLACE R.A.M.C. at & L/Cpl WELSH & to for 36 hours, between showers, the men, carried, own wounded across the open — On 12/7/16. although wounded in both arms, he cheered, under heavy shell fire in front of CATTERPILLAR WOOD, in the open, three other wounded men, wounded by the same shell as himself, one of whom had both legs blown off the knee. L/Cpl REES stepped by dressed these men, and remained with them until they could be moved to shelter — All though the attack, this man showed extra-ordinary bravery." The above was (indistinct) to us, at the time was read by the ADMS, from an (indistinct) ...	

WAR DIARY
or
INTELLIGENCE SUMMARY

(Erase heading not required.)

Army Form C. 2118.

John H Dawes
OC (30th/John) W.G. Neame Staff Capt

Place	Date	Hour	Summary of Events and Information	Remarks and references to Appendices
A 28 C.3.9	16/4/17		Visited REIGERSBURG CHATEAU and in Company with the M.O. Capt. MEADEN R.A.M.C. inspected Cook Houses of R.F.A. 122-, + Infantry stationed there, also all sanitary arrangements in this camp. — The improvements made by the same N.C.O. in charge of this unit, are maintained. — The incinerator requires rebuilding, and Cook House used by Infantry is much below standard required. — Same M.O. TROIS TOURS CHATEAU occupied by Divas reported with marked improvements in the 121st R.F.A., VII Corps Cyclists – There ofhaus Conditions of all Cook Houses, — Sanitary Arrangements are good, — a better room is required, and I have been able to obtain for them a Zinc bath — I also visited in Company of M.O. the MACHINE GUN FARM. — one Cook house is required. The others very much below Satisfactory Condition, the 17th R.W.F. now in a very Satisfactory Condition	JSHD
A 28 C 3.9	19/4/17		Visited STEENJE FARM. — The Sanitary Condition of the Camp requires early improvement much reform. — occupied by 38th T.M.B. Transferred of 119th R.F.A. This Camp has every bad approach, is ankle deep in Damage purposes and the Camp is standing in water mud. — The Kitchen hut is dirty lastly requires lime-washing. — The water supply wants further investigation. — They have no water cart. —	JSHD

WAR DIARY
or
INTELLIGENCE SUMMARY

Army Form C. 2118.

Instructions regarding War Diaries and Intelligence Summaries are contained in F. S. Regs., Part II. and the Staff Manual respectively. Title Pages will be prepared in manuscript.

(Erase heading not required.)

136th (2/5th) Field Ambulance
Lt Col Rowe . O.C.

Place	Date	Hour	Summary of Events and Information	Remarks and references to Appendices
A 23 C 2.9	20/1/17		No event, in Suss Corps -	JSHD
A 22 C 2.9	21/1/17	6 AM	Visited Loading Station at B 23 a 9.9, two Steel Dug outs (Elephants) have been erected and progress has been made in Sewa begging post. Inspected roads + trenches in this Area. - K.S. proceeded along WINDSOR CASTLE holler line, past BELMONT DUMP to Bridge 6.W. - along bank, inspected kitchen, to SUSSEX FARM. - returned via Sussex Corner. - Rfle depredn a SB.	JSHD
A 23 C 2.9	22/1/17		Visited Inspected Divisional Bomb Store Camp - Sanitary Cholera Satisfactory. Ordered a Bus Latrines. Inspected Ambulance Site.	JSHD
A 23 C 2.9	23/1/17	5.45 AM	Visited Loading Station at B 23 a 9.9 with A.D.M.S, D.A.D.M.S, who also inspected. proceeded along WINDSOR CASTLE holler, to Bridge 6.W. - Inspected FARGATE TRENCH & Sheber Site suitable for R.A.P. - returned to Bridge 6.W. remained for Site at C 13 01.2 to be used for advanced Dugout to R.A.M.C. visited SUSSEX FARM.	JSHD
A 23 C 2.9	24/1/17		Lieut H.S.A. HOGG RAMC Reported for duty, taken on strength of this Unit as from this date; Capt WATSON RAMC posted to 16 R.W.F as M.O. struck off strength of this Unit from this date.	JSHD

2449 Wt. W14957/M90 750,000 1/16 J.B.C. & A. Forms/C.2118/12

WAR DIARY
or
INTELLIGENCE SUMMARY

Army Form C. 2118.

(Erase heading not required.)

John 2nd Baron
J.G. Rowe

Place	Date	Hour	Summary of Events and Information	Remarks and references to Appendices
A23 C2.9	25/4/17	5.45 am	W.th QM. visited bathing station, and Canal Bank, made arrangements with R.E. Officer for packets & Dugout at C13c 1½. Used AD.M.S. visited from Bathing station as additional Aid Post	
A23 C2.9	26/4/17	6 AM	With Asst. Brigade visited Canal Bank — Saw G.O.C 113th Brigade, and other Officers from various Regiments to erect into Dumps & Sappers Supplementary Dug out, to be known as Fusilier Aid Post at C13 C 1.2. Also arranged for Aid Post, at C13 a 4.5.	
A23 C2.9	27/4/17		Visited & Inspected TROIS TOURS CHATEAU now occupied. Inspected all Cookhouses, latrines, ablutions, water supplies and Sanitary arrangements, all found Satisfactory. Also visited & Inspected Infantry Camp now occupied by 17th Northumberland Fusiliers. The Sanitary arrangements are Satisfactory but Cookhouse, needs to be made & cookhouse – and all drains cleared when not to be used – This Camp has been previously visited by me & Brig. J Australian found to be Satisfactory. There is no M.O. at present, but the two Dressings to be given for Emergency purposes – A supply of dressings to, has been given to him Inspection of Trench huts. Trench Toilets. Drums of this had returned.	

WAR DIARY
or
INTELLIGENCE SUMMARY

John N Bagot
Lt Col R. A. M. C.
OC 130 Fd Ambulance

Army Form C. 2118.

Place	Date	Hour	Summary of Events and Information	Remarks and references to Appendices
A 23 C 2.9	28/4/17		To A.D.M.S. Office to present instructions to medical arrangements at Canal Bank (drawing up 30th Army (S). To D.'E' Camp - Saw G.O.C. 114th Brigade - Consultation re D.'E' Camp ELVERDINGHE to G.O.C. 114th Brigade - Consultation Reported ELVERDINGHE in reference to medical arrangements. JBNR with Staff Captain	
A 23 C 2.9	29/4/17	6 AM	To Canal Bank Requested Aid Post at the WILLOWS - which I found used as Company Headquarters taking on such - arranged for the unusable housing over - inspected positions to holding lines, and told him what Visited SUSSEX Ft - Saw Officer in Charge, and had been made. - Report G O C 113th Bn Fr 35 medical arrangements. Saw C.O. of 13th WELSH. CO. 8 15 WELSH also Visited D'E Camps - Saw C.O. of 13th WELSH, and in Consultation with them, drew up lines of arrangements to the 30th T. 'S'lway	
		4 PM	L/Sgt COLI processed for duty at the WILLOWS with M.O. of 15 Welsh R.A.M.C's Roller Rances of this Field Ambulance, 129'-(25) + 131'. al 69 N.C.O's Roller Rances of this Field Ambulance, largely employed on Constructional work, Canal Bank. JBNR	

WAR DIARY or INTELLIGENCE SUMMARY

Army Form C. 2118.

Place	Date	Hour	Summary of Events and Information	Remarks and references to Appendices
A.22 C.2.9	29th 30/4/17		1 MO Field Ambce 1 RMO posted at WILLOWS with Regimental Stretcher Bearers. - 172 R.A.M.C. with an arrangement for interchange of turn Stations at A.D.S. Police S) Trolley line - WILLOWS - Barrage 6 - damage to Premises Shell holes. Afternoon of 29/4/17 - which caused a brake only, but Gas on set. where are Galts the Walls SUSSEX FARM. 3 MO's Stationed at A.D.S. Reserve R.A.M.C. Bearers at SUSSEX. One at BRIELEN, one man Dressing floor. 1 Ambulance Car Station. Barrage 12.30 A.M. - 1st wounded thro'/from WILLOW 1:30 A.M. Station at 3 A.M. - The last at 8 A.M. 1st wounded arrived main Dressing 26. Casualties admitted - 12. Severe (Abdom 2 bad) 7 Moderate, 7 Severe, 5 Septic, 2. Shell Shock. 1 Enemy Casualty, 392 Inf Regt. 15th WELSH - 12 4 — 13th R.W.F. — 3 15th R.W.F. — 3 113 Bn. M.G.C. — 113 T.M.B. 1 STRETCHER 123 R.E. 1 15th HERTS — 25	A.D.S. & Bearers at C. 13 B/S.R. Ambce.

Confidential War Diary

of the

130th (St John) Field Ambulance,
38th (Welsh) Division

From May 1st 1917
to May 31st 1917.

Army Form C. 2118.

WAR DIARY
or
INTELLIGENCE SUMMARY

(Erase heading not required.)

John B. Davoud Lt. Col. R.A.M.C.
O.C. 130' (St John) Field Amb'ce

Instructions regarding War Diaries and Intelligence Summaries are contained in F.S. Regs., Part II. and the Staff Manual respectively. Title Pages will be prepared in manuscript.

Place	Date	Hour	Summary of Events and Information	Remarks and references to Appendices
A23C.2.9	1/5/17		Capt. BURNE R.A.M.C. 16 SUSSEX A.D.S. to relieve Capt. RIDDELL, who returns to H.Q. 3 Amb'ce. Capt MELHUISH R.A.M.C. 166 to take over duties of Canal Bank Sanitary Officer relieved. Lt BANKES RAMC who returned to his Unit (129' Fd Amb'ce). A. has been in the Early morning by the 13th bd'sde and the number of Casualties admitted as a result into his Dsg Ambulance is as follows— Slight 2 Severe 3 Died 1 5 13 Lodsly — 17 } 21 of these majority severe 3 Prisoners of War admitted 5 14 RWF 2 } Slight a/c 392 Inf Reg 3 Died 1 5 124 RE 2 }	JBD
A23C.2.9	2/5/17	5.30 PM	Con'tr. G.O.C. 113th Brigade visited A.6 C.C.S. Gas Helmet instruction & drill in Respirators & P.H. Helmets Gas attack Drills & instruction of 15th Inniskilling "Shambles Hour" (9.33) immediately taken up by our Sentries.	
		9.33	Belgian Front, 1st Inniskilling Front. "gongs sounded" papers, though Camp. Sprays & observed by Sgt Squire. Begin noon.	
		9.40	Alarm given by Sprays & observed all respirators promptly & properly. Begin Relief Ken A. I found all Officers of Hen Pools. melting in— Every patient wearing bag wounded men all who Respirators in. Everyone walks up... Respirators in. Every patient wore one, in an orderly manner. Every man Gas Officer notes there were no one Spray & there Ambulance. I have reason to lay— Every thing lay— however severe. Spray & there Ambulance, I have reason to horse-bags will not lay —& so— however severe. Spray & there suffers from the Gas. Prisoners Members but — had the Jas — however severe cases Suffers from the Gas. Prisoners believe tho' none of the Personnel in Patients were completed tests in being detail, two. Res. Most out the Bullocks unit O/3rd. were Completed tests in being detail.	
			Generally — Every. however, has an Emergency Box Respirator No3 P.H. Helmet will be I have gun presence in Back Guard, for the use of assaulted. admitted patients hung up in	3/5/17 JBD

WAR DIARY
or
INTELLIGENCE SUMMARY

Army Form C. 2118.

Place	Date	Hour	Summary of Events and Information	Remarks and references to Appendices
A23 C 2.9	3/3/17	6 AM	W.L. D.A.D.M.S. visited LOADING POST at B 22 a.9.9. - Its work is now COMPLETED and capable of holding (5) 12 stretchers (cases). + 6 sitters well protected, and screened, - it extends 15 feet and would protect anything but direct hit (4) like other dug out - can be used for walking cases + wounded Lots 12 Sitting - The accommodation is (a) can be messages by stretcher of Suffolks for stretcher + (b) Seats to be erected in dug out for walking. - others from POST LOADING in prescence of Cornshelm, which will Reserve Dressing Bay. - Markers demands it. be sent up with occasion. Visited C.D. "SWB" NEW AID POST at C 13 a.3.4.5. + FUSILIER AID POST C 13 c 2.4 along COLNE VALLEY TRENCH, SKIPTON 16 NILE 16 LANCASHIRE FM - inspected TUNNELS + will visit Finding position for Aid Post. Visited and inspected SUSSEX AID POST. 38th DIVISIONAL CANAL BATHS. - 16 NEIGERSBURG CHATEAU. - with MO inspected Sanitary arrangements	✓ HD ✓ HD
A23 C 2.9	4/3/17		Attended Masking D. Ormy. Medical Society in Northumbrian Casualty Clearing Station HAZEBROUCK. - Major Sinclair R.A.M.C. opened a discussion on FRACTURED FEMURS. - Stress was laid on the importance of applying extension in these cases at the earliest opportunity, in applying THOMAS' SPLINT at AID POST. over-boot & clothing the ankles because of probability. + suspending limb later with SUSPENSION Cutting the clothing after attaching dressings.	✓ HD

Army Form C. 2118.

WAR DIARY
or
INTELLIGENCE SUMMARY

John 2ND good
war in France

(Erase heading not required.)

Place	Date	Hour	Summary of Events and Information	Remarks and references to Appendices
A23 C 2.9	5/5/17		Visited STEENJE Farm — with O.C. 38th T.M.B. There is a marked improvement in the Sanitary Conditions of this Camp since my last visit. A water cart is still being required by this Unit, there being no water Supply is obtained from the Farm house, — a Pump (well) — the ordinary stairs that they always boil this water before who occupy the Farm house, also Stagnant water there is well using — there is a midgen, and at times a bad colour, this water The supply also is limited, and I am requires too measure of bleaching powder to Chlorinate it. I am an taken for a sample to be sent for bacteriological examination outside Latrines — The well in question after drawing the water it has been in buckets. emptys it, in a large wooden tub, it from the Pump is then Pumped through the Clarifying, Chlorinating Cylinder, into a Covered water tank — these are all carefully supervised by a Corporal of this 130th Unit, and kept in a Clean Condition — Visited and inspected VIII Corps Ammunition Dump A 23 a B.1.1. This is a very Satisfactory Camp, with good Sanitary arrangements, — Excellent bit Cook-houses — Visited 113 M.G.C. A 23 C 3.7, 114th M.G.C A 23 C 3.6. been incinerator required by 114 for burning Manure, there is need for much improvement in Grease traps + Bad Pits — Mules in both Camps require cleaning 2nd MD	

Army Form C. 2118.

WAR DIARY
or
INTELLIGENCE SUMMARY

(Erase heading not required.)

JRS & Davel
W. Graves 2nd Lieut [?]

Place	Date	Hour	Summary of Events and Information	Remarks and references to Appendices
A29.C.2.9	6/5/17	9 AM	Special inspection forage of works leut, at troop Headquarters in Skeleton Pits avenue. Satisfactory turnout.	
		11.45.	Special inspection of A.S.C. & work rifle inspection. Capt. D.C.M. PAGE. R.A.M.C., reported for duty, taken on strength of unit from this day. 1099 R.A.M.C. to Canal Bank to relieve Capt. MELHUISH who returned to Headquarters. (J2 + T2)	
A.28.C.2.9	7/5/17	6.15 AM	The following casualties occurred to the following party of this unit while proceeding to duty in a car to LOADING POST at B.28.a.9.9. to complete dug out there, - between DAWSON'S CORNER, an enemy shell struck the road on the near side of MT Car wounding each of the wearers of the Car, who drove on, out of danger, the following except the driver of the Car who was not wounded. In the native of the wounds sustained (between shower glasses, no penetration) remained at Duty. 48145.Sgt. HOPKINS T.G. G.S.W. L Sgt Cheek (in hand) L.leg LIttle, L Shoulder (Serious) to 46 CCS 48103 L/Cpl DAVIES D.J. G.S.W. Compound Fracture Right ARM (Serious) Compound fracture R Elbow sub CCS 4817 L/Cpl REES G.T. G.S.W. face. Superficial. remained at Duty 18553 Pte JONES T. G.S.W. (clav) + Abdomen (Serious) this man died 3 hours after reaching 46 CCS 48157 Pte LLEWELLYN.A.M. G.S.W. Head, Compound fracture Skull - Gullet fracture left Shoulder Lumbar region. - returned at 46 CCS. Capt LORNIE RAMC 15 HQ 36th Bne 3rd Supernumerary Bn2f, Lt DICKSON RAMC 16 Re 14 RWF, Capt HONEY RAMC exceeding ontsel	

2449 Wt. W14957/M90 750,000 1/16 J.B.C.& A. Forms/C.2118/12.

WAR DIARY or INTELLIGENCE SUMMARY

Army Form C. 2118.

(Erase heading not required.)

Joseph David / W.H. Rowe O/C 1305/2 Fd Amb Oct/Nov 1917

Place	Date	Hour	Summary of Events and Information	Remarks and references to Appendices
A 28 C 2.9	8/5/17	8.30 am	To No. C.C.S. - attended burial of 46583 Pt JONES, T. of this unit, in Grd. near 46 C.C.S. PROVEN. — The O/C scrutinised conditions of this unit, found to be progressing favourably. Awarded proficiency pay to all men of this unit. Foot inspection of the personnel.	O/C 2nd HD
	9/5/17		No Event to Report.	85 HD
A 28 C 2.9	10/5/17	a.m 8.30	To LOADING POST B.23.a.9.17, and then via Windsor Cn.Rd Trolley Line to Bridge 6.W. inspected Steel Dug-out being constructed to FUSILIER MUD-BOAT to Bridge 6.D inspected Trench Elephant Dug-out in process of construction in RAMC. to form additional Aid Post. A.D.S. — visited SUSSEX A.D.S. inspected the COOK HOUSE in process of construction, inspected the Sig. and Rowel lines LAHORE. — via ESSEX to TROIS TOURS Chateau.	
		PM 3.30	Attended Conference of ADM.S "OC's FIELD AMBULANCES of VIII Corps DDMS. other subjects discussed, suggested that in the case of Minor Septic condition like the diagnosis of I.C.T. cases be substituted by such as Abrasion, boil, Cellulitis, Shallow ulcer etc. — Conference held at RED FARM 2/1 WESSEX FIELD AMB = later O/C W/Col Sayers Rams. — took us round the Field Ambces. —	85 HD

WAR DIARY
or
INTELLIGENCE SUMMARY

Army Form C. 2118.

(Erase heading not required.)

Place	Date	Hour	Summary of Events and Information	Remarks and references to Appendices
A23 C 2.9	(Continued) 10/5/17	P.M. 5.30	Lecture & practical Demonstration to N.C.O + personnel of this Field Ambulance on application of THOMAS'S THIGH SPLINT, in Out Post, in the Field, & at A.D.S. JGHD	
A 23 C 2.9	11/5/17	P.M. 2	Visited 46 C.C.S — Inspected F Camp, A16 C.8, 7 occupied by 314 R'Construction Company RE & 342 R'Construction Co. RE, also lines of 38th D.A.C. The sanitary conditions of these Camps are satisfactory, their cooked after. A storage tank for drinking water is required by the 342nd RE. The water to Ablution purposes in the case of both these units, is drawn from Stagnant Pool, which is being used by these units for the purpose of keeping horses, a Well in being sunk by these units near pool. Water for this purpose — Attended 2nd Army Medical Society Meeting, at No 2 Canadian C.C.S from 5pm to 7pm. Lectures — Aluminia — Certain interesting points were drawn attention to — especially the incidence of thrombosis in Salient especially N. of Salient JGHD	

WAR DIARY or INTELLIGENCE SUMMARY

Army Form C. 2118.

John H. David
Lt Col RAMC
OC 136 Fd Amb

Place	Date	Hour	Summary of Events and Information	Remarks and references to Appendices
A23c2.9	12/5/17		Visited Camps of 113th M.G.C. A23c3.7 & 114th M.G.C. A23c3.6. Sanitary Condition improved. Perhaps 'Soap' hoped not offered. "Gas Helmet Drill" of Personnel attached.	J.F.McD
A23c2.9	13/5/17		Ind: Paid, Capt PAGE D.C.M. to Sussex A.D.S. to relieve Lt HOGG.	J.F.McD
A23c2.9	14/5/17		D.D.M.S visited Field Ambulance, inspected wants. Visited O.C. 38th Divisional hosp, in reference to a farmer Corporal for hot meals Lt MOGG RAMC of this unit, took over temporary Medical Charge of 121st Bde RFA. in place Capt LATIMER RAMC who proceeded on leave 15/5/17	
A23c2.9	15/5/17	10.30 PM	A.D.M.S visited Head quarters of this Field Ambulance. inspected horse lines, - he approved sanitation, with the Stables lines, + H.D. L.D. + Adv Horses. Care of the horses, each Ambulance + care of Showers horn - hospital spread throughout Camp. Gas Personnel Present Gas alarm given, within a few seconds, + were inspected + found in position, 15 minutes, all use Patron.	
A23cD.9	16/5/17	11.15 AM	Visited by Officers V.C.O of Divisional Salvage - Brunshalm 9am, as to work of Ambulance - water Carts - packing of Personal + Pavents - Care of Pavents Ste Party. Scheme Shown Wharf woods, - the Sanitary + other arrangements at Cannes to Metin.	J.F.McD

WAR DIARY
or
INTELLIGENCE SUMMARY

Army Form C. 2118.

John 24 Divis 2/ce R Que
OC 130 Bde (6 R 2nd Aub Bde

(Erase heading not required.)

Place	Date	Hour	Summary of Events and Information	Remarks and references to Appendices
A.D.S.C.G	17/5/17	5.45 AM	With A.D.M.S and acting D.A.D.M.S (Capt MacDonald) visited Canal Bank SUSSEX FARM A.D.S. The new Cook-house of W of YPERLEE is nearing completion. New latrines for Officers and other ranks when this site are now complete. FUSILIER A.D.S. - This is nearing completion - the R.E. are building a concrete entrance - after which has however the two hours work will be added to four finishing layer. A new bridge has been given opposite this post by the two of this four feet wide, on same level as platform of YPERLEE. Is now sketches cases on same level, on to the hollies blink - which hollies line lines into WINDSOR CASTLE LINE.	
Puts 6 W			ST JOHN A.D.S. at Bridge 6D is nearing completion - the new only figures concrete entrance. Well the Sapper have in hand when this is completed, a building layer of thick Chateau which broken will be added. There is likely to prove a R Bat against the Dig out- in question in Comprised of 12 sections of 6 segments or 'Small Elephant' Each branch of these of these were Capt RIDDELL RAMC. 8th MD	
PutSic 6D				
A.D.S.C.G	18/5/17		Visited and inspected STEENSE FARM. occupied by 38th T.M.B. - there is normal improvement in the Camp in regard to Sanitary Conditions - a storage tank for Chlorinated water is required. Inspected B.C. 19th WELSH Coming camp of 38th T.M.B. although this Co have only recently pitched their Camp it is in a very satisfactory condition. Clean Sec. Cook-house, Latrines Urinals and Incinerator The Sanitary arrangements are also good. 8th MD	

WAR DIARY
or
INTELLIGENCE SUMMARY   No 62 4th Base
(Erase heading not required.)   J.G. Rawl

Army Form C.2118.

Place	Date	Hour	Summary of Events and Information	Remarks and references to Appendices
A23C29	10/9/17		Medical Corp Numerous Dumps. The Camp is kept in a most satisfactory condition — An improved type of grease trap is gradually being installed. Sanitary arrangements in this Camp are good. Attended 2nd Army Medical Society meeting at BAILLEUL at 2. C.C.S. when Capt. Henry Sisters R.A.M.C. read a paper on Bismuth, Iodoform, Paraffin Paste. — There was nothing new in this form of treatment nor anything that could be called an advance in surgical treatment of wound. — B.I.P.P. is composed of Bismuth Subnit. + Iodoform 2 part soft paraffin 9 i.s. to make paste. — it is laid down that no fresh quantity should be used in any one case — So that wounds of great width use in an extensive wound. — Shock antiseptic properties should be used as FB + damages muscle. Injury from contour which is then washed with Spirit — in all words a clean wound made. — B.I.P.P. is then used over the wound can often be closed — The advantages claimed over CARROLL are (1) Absence of Pain. — little assistance of frequent dressing (2) Non-Contagious, (3) Saving of time of Nurses + Sergeants (3) Saving of waste. — B.I.P.P.	

WAR DIARY
or
INTELLIGENCE SUMMARY

Army Form C. 2118.

John N David McCrae
DG 138 (?) Ross Yorks Rest

Place	Date	Hour	Summary of Events and Information	Remarks and references to Appendices
A23C2.9	19/5/17		Visited Camps of D.C. 19th Lokely, lines in good order, Cookhouse & Lantern arrangements Satisfactory. Also inspected 3rd T.M.B., transport of 119th R.F.A. — also inspected 113th, 114th M.G.C. A23C3.7 & A23C3.6. 2nd in Command visited X Camp 121st Labour Co. — Sanitary & Cookhouse arrangements most unsatisfactory. I also inspected VIII Corps Ammunition Dump — 1km in army spoilland. Camp Sennfurel Rugh — R.A.M.C. 12 ft. 13 R.W.F. N.J. — Rockchurch hut.	
A23C2.9	20/5/17		Inspection Parade called inch. — Inspection Rifles O.S.C.	JgMcD
A23C2.9	21/5/17		Gas Helmet Inspection + Drill — Service to hut. Lt Col. Rame to 114th R.W.D. Ireland. Dr Dickson posted permanently to 16 R.W.F. in place of Capt Watson N.o R.A.M.C. to 34th D.S. Lt Dickson R.A.M.C. Shook St. Strength of this unit.	JgMcD

WAR DIARY
or
INTELLIGENCE SUMMARY
(Erase heading not required.)

Army Form C. 2118.

130th Div'l R.A.M.C.
W. Col. Rawe
Oc. 13th 21st Div. Gas

Place	Date	Hour	Summary of Events and Information	Remarks and references to Appendices
A22 C3.9	22/5/17		A.D.M.S visited Thiais Bearing Station. Lecture to hut by Capt. RIDDELL – on Surgical treatments, and Retn. kit, etc. Lt. Col. Relieves from 11th R.W.F.	
A23 C3.9	23/5/17		A.D.M.S visited the Field Ambulances. Divisional Funeral Pk. 9th March – 13 Welsh 1 hy – R.A.M.C. N.E.	92 F.A. 92 F.A.
A23 C3.9	24/5/17		Capt. DAUBNEY (cope) LORNIE R.A.M.C reported from temporary duty as M.O. 38th Bn. H.Q. 93 F.A.	
A23 C3.9	25/5/17		Lt. Colt. RAMC at 38th Bn. H.Q. for temporary duty. X Camp occupied 121 Labour Batt. – 113 Queens Batt. (Bat Gnashelon Gr.) visited and Sanity Chelerous. inspected improved. since last visit Via USA STINTE F.A. and inspected 38th Bn. T.M.B. 117th R.F.A. Transport Lines and B, G & D 191st Reserves. (wilet Regiment) Also inspected – 92 F.A. VIII Corps Ammu: Camp. Dump.	
A23 C3.9	26/5/17		Visited & inspected Sanity Condition of the HQ. 129 Bngar. R.F.A. VIII Corps Signals attached to 122 Bnga X.R.F.A. also Infantry Camp at TROIS TOURS CHATEAU. 16 Collar Camp now occupied by No. 1 Worcester Pioneers (Railroad Construction) – Also 39th Div. T.M.B who occupy Stables at TROIS TOURS. also inspected 111th M.G.C. + 115th M.G.C Camps.	

WAR DIARY
or
INTELLIGENCE SUMMARY

Army Form C. 2118.

(Erase heading not required.)

Maj. T. Davy L'Estrange
O.C. 130th S. John Sub Coy

Place	Date	Hour	Summary of Events and Information	Remarks and references to Appendices
A.23.C.9.9	26/5/17 (Continued)	P.M. 5.30	Gas Drill, with Respirators, and inspection of Respirators at P.H. Network.	
			Capt. RAMC relieved Capt BURKE at SUSSEX A.D.S. Capt LORNIE relieved Capt BURKE at SUSSEX A.D.S.	JSHD
A.23.C.9.9	27/5/17	9 AM	Unit Inspection & Respirator Inspection A.S.C. rifle Inspection.	
		2 PM	Gas Drill. M.T. A.S.C. + H.T. A.S.C.	
			6 Reinforcements reported for duty.	
			Lt HOGG RAMC reported from Bethune as M.O. 122nd Brigade R.F.A.	JSHD
A.23.C.9.9	28/5/17	A.M. 11.50	Gas Alarm – Shantan Horns blown by Police. Smell of Gas faint 1.50 ams, unsafely taken up – & camp inspects, as Patrols + Personnel found properly equipped with full Respirators – all horses, with sandbag covers filled with water, were fully Respirated.	
		3.30	Wire from Signals "Masks off"	
			A.D.M.S. visited main Dressing Station	
			Capt MELHUISH R.A.M.C. & 1 Welsh for temporary duty to replace Lt ROBERTSON RAMC HD proceeding on leave	
A.23.C.9.9	29/5/17		Returned to report. Visited and Inspected X Camp occupied by 121st Labour Batt, 113th Queens Batt (Rons) Construction Co's) and Inspected F Camp occupied by 349th Road Construction Co R.E. & H.H. Road Construction Co's	
A.23.C.9.9	30/5/17		By No Event to record.	
	31/5/17		No Event	

John D Davy
Lt E Rome
OC 130(Syd) San Ambe

CONFIDENTIAL

WAR

DIARY

OF

130TH. (ST. JOHN) FIELD AMBULANCE.

From   1st. June 1917.

To   30th. June 1917.

B.E.F.

SUMMARY OF MEDICAL WAR DIARIES FOR

130th F.A., 38th Divn., 14th Corps, 5th Army.

WESTERN FRONT JUNE 1917.

--

O.C. Lt. Col. J.E.H. Davies.

SUMMARISED UNDER THE FOLLOWING HEADINGS.

Phase "D" Battle of Messines June 1917.

B.E.F.   1.

130th F.A. 38th Div. 14th Corps, 5th Army. WESTERN FRONT
O.C. Lt. Col. J.E.H. Davies.   June 1917.

Phase "D" Battle of Messines June 1917.

1917.	Headquarters. At A.23.c.2.9. Sheet 28.
June 10th.	Transfer. Unit transferred with 38th Divn. from 8th Corps, 2nd Army and 14th Corps, 5th Army.
	Medical Arrangements: Unit ran M.D.S. at A.23.c.2.9. and A.D.S. Sussex Farm C.19.c.2.6.
11th – 25th.	Operations R.A.M.C. Routine. Unit engaged in preparing A.D.Ss (Fusilier and St John) on Canal Bank.
26th.	Operations Enemy. Regular shelling of vicinity.
28th.	Medical Arrangements: M.D.S. handed over to 134th Field Ambulance.
	A.D.Ss at Sussex Farm Fusilier and St John Farm handed over to 88th Field Ambulance.
30th.	Moves: To La Tirmand – Training Area.

B.E.F.

SUMMARY OF MEDICAL WAR DIARIES FOR

130th F.A., 38th Divn., 14th Corps, 5th Army.

WESTERN FRONT JUNE 1917.

O.C. Lt. Col. J.E.H. Davies.

SUMMARISED UNDER THE FOLLOWING HEADINGS.

Phase "D" Battle of Messines June 1917.

B.E.F.

130th F.A. 38th Div. 14th Corps, 5th Army. WESTERN FRONT

O.C. Lt. Col. J.E.H. Davies. June 1917.

Phase "D" Battle of Messines June 1917.

1917.	Headquarters. At A.23.c.2.9. Sheet 28.
June 10th.	Transfer. Unit transferred with 38th Divn. from 8th Corps, 2nd Army and 14th Corps, 5th Army.
	Medical Arrangements: Unit ran M.D.S. at A.23.c.2.9. and A.D.S. Sussex Farm C.19.c.2.6.
11th – 25th.	Operations R.A.M.C. Routine. Unit engaged in preparing A.D.Ss (Fusilier and St John) on Canal Bank.
26th.	Operations Enemy. Regular shelling of vicinity.
28th.	Medical Arrangements: M.D.S. handed over to 134th Field Ambulance.
	A.D.Ss at Sussex Farm Fusilier and St John Farm handed over to 88th Field Ambulance.
30th.	Moves: To La Tirmand – Training Area.

Army Form C. 2118.

WAR DIARY
or
INTELLIGENCE SUMMARY
(Erase heading not required.)

John Power
Lt Col RAMC
OC 130 (St/h) Fd Amb

Place	Date	Hour	Summary of Events and Information	Remarks and references to Appendices
A 23 C.D.9	1/6/17	5.45 am	To LOADING-POST, – Flew on to CANAL BANK, inspected FUSILIER and Advanced Dressing Station Post "St JOHN" at Bridge G.W. – to New Aid Post "St JOHN" at Bridge 6.D. work is proceeding fast at both these posts, – although visited SUSSEX A.D.S. and inspected additions (extensions) to ward, which have now been doubled, – by digging out, and erecting 5 New Shelters. Arranged with O/C A.D.S. for further extensions to Dressing Room, and Wash-house to be completed. The Sussex Cook house completed and good work accomplished as officers billet area —	
		11.30 am	Visited & Inspected SALIENT STRENGE Fld and Camps of 38th T.M.B., 13 Coy 19th WELSH. Transport Lines of 131st R.F.A. – This Camp is in a satisfactory condition, a water cart is sent daily by was to the 38th T.M.B. also visited Camp of 152 Labour Coy R.E. (430 strong) who has just arrived, and were proceeding to construct Cookhouses, – latrines – Urinals etc. pitched their Camp – and were to resort for latrines for latrine seats etc. gave instructions, as to where to report to A.D.M.S. (Col Thompson), who arrived this day	S.H.D.
		P.M. 3.30	To Divisional Headquarters to report to A.D.M.S. (Col Thompson), who arrived this day	
		5.30	Respirator Drill and Inspections – also P.H. Helmets	
A 23 C.D.9	2/6/17		A.D.M.S. inspected Main Dressing Station Main Dressing Station visited and inspected by Surgeon-General SKINNER, D.M.S. V Army and by Col GERRARD, D.D.M.S. VIII Corps Visited Inspected the following Camps – VIII Corps Ammunition Dump, – 131st Railway Construction Coy, 116th M.G.C. – 116 M.G.C. – F. MACALLISTER, RAMC, 131st Field Amb. to Canal Bank to relieve Capt LORNIE who returned to Main Dressing Station	S2 HD
A 23 C.D.9	3/6/17	9 am	Inspection of Men in Full Marching Kit – Inspection of A.S.C. Personnel –	S2 HD

WAR DIARY or INTELLIGENCE SUMMARY

Army Form C. 2118.

(Erase heading not required.)

Place	Date	Hour	Summary of Events and Information	Remarks and references to Appendices
A23 C 2.9	4/6/17		Respirator & P.H. Helmet Inspection & Drill. Clothing Board held. Divisional Baths visited. Main Dressing Station	JgH?
A23 C 2.9	5/6/17		A.D.M.S visited Main Dressing Station. Capt Riddell R.A.M.C reported from leave	JgH?
A23 C 2.9	6/6/17		Conference at A.D.M.S's Office. D.D.M.S. VIII Corps inspected Main Dressing Station. Capt Ridder R.A.M.C to a F.S. — to relieve Capt Page R.A.M.C who returned to Headquarters	JgH?
A23 C 2.9	7/6/17		1st H.Q.'s R.A.M.C of this Unit succeeded to 12. C.C.S Sergt Jarman proceeded to report War Office in reference to Commission. Inspected Sanitary Arrangements of 8th Corps N.E. Balloon Section. (H.Q).	JgH?
A23 C 2.9	8/6/17		Capt LORNIE R.A.M.C to C.R.S. Visited & Inspected 122nd Brigade R.F.A. Three Towers,	
A23 C 2.9	9/6/17		Visited & inspected Camps of 38th T.M.B, B.G, 19th Welsh, 121 Brigade R.F.A. Houpart Line 13th Railroad Construction Co, 7th Canadian Co, VIII Corps Ammunition Dump, 36th Div Dump, 114th M.G.C, 115th M.G.C, 152 Labour Coy, D.A.D.M.S 39th Div visited Main Dressing Station.	JgH?

Army Form C. 2118.

WAR DIARY
or
INTELLIGENCE SUMMARY

John Barrel
W.Gt. Rawl. CC.135

(Erase heading not required.)

Instructions regarding War Diaries and Intelligence Summaries are contained in F. S. Regs., Part II. and the Staff Manual respectively. Title Pages will be prepared in manuscript.

Place	Date	Hour	Summary of Events and Information	Remarks and references to Appendices
A23 C.2.9 GWALIA FARM.	10/6/17		Main Dressing Station now known officially as GWALIA FM. Was had inspected in Shrapnel Rd. A.S.C. Rifle Inspection	
GWALIA FARM	11/6/17		A.D.M.S. Office moved to # VOX. VRIE Camp. – Lieutenants locates this Farm from main. DADMS visited & inspected this Ambce	
GWALIA FARM	12/6/17		Capt. LORNIE RAMC. seconded from VIII Corps Rest Station to 46 C.C.S. 3rd Div joins XIV Corps / V Army about this date. D.D.M.S. VIII Corps – Visited the Field Ambce Spoke well of work done by men of this Unit.	
GWALIA FARM	13/6/17		Respirator & P.H. helmet Inspection & Drill D.D.M.S. (Gl WAITE) DADMS XIV Corps. visited & inspected the new Dressing Station of this Ambulance, Divisional Cinema Notes this Anythg	
GWALIA FARM	14/6/17		Q.M. the Lt P.S. THOMPSON reported from leave	

Army Form C. 2118.

WAR DIARY
or
INTELLIGENCE SUMMARY

(Erase heading not required.)

Place	Date	Hour	Summary of Events and Information	Remarks and references to Appendices
GWALIA FARM A22C2.9	15/6/17	5.AM	Lt. acting ADMS, +DADMS visited ROEBUCK LOADING Post, — St JOHN, FUSILIER, & SUSSEX A.D.S's also inspected trenches in front of this area —	
		3 PM	The Main Dressing Station visited and inspected by D.D.M.S. XVIII Corps. A.D.M.S. 39' Division, + Capt. BROWN. H.M. R.A.M.C. reported for duty then placed on strength of this unit on from this date —	39Div 39Div
GWALIA FARM A22C2.9	16/6/17		DaDmS visited Main Dressing Station visited 9th Field Ambulance	9FA
GWALIA FARM A22C2.9	17/6/17		Visited by OC 134th Field Ambulance	134FA
GWALIA FARM A22C2.9	18/6/17		Lo/Sergt K Jepost — 17/6/17 Capt. GROVE.(F.P) R.A.M.C. reported to duty & put on Strength of this unit.	
GWALIA FARM A22C2.9	19/6/17		Acting ADMS. + DaDmS visited Main Dressing Station, to Prepare Evacuation for P.B. —	39Div

WAR DIARY or INTELLIGENCE SUMMARY

Army Form C. 2118.

John J Renal
W.G. Rawle
Do 135 Sept Jolin Worth

Place	Date	Hour	Summary of Events and Information	Remarks and references to Appendices
GWALIA FARM A23 c.2.9	20/6/17		Capt BROWN, R.A.M.C. to A.D.S., 12 Cases of Malaria, Tarassa War. Continued admissions.	J.L.M.R.
GWALIA FARM A23 c.2.9	21/6/17		Visited H.Q. No news to report.	J.L.M.R.
GWALIA FARM A23 c.2.9	22/6/17	5 AM	Capt Riddell Round to dressing Post, also on to Lt John A.D.S., Sussex A.D.S. Sussex A.D.S.	J.L.M.R.
	22/6/17		1 Sergt. 30 other ranks 13/81 Fld Ambulance reported for duty at Canal Bank 9 am. No news to report.	J.L.M.R. 95 HD
GWALIA FARM A23 c.2.9	24/6/17		4 Cases of Pneumonia admitted from Jamaica War Contingent — Infection of throat, in stretcher by Rifle musketry Drill — Infection of Pte T. Allen, Pte Chase, Pte T Allen, both of Aug 17 R.W.9. Pte J. NEWMAN, both of 2nd W. Commans	J/L/H/R
GWALIA FARM A23 c.2.9	25/6/17	3.30 am	Proceeded on leave, — after handing over to Capt. Russell Ramc 2nd W Commans	J.L.M.R.

WAR DIARY or INTELLIGENCE SUMMARY

Army Form C. 2118.

Remarks: Relieved Captain Osborne acting O/C 130th F.A. (St John)

Place	Date	Hour	Summary of Events and Information
RWALIA FARM	25/6/17		In the morning Officer i/c 134 F.A. reported to take over from me within the Camp. Having no orders to do so we communicated with the A.D.M.S. who ordered to the allotment of ground. F.A. in the afternoon pitched on the site. That evening A.D.M.S. summoned me to a conference, when I received orders to hand an Officer to the new arrivals next day for P.B. or P.C. A.D.M.S. held inspection — were recommended for P.B or P.C.
do. do.	26/6/17		D.A.D.M.S. was also present. Seeing in the vicinity had been regular. In the afternoon the D.D.M.S. XIV Corps visited the camp and was very pleased at its appearance. We were ordered by him that on receipt of orders to move all B.R.C.S. material in Canada Farm.
do. do.	27/6/17		On morning of O/C 134th F.A. and I communicated on the phone. He spoke to B.R.C.S. He reported on his starting to move to Reception the B.R.C.S. stores at once forwarded to the office to remove all B.R.C.S. to obtain orders and shewn to Col. Atkinson. I interviewed the A.D.M.S. This was returned and ordered me to remove the A.D.M.S. that evening to allow me to remove A.D.M. S. XXXVIII Div D.A.D.M.S. the refused. D.D.M.S. XIV Corps together with A.R.C.S. materials to Canada Farm to D.D.M.S. Divl Office inspected. The B.R.C.S. were all ready for Col. to have and ordered to move the morning. We temporarily that evening to Canada relieve the morning A.D.S. from Suchene.

Army Form C. 2118.

WAR DIARY
or
INTELLIGENCE SUMMARY

(Erase heading not required.)

Remarks and references to Appendices: A.P. Riddell Acting O/C Cap R.A.M.C. 130 F.A (SrlA.)
Cap.R.A.M.C.

Place	Date	Hour	Summary of Events and Information
RAWALIA FARM	27/6/17		(Continued) Orders received to hand over the Camp to 134 F.A. also to hand over A.D.S on Canal bank i.e. Essier, St John, Roebuck, Sussex, to an Ambulance of the 29th Div. Appr.
Do Do	28/6/17		A.D.M.S & D.A.D.M.S. visited camp in the morning and remained for all B.R.C.S. stores were removed to Canada Farm, A.D.M.S. & O/C 134 F.A had a conference. D.A.M.S was present. Appr. Officers of the 66th F.A arrived to take over Art Posts, and construction was made in connection with them. A A.D.S departments were handed over to at 2.30 p.m. the wards and A.D.D departments were handed over to the 134 F.A. A.D Posts handed over and relief completed by 10-30 p.m. at Centre.
Do Do	29/6/17		Transport departed at 7 A.M. for Centre at 9 A.M. Personnel entrained for Centre and relief completed by 9-30 Everything handed over at 12 noon. Appr. Transport arrived at Centre at 11 " " Unit "
Do Do	30/6/17		Transport departs from Centre at 6.A.M. Then Personnel marches to La Brande 2½ miles from Centre to La Timana, entrained for Entree Blanche. On arrival marched about 3½ miles Transport arrived at

A.P. Riddell Col
W.G. Thompson Col
Wards 38 Mos

CAPTAIN,
R.A.M.C.

CONFIDENTIAL

WAR DIARY

OF

130th (St John) FIELD AMBULANCE

From July 1st 1917
To July 31st 1917

B.E.F.

130th F.A. 38th Div. 14th Corps, 5th Army.   WESTERN FRONT.

O.C. Lt. Col. J.E.H. Davies.   July- '17.

Phase "D" 1. Passchendaele Operations July-Nov. 1917.

(a) Operations commencing 1st July 1917.

1917.	Headquarters. At La Tirmand.
July 1st- 15th.	Operations R.A.M.C. Training.
16th. 18th.	Moves: To Proven.
19th.	Moves Detachment: 1 and 5 advance party took over Mordacq Farm and Roebuck Loading Post from 88th Field Ambulance.
21st.	Moves: F.6.a. (Sheet 27.a.) Sefton Camp.
	Casualties R.A.M.C. 0 and 1 wounded.
26th.	Casualties Gas. 53 cases admitted.
28th.	Moves: To Coppernolle A.17.a.2.9. (Sheet 28)
	Moves Detachment: 0 and 31 to Canal Bank to relieve party of 129th Field Ambulance.
	Moves Transport. All available M. Ambulances sent to 131st Field Ambulance Canada Farm.
30th.	Moves Detachment: 2 and 56 to Canada Farm.
	1 and 12 to C.W.W. Coll. P. Mouton Farm.
31st.	Operations. Zero.
	Casualties R.A.M.C. Capt Renwick attached 17th R.W.F. wounded.
	Moves Detachment: 0 and 10 to Canal Bank as S.Bs.

Aug. 6th.   Moves: To Priory Camp F.10.c.8.6.

15th.   Decorations.   Cpl. Sweeting and L/Cpls. Samuel and Thomas awarded M.M.

B.E.F.   1.

<u>130th F.A. 38th Div. 14th Corps, 5th Army.</u> <u>WESTERN FRONT.</u>
<u>O.C. Lt. Col. J.E.H. Davies.</u>   <u>July-Aug. '17.</u>

<u>Phase "D" 1. Passchendaele Operation July-Nov. 1917.</u>
<u>(a) Operations commencing 1st July 1917.</u>

1917.	<u>Headquarters.</u> At La Tirmand.
July 1st- 15th.	<u>Operations R.A.M.C.</u> Training.
16th. 18th.	<u>Moves:</u> To Proven.
19th.	<u>Moves Detachment:</u> 1 and 5 advance party took over Mordacq Farm and Roebuck Loading Post from 83th Field Ambulance.
21st.	<u>Moves:</u> F.6.a. (Sheet 27.a.) Safton Camp.
	<u>Casualties R.A.M.C.</u> 0 and 1 wounded.
26th.	<u>Casualties Gas.</u> 53 cases admitted.
28th.	<u>Moves:</u> To Coppernolle A.17.a.2.9. (Sheet 28)
	<u>Moves Detachment:</u> 0 and 31 to Canal Bank to relieve party of 129th Field Ambulance.
	<u>Moves Transport.</u> All available M. Ambulances sent to 131st Field Ambulance Canada Farm.
30th.	<u>Moves Detachment:</u> 2 and 56 to Canada Farm.
	1 and 12 to C.W.W. Coll. P. Mouton Farm.
31st.	<u>Operations.</u> Zero.
	<u>Casualties R.A.M.C.</u> Capt Renwick attached 17th R.W.F.W. wounded.
	<u>Moves Detachment:</u> 0 and 10 to Canal Bank as S.Bs.

WAR DIARY or INTELLIGENCE SUMMARY

Army Form C. 2118.

John B. Baird Lieut Colonel
V/Cr RAMC
OC 130 St John Amb[?]

Place	Date	Hour	Summary of Events and Information	Remarks and references to Appendices
La Tirmand	1/7/17		The marquees & Tents were pitched in the morning, and collection of the sick of the 114 Byde commenced. Capt Page R.A.M.C. returned to duty from the 134 Field a. R.F. Capt Brown proceed to take up duties at XIV Corps School in place of Capt J.E. Davies. Capt Davies & Capt Reynolds — The latter from the Reinforcement Camp — returned by armr. car to the 131 F.A.	
do do	2/7/17		I visited training ground in the morning, and found things only in a preparatory state. Visited A.D.m.S. in the evening about cars for the O/c and regarding Officers to Temporally relieve the M/O's ? 10th & 13th Welsh - proceeding on leave, I also conferred as to course of training.	
do do	3/7/17		Inspected unit in Skeleton Kit. There was an inspection of Box Respirators & P.H. Helmets. There were Company Drill, Stretcher Drill and Route march	

Army Form C. 2118.

WAR DIARY
or
INTELLIGENCE SUMMARY.
(Erase heading not required.)

John Purcell L/Cpl RAMC

Instructions regarding War Diaries and Intelligence Summaries are contained in F. S. Regs., Part II. and the Staff Manual respectively. Title pages will be prepared in manuscript.

Place	Date	Hour	Summary of Events and Information	Remarks and references to Appendices
LA TIRMAND	3/7		(continued) Capt Evans proceeded to Temporary Duty with the 105 Welsh. Capt Page proceeded to Temporary Duty with the 135 Welsh. JPR	
do	4/7		Visited Training area to select points. Clow proceeded Headquarters (114) for full instructions. Arranged about B.Ths. A.D.Ss to D.A.D.m.S. visited camp and found everything satisfactory. JPR	
do	5/7		80 men bathed in the afternoon at Fleckinelles, remainder route marches. Visited Training area. O/C returned from 10 days leave. JPR	
LA TIRMAND	6/7/16		Visits A.D.M.S. Office to report. Visits 114th H.Q. - Physical Science Stretcher Drill thanks JPR	
LA TIRMAND	7/7/16		Conference of O.C. Bn.O. Coys Bns at A.Dm.S Office. Physical Exercises Conference, Stretcher Drill, Lectures, Practice JPR	

A6945 Wt. W11417/M1160 350,000 12/16 D. D. & L. Forms/C./2118/14.

WAR DIARY
or
INTELLIGENCE SUMMARY.
(Erase heading not required.)

Army Form C. 2118.

John Anderson
LtCol. Bays
OC 136th (1) John Bn Lab Aube Coy

Place	Date	Hour	Summary of Events and Information	Remarks and references to Appendices
LA TIRMAND	8/7/17		Inspection of Unit. - Inspection Rifles ABC. - Route March visited HQ 114th Brigade. (J.S.HQ)	
LA TIRMAND	9/7/17		Gun Drill - Foot Inspection - Visited HQ Brigade. Later Inspects huts Camp area. (J.S.HQ)	
LA TIRMAND	10/7/17		Respirators P.H. Helmet Drill, Inspection Stretcher Bearers under Capt MELHUISH Lt. COLT. visits Training ground (J.S.HQ)	
LA TIRMAND	11/7/17		Stunned War recommenced for P.B. at the Sous Aubee and at 136th Sous Aubee for ADWR. (J.S.HQ)	
LA TIRMAND	12/7/17		Divisional Gold Day - Parade 5.45 AM - 3 Groups of S.B's to HQ number of 104 Parades under LtGn. of this Unit, + proceeded to form Report to OC 129th B.W.Ans.Fr. One 3rd Sub-Division under Capt RIDDELL formed Divisional Collecting Station for walking wounded walking wounded al	

WAR DIARY
or
INTELLIGENCE SUMMARY

Army Form C. 2118.

Place	Date	Hour	Summary of Events and Information	Remarks and references to Appendices
LA TIRMOND	12/7/19 (continued)		LA FLECHINELLE - 1st SB's were attached to Infantry Units of 111th Brigade, and reported at HQ at 5.15 P.M.	JSND
LA TIRMOND	13/7/17	7.9 am	OC Inspection of Unit	
		10.15	Foot Inspection	
		2 PM	Rifle Inspection ASC (HT)	JSND
		2.1130	Route march.	
LA TIRMOND	14/7/17		Arrangements made to move on 16/7/17 - Route march, Inspection of Box Respirators, Iron Rations, visited 111th Brigade HQ.	JSND
LA TIRMOND	15/7/17		OC Inspection, Church Parade 10 am & 4.30, No Parad to report	JSND
LA TIRMOND	16/7/17	5 AM	Reveille, Parade 7.30 am, moved off 7.45 am, units own arrangements about the AUREANT via LINGHEM, ROMBLY, LAMBRES, AIRE, BOESEGHEM.	

WAR DIARY or INTELLIGENCE SUMMARY

Army Form C. 2118.

John Ridge
Lt. RAMC

Place	Date	Hour	Summary of Events and Information	Remarks and references to Appendices
LA TIRMOND	16/7/17		(Continued) 16 STEENBECQUE arriving 1.15 P.M. + Good relgrin Billets for Billets. Reported to H.Q. 114th Brigade. Visited M.O's & units	
STEENBECQUE	17/7/17	5:30 am	Reveille, Parade 7.45 am, Marched off via MORBECQUE, HAZEBROUCK, LE BREARDE, to HONDEGHEM, arrived 12.30 P.M. Billets good, but very scattered. Gas alert. - Capt GROVES RAMC reported for duty, with 1 Welsh, Capt PAGE from 13 Welsh Reported to H.Q. 114th Brigade. Visited MO's & units	
HONDEGHEM	18/7/17	2:30 AM	48106 Pte DAVIES D.J. 125628 Pte PARNIN T. to 15 CCS from this unit. Reveille, Parade 3.50 am, Marched via LE BREARDE, CAESTRE, EECKE, 6.50 - 8 AM Breakfast, - GODEWAERSVELDE, WATOU, to PROVEN, arriving at 11.30 AM. Picked Camp, - two poor barns as billets	
PROVEN	19/7/17		48190 Pte SMITH. W.H. 76757 Pte WARR J.W. of This Unit Evacuated to 63 CCS Box Respirator + P.H. Helmet Inspection. Visited x 70 (final ?) 87 Field Amb/c to whom others where possessed to take over from. Visited A.D.M.S. office. Capt RIDDELL RAMC of this Unit with 1 Sergt + 14 other ranks + Motor Dispatch	

WAR DIARY or INTELLIGENCE SUMMARY

Army Form C. 2118.

Place	Date	Hour	Summary of Events and Information	Remarks and references to Appendices
PROVEN	19/7/17 (Contind)		Proceed to Advanced Post to take over MORDACQ FARM, ROEBUCK LOADING POST from a Field Ambce 27 27' Div. (88' Fld Amb')	JSMD
PROVEN	20/7/17		Visited HQ 115 Brigade, with whom the Unit is attached, during move from present area, to Corps Staging Area, Moved Camp from E 16 6 3.5 to E 16 6 7.2 Evacuated No 48122 Pte Hayburn J. Wounded to C.C.S	JSMD
PROVEN Camp F6a.	21/7/17	7.30 am	Moved off from E 16 6 7.2 with 115' Brigade to SEFTON Camp F6a in Staging Area. Arrived 9.30 AM. Pte DRAPER wounded evacuated to No 4 CCS	
Camp F6a Seal 27	22/7/17		A.D.M.S + DADMS visited Camp - Interpreter W. DAMMAN reported. DDMS XIV Corps visited Camp - Capt. Grove relieved Capt Ross MORDACQ FARM	JSMD
Camp F6a	23/7/17		LCpl SLAUGHTER of this Unit evacuated to CCS Visited ADMS office 4 CCS. Received 3rd Div Medical arrangements (Operation No I)	JSMD

WAR DIARY
or
INTELLIGENCE SUMMARY

Army Form C. 2118.

W ASH Davies
Lt Col RAMC
OC 130th Field Ambulance

Place	Date	Hour	Summary of Events and Information	Remarks and references to Appendices
Camp F6a SEFTON	24/7/17		A.D.M.S. in Charge of Divn'L Visited ADMS Office for Conference Respecting 9th Welsh Div. Forman S. Lieut	
Camp F6a SEFTON	25/7/17		Visited Brigade HQ — Lecture to Unit on Gas Poisoning. — Drill in hand in Alphabet. Visited 10 SWB. Examined 1 Officer + 63 other ranks all alleged suffering from "effects of Lacrymatory Gas" (? Mustard Gas) Notified ADMS. Respirators inspected for instructions 92 HR	Respirator PH helmet
Camp F6a SEFTON	26/7/17		Instructions received from ADMS to count for observation "Slight" Gassed Cases — 53 admitted. Visited Bn' COPPERNOLLE	
Camp F6a SEFTON	27/7/17		Order issued to be prepared to move on one hour's notice. ADMS visited Field Ambulance and Standard MBW Examined. Co. P.B. Received A.D.M.S. General orders No 2 Order issued to move forthwith to COPPERNOLLE and remain parked there. Moved off 4 P.M. arrived 5.30 P.M.	

WAR DIARY
INTELLIGENCE SUMMARY

John A Roos
Lt Col. R.A.M.C.
od 130 St John Amb Amb

Army Form C. 2118.

Place	Date	Hour	Summary of Events and Information	Remarks and references to Appendices
COPPERNOLLE A 17a 2.9 (Sheet 28)	28/7/17		Bivouac Camp, in conjunction with 129th Field Ambce, ADtuS visited Camp	
			Visited ADMS Office	
			1 N.C.O. 30 O.R. proceeded to Canal Bank to relieve a similar number from 129th (who returned to rest in transport lines	
			All Water Ambulance available south 131st Field Ambulance CANADA FARM.	
			Visited OC 131st CANADA FARM	J8.H2)
COPPERNOLLE A 17a 2.9	29/7/17		Received Operation orders No 2 addendum No I -	
			10.15 ADMS visited MORDACQ Fm area, with intermittent shell fire, also visited MOUTON FARM. (See XIV Corps Collection Station for walking wounded.)	
			Operation orders No 2 addendum No II issued	JE H2
COPPERNOLLE A 17a 2.9	30/7/17		Capt. Riddell to MORDACQ to relieve Capt. Grove. Erected walking wounded directing signs — 3 routes from Canal Bank to MORDACQ, - 1 by shortest route MORDACQ Fm MOUTON. Fm.	
			Continued.	

Army Form C. 2118.

WAR DIARY
or
INTELLIGENCE SUMMARY
(Erase heading not required.)

Place	Date	Hour	Summary of Events and Information	Remarks and references to Appendices
COPPERNOLLE	30/7/17	4.15 AM	D. Officers 36. DR proceeded to CANADA F™ on route to CANAL BANK.	
A.17.a.2.9		2.30 PM	Capt. PAGE R.A.M.C. & Clerks & O.R. proceeded to MOUTON F™ & MORDACQ F™	
			2nd Cars reported to O.C. CANADA FARM	J.S. H-Q
COPPERNOLLE	31/7/17	3.40 AM	ZERO.	
A.17.a.2.9			Lt.C. A.D.M.S. visited XIV Corps Main Dressing Station CANADA FARM, XIV Corps Collecting Station for Walking Wounded MOUTON F™, Divisional Collecting Post for walking wounded MORDACQ F™, the A.D.S. at SUSSEX, FUSILIER, Battn.R.A.P. at C.13.d.60.30.	
		2.15 PM	Capt. GROVE of this unit proceeded to CANAL BANK to be posted temporary 15. 17'. R.W.F. in place of Capt. RENWICK wounded in action.	
			10 O.R. TD4 Sub-division reported for duty to act as S.B's CANAL BANK	
			Motor Car No. 1550 from D.W. Workshops reported to O.C. 131. 2nd Amb. at CANADA F™.	

JMcBrazil 2/Lt R.A.M.C.
L/Cpl. R. Owe
OC 130(St.John) 3rd Amb
38ᵈ (Welsh) Div

JMcBrazil 2/Lt R.A.M.C.
O.C. 130 (St.John) 3rd Field Amb.
38ᵈ (Welsh) Div.

CONFIDENTIAL

Vol 21

War Diary

of

130th (St John) Field Ambulance

from

1st August 1917 to 31st August 1917

COMMITTEE FOR THE
MEDICAL HISTORY OF THE WAR
Date   −5 NOV. 1917

B.E.F.

SUMMARY OF MEDICAL WAR DIARIES FOR

130th F.A., 38th Divn. 14th Corps, 5th Army.
To 11th Corps, 1st Army from 13.9.17.

WESTERN FRONT ~~JULY~~ Aug.- ~~SEPT~~ 1917.

O.C. Lt. Col. J.E.H. Davies.

SUMMARISED UNDER THE FOLLOWING HEADINGS.

Phase "D" 1. Passchendaele Operations July.-Nov. '17.

(a) Operations commencing 1st July 1917

B.E.F.

130th F.A. 38th Divn. 14th Corps, 5th Army. WESTERN FRONT

O.C. Lt. Col. J.E.H. Davies.   Aug. Sept. 17

Phase "D" 1. (a) (Cont.)

1917.

Aug. 18th.   <u>Moves:</u> To Sussex Farm, (A.D.S.)

<u>Decorations.</u> Pte. Allison A.S.C. awarded M.M.

19th.   <u>Casualties R.A.M.C.</u> 0 and 2 wounded.

21st.   <u>Medical Arrangements.</u> Eestablished Advanced A.D.S. at Cement House U..28.c.3.2.

22nd.   <u>Decorations.</u> Sgt. King R.A.M.C. awarded D.C.M.

24th.   <u>Moves:</u> To Fusilier A.D.S. C.13.c.1.2.

27th.   <u>Operations.</u> Severe and prolonged bombardment commenced 1.55 p.m.

28th.   <u>Evacuation: Casualties:</u> Arrangements for evacuation worked smoothly. Casualties passed through to 12.30 p.m. 213.

B.E.F.

130th F.A. 38th Divn. 14th Corps, 5th Army. WESTERN FRON[T]
O.C. Lt. Col. J.E.H. Davies.   Aug. Sept. [

Phase "D" 1. (a) (Cont.)

1917.

Aug. 18th.   Moves: To Sussex Farm, (A.D.S.)

             Decorations. Pte. Allison A.S.C. awarded M.M.

19th.   Casualties R.A.M.C. 0 and 2 wounded.

21st.   Medical Arrangements: Established Advanced A.D.S.
             at Cement House U..28.c.3.2.

22nd.   Decorations. Sgt. King R.A.M.C. awarded D.C.M.

24th.   Moves: To Fusilier A.D.S. C.13.c.1.2.

27th.   Operations. Severe and prolonged bombardment commenced
             1.55 p.m.

28th.   Evacuation; Casualties: Arrangements for evacuation
             worked smoothly. Casualties passed through to
             12.30 p.m. 213.

WAR DIARY or INTELLIGENCE SUMMARY

Army Form C. 2118

John S. Rawe
Lt Col RAMC
O. 130th (St John) Fld Amb

Place	Date	Hour	Summary of Events and Information	Remarks and references to Appendices
COPPERNOLLE	1/8/17		Visited CANAL BANK ADSs of SUSSEX & FUSILIER, a number of wounded still coming in.	
A.17 a 2.9			Insp: Stretcher Cases	
			Visited MORDACQ - 57th Casual has now been back.	I.S.H.D
COPPERNOLLE	2/8/17		With ADMS visited MORDACQ, arranged to open as Fwd Amce Post, for sick.	
A.17 a 2.9			6 Clertes reported from XIV Corps Clearing Station to Dressing Wounded, 1FA	
			Station is now closed (12 noon) -	
			2 Ambulance Wagons sent to MORDACQ	JE H.D
COPPERNOLLE	3/8/17		Visited CANAL BANK "DS" at SUSSEX & FUSILIER - Canal Bank Fwd Amce	
A.17 a 2.5			Stalled	
			Fwd Amb Co 56/13/5'. Sent to the Ambce Designed by Col S Evans EVERDINGE -	
			BOESINGHE Road - Personnel in jured	JE H.D
COPPERNOLLE	4/8/17		Fwd Opn. No 33 issued. Clearance park by 1 Officer + 6 OR. to Central	
A.17 c 2.5			Site of 61 Fd Amb. at F.10.c.8.6 (Map 27)	JS H.D

Army Form C. 2118.

WAR DIARY
or
INTELLIGENCE SUMMARY.
(Erase heading not required.)

John ?? and Lt Col. Parsons
OC 130 (SD) Field Amb

Instructions regarding War Diaries and Intelligence Summaries are contained in F. S. Regs., Part II. and the Staff Manual respectively. Title pages will be prepared in manuscript.

Place	Date	Hour	Summary of Events and Information	Remarks and references to Appendices
COPPERNOLLE	5/8/17		LOADING POST at MORDACQ relieved by party from 60° Fd Amb. 20 O.Rs.	
			The following Officers posted to/from 8th Shrops. & 1st Fd Ambulance. Capt F. DOYLE	
			STANLEY PARSONS	SMO
			RAMC King's Company returned from Canal Bank	
COPPERNOLLE	6/8/17	6.30 am	Moved off to Camp F.10.c.6.6. — Some delay due to other transport.	
			Arrived new Camp 8.15 am — 130 Fd Ambulance Supplies	SMO
PRIORY CAMP	7/8/17		Been hospital for inspection by Patients	
F.10.c.6.6			Capt J.A. PARSONS RAMC reported for duty	
			Capt C.W. STANLEY RAMC transferred to 13 RWF taking off Shrops for duty	
			Visited HQ 114 L Brigade — Inspection of lines	
PRIORY Camp	8/8/17		No work to report — Inspection of Regulators & P.H. Helmets	
F.10.C.8.6			Medical Inspection of lines —	

A6945 Wt. W11442/M1160 350,000 12/16 D.D.&L. Forms/C./2118/14.

WAR DIARY
or
INTELLIGENCE SUMMARY

Army Form C. 2118.

Place	Date	Hour	Summary of Events and Information	Remarks and references to Appendices
PRIORY CAMP F10 c.8.6.	9/8/17		Congratulations received for work of unit, from G.O.C., A.D.M.S., also copy of Congratulatory letters from Corps Commander XIV Corps, & Congratulations from General PLUMER & Staff 2nd Army. /EDWARD, P. HQ XIV Corps. Capt P.A. DOYLE. R.A.M.C. left & reaches 15 15 R.W.F. Sit Report. has been taken of Strength of 15 36 D.A.C. in Reduction of Establishment, Authority O.B. 2035 19/7/17 on Reduction.	
PRIORY CAMP F10 c.6.6	10/8/17		A.D.M.S. visited Ambulances. h. accompanied with A.D.M.S. withdrawing visited forward Area - watching the MORDACQ FARM, then proceeded to Canal Bank and followed Trolley Line (Louvahoe Farm) above Bridge G. 15 C.8 Central, crossing the YPRES-PILCKEM Road, this road is under fire & and it would be impossible at the present line 15 later after - and it would be impossible at the present line Ambulances up to GALLWITZ FARM. This spot when present had has very little protection. ADMS on forward ADS G.O.C. 36. Div visits the Camps. Expressed his approval to Real John Ralston with the Ambulances Carrying out of the search He also called personally to Congratulate by the O.C. Officers N.C.O's. Men & & the men. of special operations.	

WAR DIARY
or
INTELLIGENCE SUMMARY
(Erase heading not required.)

Army Form C. 2118.

Place	Date	Hour	Summary of Events and Information	Remarks and references to Appendices
PRIORY CAMP F10c 8·6	11/8/17		Again visited CANAL BANK. followed new road running N.N.W. in the direction of CANDIN Fm. Pontje 6.W. but found road + surrounding area was as that was heavily shelled by its enemy, my line was taken up with seeing some D.H. horses. I almost proceeded beyond NIEL COTTAGE - returned to Canal Bank to Trolley line which run past GLIMPSE CROSS, CROSSES Pontje 6·W. Capt. MELHUISH reports from 14. R.W.F. Taken on Strength 92HD	92HD
PRIORY Camp F10c 8·6	12/8/17		Lieut Trafzelon (O.C.) Divnt Baths attended baths at COUTROVE All run.	92HD
PRIORY Camp F10c 8·2	13/8/17		No event to report — Respiralor Dress — by Gas Officer	
PRIORY Camp F10c 9·2	14/8/17		A.D.M.S. visited Ambulance — Lieut Trafzelon —	
PRIORY Camp F10c 8·2	15/8/17	7. am	Visited Forward Area, with A.D.M.S. outposts found easy + A.D.S. posts held by 20th Div. also later posts, and A.D.S. + Advanced A.D.S. at GALLWITZ FARM	92HD

WAR DIARY or INTELLIGENCE SUMMARY

Army Form C. 2118.

John B.H. Dauga
L/Cpl. R.A.M.C
to 130th Coy Sth Division

Place	Date	Hour	Summary of Events and Information	Remarks and references to Appendices
FRIDAY Camp F10 C & 6	(cont) 15/8/17		Received following copy from "O" Corps Commander has awarded MILITARY MEDAL to 48197 Cpl. (A/Sgt.) E SWEETING, 48186 Lce. Cpl. D.J. SAMUEL, 48196 Lce. Cpl. W.G. THOMAS. Please convey Corps & Divisional Commander's Congratulations — "I have great pleasure in forwarding you copy of OC 130th Field Amb. I wish to congratulate yourself on my behalf on above, and wish you to congratulate yourself on my behalf." — Signed. A.G. Thomson, a Brig. 38th Div. — The following is the reports of acts of gallantry & devotion to duty reported by OC Brmard. 48186 L/Cpl. DAVID JOHN SAMUEL — whilst from 30/7/17 to 5/8/17 while acting as one of the advanced stretcher bearers this L/Cpl. repeatedly made journeys across the open under intense shell fire to bring in wounded, and at times to greatest coolness, endurance, courage, and set a splendid example to all with him. He was to have to volunteer after several days heavy work, to clear the roads at JOLIE & STRAY FMs, and during the entire attack & barrage on afternoon of 11/8/17 he guided stretcher squads conveying wounded through his RAMC — Coolu Coo, great — Encouraged often bearers. — #81492 Cpl. (A/Sgt) ERNEST SWEETING — from 30/7/17 to 5/8/17 this N.C.O. was in charge of an advanced stretcher bearer party, he at once proceeded	

WAR DIARY
or
INTELLIGENCE SUMMARY

Army Form C. 2118.

John En Basal
W. G. Rawe

Place	Date	Hour	Summary of Events and Information	Remarks and references to Appendices
	15/9/17 (cont)		"B" discover a route, to Evacuate wounded, as the tracks allotted, for this purpose had been completely destroyed, the NCO Evacuated at July 5 5/8/17. — Showed great Courage, Coolness, judgement + Determination, + proved himself to be a Reliable Bearer of NCO. JETR 48196. L/Corp. W.G. Thomas from 30/7/17 to 3/8/17 while acting as one of two advanced Stretcher Bearers working from JOLIE Fm to R. Bassee Outpt, then Conf. showed conspicuous gallantry + devotion to duty, in that he repeatedly made journeys across the open to bring in wounded men (very often Regimental Aid Post, for 3½ days, — he was one of the first always to volunteer, and showed great Courage, Coolness, + Determination of the kind hardest to XIV Corps Offrs Rest Station Capt MELHUISH. JETR	
PRIORY Camp F100 6.6	16/9/17		Warning order from ADMS that 38ᵗʰ Division probably be leaving 20ᵗʰ Div Comdg 17/9/17 - preparations therefore made, to be able to move off within an hour's notice. JETR	

WAR DIARY
or
INTELLIGENCE SUMMARY

Army Form C. 2118.

John G H Barrey
W/Gr R.A.M.C. (T.) OC
OC 130/131 Fd Amb (?)

Place	Date	Hour	Summary of Events and Information	Remarks and references to Appendices
PRIORY CAMP. F10 CC 6.	7/9/17		Recd. Medical Arrangement No1 (Orders) dated 15/8/17 in Raid J 32 Dig Infantry. 20 Other Ranks preceded to Canal Bank for the purpose of making an advance Dressing Post from 61st Field Amb. 50 Other Ranks sent up same night — An advance party of 1 Officer + 8 O.R. reported Priory Camp. 60 Fd. Amb. to take over.	JSHD
PRIORY CAMP F10 CC 6	16/8/17	5 am	Transport under Lt. Thompson proceeded in accordance with time table to PELISSIER Fm B21a0.2 sheet 28.	
		7 am	Remainder of unit, after handing over S/G moved to above Fm under Capt BURNE. A.D.S. at SUSSEX FUSILIER, also an advanced posts took one. Completed by 3.45 P.M. Notified that Corps Commander has awarded the MILITARY MEDAL to 70485 71 Private G.W. ALLISON A.S.C. attached to this Unit, for brave conduct. Capt PARRY R.A.M.C.(T) Capt. BROWN 129 Fd Amb reported for duty with this Unit (temporary) CAPT. BROWN relieved M.O. S.W.B. released by Lt DICKSON.	JSHD

Army Form C. 2118.

WAR DIARY
or
INTELLIGENCE SUMMARY
(Erase heading not required.)

John A Deval
Lt Col RAMC OC 130 9 Amb

Place	Date	Hour	Summary of Events and Information	Remarks and references to Appendices
SUSSEX F⁺ (13 Bn, D.S. FUSILIER A.D.S. (C.13.C.1.2) ST JOHN A.D.S. (C.13.4.2.3)	19/8/17		Visited GALLWITZ F⁺ which I found had been (10 hours from Zero, on the day, 19, then called) wounded by 6/Gloster Querie of 20⁺ Dis⁺ on account of Enemy Shellfire. — CORNER HOUSE, CORK HOUSE, BURNT F⁺ & CEMENT HOUSE — used as relay posts. Number of casualties of 20⁺ Dis. + Wounded (Tournai passed through) J.E.A.D	
			The FUSILIER SUSSEX 45099 Pte CHURCHILL W. + 45619 Pte YATES F — wounded Shellfire — Strength of platoon — 35 cases passed through SUSSEX + FUSILIER A.D.S's	J.E.A.D
SUSSEX F⁺ (C.15.C.6)	20/8/17	7am	With A.D.M.S. inspected posts Waterlines to beyond. STEENBECK. Visiting relay posts — 25 casualties passed through SUSSEX + FUSILIER Report	J.E.A.D
SUSSEX F⁺ (C.15.C.2.6)	21/8/17		Selected CEMENT HOUSE otherwise known as BURNT F⁺ U.28.C.3.2 as advanced A.D.S. Reported to that effect to A.D.M.S. — It is near main PILKEN — LANGEMARCK road, and at any distance from TROLLEY LINE — Consists of 2 rooms — with concrete walls, and has been used as German A.D.S. — Its larger room is capable of holding 16 stretcher cases. Its smaller, an annexion or dressing room, can hold 2 Stretcher Cases at one time — Its walls & flushes are 4ft in thickness with roof 7¼ thick — arranged for the Sand-bagging of windows & Door — Capt RIDDELL D.C Reserve, moving from Corner H⁰ & CEMENT F⁺. CORNER H⁰ held as R.A.P for R.F.A.	J.E.A.D

WAR DIARY or INTELLIGENCE SUMMARY

Army Form C. 2118.

John Shortall
Lt Colonel
OC 130th (St John) Field Amb

Place	Date	Hour	Summary of Events and Information	Remarks and references to Appendices
SUSSEX A.D.S. C.19.c.2.6.	21/8/17	(Continued)	Major Carter T.M. 12 RAMC reported for duty and put on strength of this F.A. from 22nd. JSMD	
SUSSEX A.D.S.	22/8/17		2 Stafford Steel Dug outs drawn from R.E. and sent on holiday in direction of CEMENT H°. TROLLEY line damaged by enemy, near shop - Ft 20 Steel Shelter dumped there. Notified that Commander in Chief has awarded the following decoration: D.C.M. to No 45068 Serj F.T. KING of this unit. The Corps D. wounded Commander Congratulations as well as those of the A.D.M.S. were conveyed to Serj. King. JEHD	
SUSSEX A.D.S.	23/8/17		Medical Arrangements - operation order No.4 issued.	
SUSSEX A.D.S.	24/8/17		O.R.s & 1 Corporal SUSSEX F. A.D.S. moved up H.Q.s. to FUSILIER F. Further FUSILIER A.D.S. C.13.c.1.2. - Leaving a holding party at SUSSEX. Medical Arrangements operation Order No 4 Amendment No1 issued, which reads as follows "Delete SUSSEX from list of A.D.S's —"	
FUSILIER A.D.S. C.13.c.1.2.				

WAR DIARY
or
INTELLIGENCE SUMMARY.

(Erase heading not required.)

Army Form C. 2118.

John H Davis
Lt Col RAMC
OC 1/3rd 2/Field Ambulance

Place	Date	Hour	Summary of Events and Information	Remarks and references to Appendices
FUSILIER ADS	25/9/17		Medical Arrangements of evacuation of sick No. 4. Austrian H. 2. Received	
C.13.C.1.2.			Received 38th Div ADMS visited ADS	
			Capt Rodon to CEMENT HOUSE to relieve Capt Burke RAMC	
FUSILIER A.D.S.	26/9/17		Arrangements made for light railway to carry wounded from GALLWITZ Ft	
C.13.C.1.12.			to SOLFERINO calling at CHEAPSIDE with walking wounded	
Advanced ADS at			CAPT MELHUISH reported from C.R.S. for Orders – discharged to Duty	
GALLWITZ Ft.			Orders received for Austrian Shelter Prepared to relieve to their Lieut (Colonel)	
CEMENT Ft.				
FUSILIER ADS	27/9/17		Wrote Orders visited - GALLWITZ A.D.S. each R.M.P. supplied with 36 Field Dressings	
C.13.C.1.12.			Bombardment of Enemy Positions 1.55 P.M. (ZERO) Severe Barrage	
			first wounded around CEMENT Ft (Advanced ADS) shortly after 4.P.M – (Walking Wounded)	
			a large number up to midnight	
FUSILIER ADS	28/9/17		Large number of Stretcher Cases brought into Advanced ADS or Dawn – These	
C.13.C.1.2.			were invalidly prepared to be for warded, after being made comfortable, were	
			covered with blankets were fed, with hot Drinks, Sandwiches, were Rapidly	

WAR DIARY
or
INTELLIGENCE SUMMARY

Army Form C. 2118.

Place	Date	Hour	Summary of Events and Information	Remarks and references to Appendices
FUSILIER A DS	Continued 28/8/17		Placed on (alert) & taken down to GALLWITZ Ft ADS. There inspected by the O.C. 129th Fieldamb who arranged work in connection with the loading & arrangements for the Fourth evening. Crateful supply of Dressing Vans (very few required such) passed only of essentials, bar, fed, & loaded on Travois - via to SOLFERINO. - CHEAPSIDE	
CEMENT Ft				
GALLWITZ Ft		9.30 am	Visited GALLWITZ, CEMENT HOUSE, relay posts CORK HOUSE, STRAY FARM all running smoothly, wounded rapidly evacuated, - O.C. advanced	
		11 AM	Guard reports at 12.30 am. that all the AD Post. Clear, that only a few Walking Casualties stretchers -	
			number of wounded which passed through A.D.S.'s were in command.	
			from 2 PM 27/8/17 to 12.30 P.M. 28/8/17	
			CEMENT Ft: GALLWITZ Ft (Advanced ADS's) 181	
			FUSILIER ADS 32	
			Total - 213	
			There seems little in all the arrangements: - no shortage of supplies for Rations - Asprts, Rum, Board even Officer (Military)	

WAR DIARY
or
INTELLIGENCE SUMMARY

Army Form C. 2118.

J.O.S.H. Davis
W.G. Raue

Place	Date	Hour	Summary of Events and Information	Remarks and references to Appendices
FUSILIER RDS	28/8/17		OC 194 Fd Ambce Wishaw were ambulance help NCOs & men of the 3 Fd Ambulances worked splendidly. very valuable work was done by Capt RODELL of this unit in charge of Advanced Posts, who at great risk, visited [erased] the RAP & Posts in Contrd Trench when the Rnd's & 1st Dressing Station — This often showed fine pluck good leadership, thoroughness & Resource Powers of Endurance. JSHD	
CEMENT F"				
GALLWITZ F"				
ADVANCED ADS				
FUSILIER RDS	29/8/17		The work of erecting two Steel Shelters at CEMENT F" Commenced a number of R.A.M.C leaves were withdrawn. JSHD	
CEMENT F"				
GALLWITZ F"			Visited GALLWITZ, Bde	
FUSILIER RDS	30/8/17		Whitewashing of Dressing Rooms at FUSILIER commenced. Shales. Major CARTER RAMC i/c this unit took a Sanitary Officer — to inspect area on Canal Bank —	
CEMENT F"				
GALLWITZ F"			ADMS visited ADS — JSHD	

Army Form C. 2118.

WAR DIARY
or
INTELLIGENCE SUMMARY.
(Erase heading not required.)

John Davies
J. Gerome

Instructions regarding War Diaries and Intelligence Summaries are contained in F. S. Regs., Part II. and the Staff Manual respectively. Title pages will be prepared in manuscript.

Place	Date	Hour	Summary of Events and Information	Remarks and references to Appendices
FUSILIER ADS	31/8/17		Visited GALLWITZ Fm ADVANCED ADS	
CEMENT Fm				
GALLWITZ Fm				

J. Davies
Lt Col
O.C. 130TH (ST. JOHN) FIELD AMBULANCE

J. Humphreys
Capt
28th WELSH DIVISION

A6945 Wt. W14422/M1160 350,000 12/16 D. D. & L. Farms/C./2118/14.

Confidential

War Diary

of

130th (St John) Field Ambulance

From 1st September 1917

To 30th September 1917

B.E.F.

SUMMARY OF MEDICAL WAR DIARIES FOR

130th F.A., 38th Divn. 14th Corps, 5th Army.
To 11th Corps 1st Army 13.9.17.

WESTERN FRONT ~~JULY~~ SEPT 1917.

O.C. Lt. Col. J.E.H. Davies.

SUMMARISED UNDER THE FOLLOWING HEADINGS.

Phase "D" 1. Passchendaele Operation July.-Nov. '17.

(a) Operations commencing 1st July 1917

Sept. 2nd		<u>Operations Enemy</u>: <u>Casualties R.A.M.C.</u> A.D.S. at Gallwitz Farm heavily shelled, 0 and 1 wounded.
3rd.		<u>Operations Enemy</u>. Gallwitz Farm again shelled.
4th.		Canal Bank heavily shelled. Dugout and cookhouse at St. Johns destroyed. <u>Casualties R.A.M.C.</u> 4 and 0 wounded.
9th.		<u>Decorations</u>: Cpls. Probert and Young awarded M.M.
10th.		<u>Moves</u>: To Pelissier Farm. Priory Camp F.10c.8.6.

130th F.A. 38th Divn. 14th Corps, 5th Army WESTERN FRONT

O.C. Lt. Col. J.E.H. Davies. Sept., 1917.

Phase "D" 1.(a) (Cont.)

1917.
Sept. 13th. Moves and Transfer.   To Eecke area on transfer to 11th Corps 1st Army.

Sept.	2nd	<u>Operations Enemy:</u> <u>C</u>asualties R.A.M.C. A.D.S. at Gallwitz Farm heavily shelled 0 and 1 wounded.
	3rd.	<u>Operations Enemy.</u> Gallwitz Farm again shelled.
	4th.	Canal Bank heavily shelled. Dugout and cookhouse at St Johns destroyed. <u>Casualties R.A.M.C.</u> 4 and 0 wounded.
	9th.	<u>Decorations:</u> Cpls. Probert and Young awarded M.M.
	10th.	<u>Moves:</u> To Pelissier Farm. Priory Camp F.10c.8.6.

130th F.A. 38th Divn. 14th Corps, 5th Army WESTERN FRONT
O.C. Lt. Col. J.E.H. Davies.   Sept. 1917.

Phase "D" 1.(a) (Cont.)

1917.
Sept. 13th.   Moves and Transfer.   To Eecke area on transfer to 11th Corps 1st Army.

Army Form C. 2118.

WAR DIARY
or
INTELLIGENCE SUMMARY.
(Erase heading not required.)

John Drose
Lt-Col. R.A.M.C.
OC 130 (St Jn) Fd. Amb.

Place	Date	Hour	Summary of Events and Information	Remarks and references to Appendices
FUSILIER ADS	1/9/17	7.30 am	Visited GALLWITZ Fm ; CEMENT HOUSE ; Brigade HQ² at STRAY Fm one 'Shed Shelter' Completed at CEMENT HOUSE	
FUSILIER ADS	2/9/17		Visited GALLWITZ & ADMS' Office. Pte BULLS of this unit wounded. Spare Shelter P'torm GALLWITZ Fm. Lewis Stated. ASMD	
FUSILIER ADS	3/9/17		Visited by OC 60 Sard Ambce who came to take over. CAPT DOYLE R.A.M.C. wounded. Evacuated to 46 CCS Visited 4th M.A.C. GALLWITZ Fm Lewis Shelter. — Capt Stanley R.A.M.C. — 13 R.W.F wounded. Capt PAGE 1/13 R.W.F. & MD	
FUSILIER ADS	4/9/17	6 AM	Will be be to 60 Fd Ambce visited GALLWITZ Fm, CEMENT HOUSE, H/R of Latter. Report Progressing . 2 Shed Shelters Completed. CANAL BANK H'qurs. Stelles - Dug-out - Cookhouse at St JOHN's destroyed by enemy Shellfire. Capt WOODHOUSE R.A.M.C. 10 WELSH. wounded (shrapnel wound Side) whilst proceeding up Line with his unit. Evacuated through XIV Corps MDS to 64 CCS — & MD Capt. RIDDELL R.A.M.C. relieves Capt. BURKE R.A.M.C. at CEMENT H⁰ Joined ADS. — 1 H.D. Horse Killed, Evacuated (4 H.D - I L.D) + Shoer S/6 Sheryth	

Army Form C. 2118.

WAR DIARY
or
INTELLIGENCE SUMMARY.
(Erase heading not required.)

John B Prass
J Belrowe O.C. 135 Field Amb

Place	Date	Hour	Summary of Events and Information	Remarks and references to Appendices
FUSILIER ADS CASC 11.2	5/9/17		Visited ADMS Office. - Transport Lines, DOZINGHEM.	
			Lt. DUNN RAMC 129- 7th Amb posted Capt PAGE RAMC 13 Rust.	
			who was losing Adv Post for 10th WELSH at ALOUETTE try. (JBD)	
		9 PM	Lt DUNN RAMC Killed by Shell at Batt. HQ ALOUETTE F. Sele (JBD)	
			entering dug-out.	
			R.A.P's at ALOUETTE Fm - STEEBECK Evacuated + re-established at	
			CEMENT (+ D (D)) BURNT FARM (JBD)	
			Operation Order 36. received.	
FUSILIER R ADS CASC 11.2	6/9/17	8.30	Visited Proceeded by Car to reconnoitre new area, reported to A.D.M.S.	
		am	57 Div at CROIX DE BAC - 11.A.M - with D.A.D.M.S. 57 Div. OC 129 7 amb	
			Visited MAIN DRESSING STATION of 3rd W/ Lancs F.d Amb at SAILLY sur la LYS and	
			ADS at BOIS GRENIER - Visited RAP's - the RELAY POSTS	
			The frontage of new Line is 15000 yards	
			Visited PELISSERIE - inspected 5 H.D. horses, - put on our strength, head thin. Dairy	
			to replace Cavaller - Visited ADMS Office. (JBD)	

WAR DIARY
or
INTELLIGENCE SUMMARY.

Army Form C. 2118.

JohnSmDavies
L/Col Rawe

Place	Date	Hour	Summary of Events and Information	Remarks and references to Appendices
FUSILIER A.D.S. C.13.C.1.2	7/9/17	9 AM	The A.D.M.S. visited A.D.S., GALLWITZ Fm, CEMENT H". Attended funeral of Capt WOODHOUSE, RAMC at Buliah Cemetery, near 64 CCS. (Lt WOLSTENHOLME SC) A.D.M.S return	JSMD
FUSILIER ADS C.13.C.1.2	8/9/17		Advance Party of 60th Field Amb.ce 20th Div. reported for the purpose of takeing over Advance Ads's at GALLWITZ, CEMENT H". Capt H. BROWN. RAMC - Struck off Strength, - on Strength of XIII Corps School of Instruction	JSMD
FUSILIER ADS C.13.C.1.2	9/9/17	2 PM	Lt R.M. DAVIS U.S. MORC. reported for duty taken on Strength. Handed over FUSILIER A.D.S., + St JOHN A.D.S. 16 60th Field Amb.ce 20 Div. Lieut proceeded to Kortepyp Cnr on of PELLISSER Fm MILITARY MEDALS awarded a/c Cpl W.J. PROBERT, OLIVER YOUNG of this Unit	JSMD
PELLISSER Fm	10/9/17	6.30 AM	Transport with Capt MELNUISH proceeded to PRIORY Camp (Dragon Area) F10.C.8.6 - Unit proceeded with Major Carter Rawe retained Sterenhoff - RAMC Diagram No 37 Copy 2 Bound -	JSMD

WAR DIARY
or
INTELLIGENCE SUMMARY.
(Erase heading not required.)

Army Form C. 2118.

JOHN H DAVID
Lt Col RAMC

Instructions regarding War Diaries and Intelligence Summaries are contained in F. S. Regs., Part II. and the Staff Manual respectively. Title pages will be prepared in manuscript.

Place	Date	Hour	Summary of Events and Information	Remarks and references to Appendices
PELLISIER F	10/9/17	10.0	Took over PRIORY CAMP from 20 Div (60th Field Amb ce)	
PRIORY Camp			Received 114th Inf/Brigade Order No 123, Appx No 9	
F 10 C 8.6			Capt R. FRIEL R.A.M.C. reported for duty. Taken on Strength	
			Visited Brigade HQ's	JE+O
PRIORY Camp	11/9/17		Men of unit attended delousing station	
F 10 C 8.6		9 am	Inspection of unit	
			Visited Brigade HQ's	JE+O
PRIORY Camp	12/9/17	9 am	Capt R. FRIEL RAMC to 15th 13th Bn to relieve Capt D.C.M. PAGE who	
F 10 C 8.6			proceeded on leave — Inspection in full marching order of unit	
			Copy of No 16 57th Div Orders received	
			P.H. + Box respirator Inspection — 114th Inf/Brigade Order 124 received Appx 9	95+D
PRIORY Camp	13/9/17	9.0 am	unit defeated —	
F 10 C 8.6		11.0	moved off — to starting point Reached 12.20 PM arrived ECCKE area	
		4 PM	good billets in farms	JE+O

Army Form C. 2118.

WAR DIARY
or
INTELLIGENCE SUMMARY. John D. 296 Rams
(Erase heading not required.)

Instructions regarding War Diaries and Intelligence Summaries are contained in F.S. Regs., Part II. and the Staff Manual respectively. Title pages will be prepared in manuscript.

Place	Date	Hour	Summary of Events and Information	Remarks and references to Appendices
EECKE	14/9/17		Fallen 10 a.m. Reached Starting Point 10.41 A.M. Proceeded by ST. SYLVESTRE + HAZEBROUCK to MORBEQUE AREA arriving 2 P.M. LA CUNEWELE. W. Coy. sent to Brigan Comp. to Report. Staff Capt. 36th Bde. Cullerly. Rec'd 114 Brigade Orden 125. Copy No 14 - Rec'd 114 Brigade Orden 126 Major CARTER R.A.M.C. proceeded to SAILLY with 1 Sergt. 19 O.R. to take over div. Advance A.D.S. traps in new area -	
MORBECQUE	15/9/17	a.m. 9.0	Battn. reached Starting Point 9. 44 am. Proceeded via HAZEBROUCK LE TIR ANGLAIS, LA MOTTE, MERVILLE to ESTAIRES arriving 2.10.P.M. Billeted in School.	
ESTAIRES	16/9/17	9.0	Battn. 9.30 moved off to SAILLY G17a 8.4 Relieved 3/3 WEST LANC'D 2 amb. all reliefs completed 12. noon - Capt. HY.RIDDELL - ace. Postal Informed and handed over duties to Advanced Surgical Centre. Div. 5th C.C.S. Church St. Sailly.	
SAILLY G.17 a 8.4	17/9/17		Conference O.R.U.S officer	

WAR DIARY
or
INTELLIGENCE SUMMARY.
(Erase heading not required.)

Army Form C. 2118.

Place	Date	Hour	Summary of Events and Information	Remarks and references to Appendices
SAILLY G.17a8.4.	18/9/17	a.m 9.0 P.M 2.0	Inspection of units - run-120 Inspection A.E.C. Rifles Clothing Boots -	JSNZ
SAILLY G.17a8.4.	19/9/17	9.0	Inspection of unit 1st DAVIS 16 A.D.S.	JSNZ
SAILLY G.17a8.4.	20/9/17		G.O.C. + Acting A.D.M.S. inspected Hospital. approved of Regimid alterations. recommends to its site Visited HQ's	JSNZ JSNZ
SAILLY G.17a8.4.	21/9/17		Visited A.D.S. inspected Aid Posts.	JSNZ
SAILLY G.17a8.4.	22/9/17		P.H. - Restandin Inspection -	JSNZ

Army Form C. 2118.

WAR DIARY
or
INTELLIGENCE SUMMARY.
(Erase heading not required.)

John Doval L/Gt. Raue
OC 130 Fold Aub.

Place	Date	Hour	Summary of Events and Information	Remarks and references to Appendices
SAILLY	23/9/17		Capt MELHUISH of this Unit temporarily posted 15 15th WELSH, 15 relieve Lt. ROBERTSON	
G 17a 8.4			reporting to Coen Office at S+ bretion of Onriet	
			Capt. BURKE 16 A.D.S. 15 relieve MAJOR CARTER. J.F.H.D.	
SAILLY	24/9/17		No event to report. — a large amount of Shrapnel alterations completed	
G 17a 8.4			Visited A.D.S. at BOIS GRENIER & R.A.P. at SHAFTSBURY AVENUE J.S.H.D.	
SAILLY	25/9/17		D.D.M.S. XI Corps — Col Army Col WRIGHT was at lulu Blachi Zaskus visited J.S.H.D	
G 17a 8.4			Visited Site of new Dressing Station.	
SAILLY	26/9/17		Attended with 60 O.R. of this Unit, Demonstration of THOMAS' SPLINT at 129th F. Amb.	
G 17a 8.4			Capt. FRIEL returned from duty with 13 R. W. S — J.S.H.D	
		8 AM	C.I. + Respirator Inspection —	
SAILLY	27/9/17		Visited A.D.S. at BOIS GRENIER, meet C.O 15th WELSH at WYE FARM A.D.S R.A.P.	
G 17a 8.4			in reference to new position for R.A.P. — Visited ELBOW FARM. J.F.H.D	
		PM 5.30	took Inspection of Unit —	

WAR DIARY
or
INTELLIGENCE SUMMARY.

Army Form C. 2118.

John Davies Lt Col RAMC
OC 130 (St Pal) Field Amb.

(Erase heading not required.)

Place	Date	Hour	Summary of Events and Information	Remarks and references to Appendices
SAILLY SUR LA LYS G.17.a.8.4	28/9/17		Visited HQ Div Train – Visited A.D.S. No news to report	JSD
SAILLY SUR LA LYS G.17.a.8.4	29/9/17		Capt. MELHUISH RAMC of this unit struck off strength to Troopships 15 WELSH Lt DAVIS to A.D.S. BOIS GRENIER	JSD
SAILLY SUR LA LYS G.17.a.8.4	30/9/17	9 am 12 noon	O.C. inspection in Skeleton R.L. Inspection Rifles etc. No news to report	JSD

John Davies Lt Col RAMC
OC 130 Field Amb.

Confidential

War Diary

of

130ᵗʰ (St John) Field Ambulance

From 1ˢᵗ October 1917

To 31ˢᵗ October 1917

COMMITTEE FOR THE MEDICAL HISTORY OF THE WAR
Date -8 DEC. 1917

Army Form C. 2118.

WAR DIARY
or
INTELLIGENCE SUMMARY.

(Erase heading not required.)

Page 1

102nd Divis. H.Q. R.A.M.C.
O.C. No. 3 (S. Af.) Fd. Amb.

Instructions regarding War Diaries and Intelligence Summaries are contained in F. S. Regs., Part II. and the Staff Manual respectively. Title pages will be prepared in manuscript.

Place	Date	Hour	Summary of Events and Information	Remarks and references to Appendices
SAILLY Sur La LYS G17a 8.4.	1/10/17		Lt.K. A.D.M.S. visited A.D.S. BOIS GRENIER and R.A.P's at SHAFTSBURY AVENUE	
			ELBOW F.H. WYE F.H. + WHITE CITY	
			MAJOR CARTER of this Unit proceeded on Leave	JS HD
SAILLY Sur La LYS	2/10/17		A.D.M.S. visited Main Dressing Station	JS HD
SAILLY Sur La LYS	3/10/17		Visited 129th Fd. Amb.	JS HD
SAILLY Sur 4/10/17 La LYS			No event to report	JS HD
SAILLY Sur La LYS	5/10/17		Inspection Gas Boots, Conference with A.D.M.S. at 131st Fd. Amb.	JS HD
SAILLY Sur La LYS	6/10/17		No event to report.	JS HD
SAILLY Sur La LYS	7/10/17		O.C. Inspection of Unit, Inspection Rifles &c.	JS HD

Army Form C. 2118.

WAR DIARY
or
INTELLIGENCE SUMMARY.   John J. Dowd
(Erase heading not required.)   W. Lt. Rame.

Place	Date	Hour	Summary of Events and Information	Remarks and references to Appendices
SAILLY Sur La Lys G.17.a.8.b.6	8/10/17		16 Casualties reported. 4 bombs dropped nr. BAC ST MAUR. Western Junction Seven	JJH.
SAILLY Sur La LYS	9/10/17		11 Casualties reported mostly Hun. — Capt BURNE of the unit proceeded on leave. 10'-24" Capt FRIEL to 58 C.C.S. — Lt. DICKSON from 129th Fd. Amb. reported for duty. Leave of Shrapnel. — Lt. DAVIS to ADS S.P.R won reported to replace 5' Belgian A.S.C.	JJH.
SAILLY sur LYS	10/10/17		Lt GOODMAN R.A.M.C. reported for duty. Taken on strength.	JJH.
SAILLY sur la LYS	11/10/17		4 A.S.C. wgn proceed to base — D.A.D.V.S. inspected stores — states they were in better Condition than any A.D.M.S visited the D.S. A.D.M.S. forwarded following copy of report from water testing reporter from DC No 3 mobile laboratory "The Sauto of the Reserve Water Supply has June better less. The Water Contains "no" slightly well. h.d.s. awaiting of the Sample to serve as a model for other Funds"	JJH.

Army Form C. 2118.

WAR DIARY
or
INTELLIGENCE SUMMARY.
(Erase heading not required.)

Instructions regarding War Diaries and Intelligence Summaries are contained in F.S. Regs., Part II. and the Staff Manual respectively. Title pages will be prepared in manuscript.

Place	Date	Hour	Summary of Events and Information	Remarks and references to Appendices
SAILLY SUR La LYS	12/10/17		A.A.Q.M.G. D.A.A.M.G. D.A.D.M.S visited Main Dressing Station	
			A.D.M.S. visited M.D.S.	
			Divisional Baths visited site	
			Major CARTER reported from Base	824/3
SAILLY SUR La LYS	13/10/17		Lt. DAVIS attached for temporary duty (5 14th WELSH) to relieve Capt BATEMAN R.A.M.C. - who proceeds to England	
			Lt. DICKSON R.A.M.C. to A.D.S.	82H3
SAILLY SUR La LYS	14/10/17	8:30 am from 12	Inspection of huts. Inspection A.S.C. -	82H3
SAILLY SUR La LYS	15/10/17		No events to report	8943
SAILLY SUR La LYS	16/10/17		No event to report	8548

WAR DIARY
or
INTELLIGENCE SUMMARY.
(Erase heading not required.)

Army Form C. 2118.

JD McDonal
W.B. Raine
Lt 130 Field Amb.

Place	Date	Hour	Summary of Events and Information	Remarks and references to Appendices
SAILLY Sur La LYS	17/10/17	2.30 PM	Conference O/D M.S. Office A.D.M.S. visited M.D.S.	J.S.McD
SAILLY Sur La LYS	18/10/17		No Report - Major Carter visited ADS RAP's RP	J.S.McD
SAILLY Sur La LYS	19/10/17		No report to report	J.E.H.D
SAILLY Sur La LYS	20/10/17		Visited A.D.S. BOISGRENIER and RAP's WHITE CITY, WYE F^m A.D.M.S. visited M.D.S. Lt GOODMAN to A.D.S. to relieve Lt B. DICKSON.	J.E.H.D
SAILLY Sur La LYS	21/10/17	9. AM	Lt DICKSON proceeded to 33rd Labour Company. Inspection of Unit. visited 129^t Fd Amber	J.S.McD
SAILLY Sur La LYS	22/10/17		Major Carter visited ADS. M Army Inspector of Quering visited M.D.S. with A.D.M.S. Insp	J.S.McD

WAR DIARY
or
INTELLIGENCE SUMMARY.

(Erase heading not required.)

Army Form C. 2118.

Thos M Caylie
Major RAMC
O/c 130th Field Ambulance

Place	Date	Hour	Summary of Events and Information	Remarks and references to Appendices
SAILLY sur la LYS	23/10/17		Lt Col. J.E.H. DAVIES proceeded on leave. (24/10/17 - 23/11/17)	Jmb
SAILLY sur la LYS	24/10/17		CAPT J. BURKE returned from leave.	Jmb
SAILLY sur la LYS	25/10/17		No report.	Jmb
SAILLY sur la LYS	26/10/17		No report.	Jmb
SAILLY sur la LYS	27/10/17		Visited A.D.S. and R.A.P's on left Sector - WHITE CITY - SHAFTESBURY AVENUE - and site of proposed new R.A.P on road near the end of TRAMWAY AVENUE - accompanied by DIVISIONAL GAS OFFICER.	Jmb
SAILLY sur la LYS	28/10/17		Inspection of R.A.M.C. personnel 8.30 a.m. Inspection of A.S.C. personnel attached 12 noon.	Jmb
SAILLY sur la LYS	29/10/17		No report	Jmb
SAILLY sur la LYS	30/10/17		Medical Examination of R.A.M.C. personnel for Category Classification. 13 "A" Class. 49 "B" Class.	Jmb
SAILLY sur la LYS	31/10/17		Capt. BURKE relieved LIEUT GOODMAN at A.D.S. LIEUT GOODMAN returned for duty to M.D.S.	Jmb

J.G. Gaunt
COLONEL.
A.D.M.S. 38TH (WELSH) DIVISION.

Thos M Caylie
Major RAMC
O/c 130th (St John) Field Ambulance.

Confidential

War Diary

of

130th (St John) Field Ambulance

From 1st November 1917

To 30th November 1917

Army Form C. 2118.

WAR DIARY
or
INTELLIGENCE SUMMARY.
(Erase heading not required.)

Thompson Major R.A.M.C.
o/c 130th Field Ambulance

Instructions regarding War Diaries and Intelligence Summaries are contained in F. S. Regs., Part II. and the Staff Manual respectively. Title pages will be prepared in manuscript.

Place	Date	Hour	Summary of Events and Information	Remarks and references to Appendices
SAILLY sur LYS	1/1/17		Brigadier Gen'l A.R. HARMAN D.S.O. O/c 114 Bde Inf. visited M.D.S. Capt C.D. FAULKNER reported for duty	July
SAILLY sur LYS	2/1/17		D.D.M.S. 11th Corps with ADMS visited ADS. attended ADMS's Conference at 131 Field Ambulance Inspection of personnel and rifles	July
SAILLY sur LYS	3/1/17		Brig. Gen. E.W. ALEXANDER V.C. Cmg. O/c 38th Division visited M.D.S. accompanied by A.A. & Q.M.G. Lt.Col. A.M. PRYCE-JONES.	July
SAILLY sur LYS	4/1/17		Visited ADS with ADMS to decide site for new R.A.P.	July
SAILLY sur LYS	5/1/17		No report.	July
SAILLY sur LYS	6/1/17		Attended Demonstration on "Humphries" at 113 Brigade School. ADMS visited & inspected M.D.S.	July
SAILLY sur LYS	7/1/17		Visited A.D.S. and WYE FARM R.A.P. Two cars detailed for Service with 131 F.A. to assist in evacuation of casualties in intended raid.	July
SAILLY sur LYS	8/1/17		No report.	July

Army Form C. 2118.

WAR DIARY
or
INTELLIGENCE SUMMARY.

(Erase heading not required.)

T.W. Carli
Major RAMC
O/c 130 Field Ambulance

Instructions regarding War Diaries and Intelligence Summaries are contained in F.S. Regs., Part II. and the Staff Manual respectively. Title pages will be prepared in manuscript.

Place	Date	Hour	Summary of Events and Information	Remarks and references to Appendices
SAILLY sur la LYS	9/11/17		Kit inspection of R.A.M.C personnel.	Jmb
SAILLY sur la LYS	10/11/17		No report.	Jmb
SAILLY sur la LYS	11/11/17		Inspection of Personnel and rifles. Kit inspection of M.T. and H.T. A.S.C. attached personnel.	Jmb
SAILLY sur la LYS	12/11/17		A.D.M.S. visited + inspected M.D.S. Electrical Engineer (of Army) inspected Dynamo + plant.	Jmb
SAILLY sur la LYS	13/11/17		Visited A.D.S and R.A.P's WHITE CITY + SHAFTESBURY AVENUE. D.D.M.S. XI Corps inspected M.D.S.	Jmb
SAILLY sur la LYS	14/11/17		A.D.M.S visited M.D.S. CAPT C.D. FAULKNER relieved CAPT BURKE at A.D.S. The latter returned for duty to M.D.S.	Jmb
SAILLY sur la LYS	15/11/17		No report.	Jmb
SAILLY sur la LYS	16/11/17		LIEUT H. GOODMAN evacuated to No 54 C.C.S. CAPT. G.Q. GRIFFITHS C.F. attached for billetting + rations	Jmb

Army Form C. 2118.

WAR DIARY
or
INTELLIGENCE SUMMARY.
(Erase heading not required.)

Tho McCarter
Major RAMC
O/C 130 St John Field Ambulance

Place	Date	Hour	Summary of Events and Information	Remarks and references to Appendices
SAILLY sur la LYS	17/11/17		No report.	
SAILLY sur la LYS	18/11/17		Inspection of RAMC personnel 9am. Inspection of ASC personnel + of rifles 12 noon.	Ditto.
SAILLY sur la LYS	19/11/17		Divisional Band visited M.D.S. and played from 2.30–4 and 5–6 p.m.	Ditto.
SAILLY sur la LYS	20/11/17		No report.	Ditto.
SAILLY sur la LYS	21/11/17		A.D.M.S. visited ADS at BOIS GRENIER.	Ditto.
SAILLY sur la LYS	22/11/17		Visited A.D.S.	Ditto.
SAILLY sur la LYS	23/11/17		Reported from leave.	1st ND
SAILLY sur la LYS	24/11/17		A.D.M.S. visited inspected M.D.S.	ditto

WAR DIARY
or
INTELLIGENCE SUMMARY.

Army Form C. 2118.

(Erase heading not required.)

John H Rawl
Lt Col RAMC
OC 130 Fd Amb 3rd Div Amb.

Place	Date	Hour	Summary of Events and Information	Remarks and references to Appendices
SAILLY sur la LYS	25/11/17	9 AM	Inspection R.A.M.C. personnel. — 12 noon. Inspection A.S.C. H.T. Rifle Drill + Inspection of Rifles	
			Visited XV C.R.S.	
			Acting DDMS XV Corps visited, + ADMS visited M.D.S.	38MD
SAILLY sur la LYS	26/11/17		Visited XV C.R.S. CORPS. C.S.D. Six men detected for inoculation in water bath	
			Visited ADS at BOIS GRENIER	32 MD
SAILLY sur la LYS	27/11/17		ADMS visited inspected MDS. — visited ESTAIRES inspected various sites. No provision for Horse Transport	
			visited inspected ADMS at D.HQ — 19 O.R. proceeded for duty to 54 C.C.S.	32MD
SAILLY sur la LYS	28/11/17		Acting DDMS. XV Corps visited M.D.S.	13MD
SAILLY sur la LYS	29/11/17		Lt R.N.Davis, U.S. M.O.R.C. posted to 1st Welsh, visited HQ Shaft of the unit from this Day	35 MD
SAILLY sur la LYS	30/11/17		G.O.C. 38th Div. visited M.D.S.	13MD

J Stansfeen Col
ADMS
38 Div

John H Rawl
Lt Col RAMC
OC 130 Fd Amb 3rd Div Amb.

Confidential

War Diary

of

130th (St John) Field Ambulance

From 1st December 1917

To 31st December 1917

WAR DIARY or INTELLIGENCE SUMMARY

Army Form C. 2118.

John H. Dansk, DGR RMC
OC 130th (2nd Co.) Field Ambulance

Place	Date	Hour	Summary of Events and Information	Remarks and references to Appendices
SAILLY Sur la LYS	1/XII/17		AA Q.M.G. + DDMS XV Corps visited MDS — visited Advanced Dressing Stn SINCEAL Gabr ESTAIRES, with views to taking over as Field Ambulance site — visited A.D.M.S. reported on self	JND
			Examined 6 men, under training at the MDS for stretcher bearers	JND
SAILLY sur la LYS	2/XII/17		Inspected site at L27b 1.6 but 36th to transfer over, proposed to 6 Adv Dress power of most	JND
			DAQMG 36th Div visited MDS	
SAILLY Sur la LYS	3/XII/17		Lt Col. A.D.M.S. RCC 129th Brist Amb visited DDMS HQ XV Corps. Lt Col. DICNSON RAMC struck off Strength	JND
SAILLY Sur la LYS	4/XII/17		No report.	JND
SAILLY Sur la LYS	5/XII/17		DDMS XV Corps ADMS 36 Div visited MDS	JND
SAILLY Sur la LYS	6/XII/17		Capt. J BURNE RAMC Office hurt wished to July late 131st Field DDMS.-sky. H. C.E.P.? inspected site.	JND

Army Form C. 2118.

WAR DIARY
or
INTELLIGENCE SUMMARY.
(Erase heading not required.)

10th Draward
Lt.Col. Raue
at 130(S)F.A. > F.A.N.Amb

Place	Date	Hour	Summary of Events and Information	Remarks and references to Appendices
SAILLY sur LYS	7/XII/17		Visited Sites at ESTAIRES.	JS#D
SAILLY sur LYS	8/XII/17		In accordance with R.A.M.C. order No 35. O.D.S. BOIS GRENIER this day handed over to 129'FDA Amb.	JS#D
SAILLY sur LYS	9/XII/17		2. Sections proceeded to ESTAIRES. took over site for billets at PENSIONNAT DES JEUNES FILLES, RUE DE L'HOSPICE, + to Advanced Surgical Centre RUE DE COLLEGE when site was opened for admission at 5a.m. the same Day at Noon.	JS#D
ESTAIRES L29 b 6.6	10/XII/17		Handed over M.D.S. at G17 Q&L/Sailly sur la LYS 1 to C.E.P.90 at 3 P.M. A.D.M.S. visited New Hospital Site	JS#D
ESTAIRES L29 b 6.6	11/XII/17		Capt FRIEL R.A.M.C. relieved Capt FAULKNER R.A.M.C. two 15" WELCH 156/6(Canes) brund. A.D.M.S. visited N.D.S. - billets	JS#D
ESTAIRES	12/XII/17		D.D.M.S. to XV Corps visited hospital Site	JS#D

A6945 Wt. W11422/M1160 350000 12/16 D.D.&L. Forms/C/2118/14

WAR DIARY
or
INTELLIGENCE SUMMARY.

(Erase heading not required.)

Army Form C. 2118.

Allen Daniel
W. G. Crame

Place	Date	Hour	Summary of Events and Information	Remarks and references to Appendices
ESTAIRES	13/XII/17		Inspection of Stoke Jones	JSHQ
ESTAIRES	14/XII/17		Major Gen. Sir A. Poulton CMG. Consulting Surgeon 1st Army inspected Divisional Surgical Centre	JSHQ
ESTAIRES	15/XII/17		ADMS. Works inspected. Foot inspection for trench —	JSHQ
ESTAIRES	16/XII/17		1 N.C.O. & 26 O.R. to 54 C.C.S. P.H. & Box Respirators inspection of Drill. O.C. inspection of Strait	JSHQ
ESTAIRES	17/XII/17		No Event to Report.	R.M.O.
ESTAIRES	18/XII/17		DDMS (Col Luton DSO) visited various Ambulance Stns. Conference of Officers at 13th F. Amb. Capt FRIEL RAMC transferred to 15WFLSH 1st Shock of Staff, Capt. MELLUISH RAMC reported taken on Strength this day.	JSHQ
ESTAIRES	19/XII/17		ADMS visited Subjects. Capt SPITERI RAMC. taken on Strength this day	JSHQ

A6945 Wt. W11422/M1160 350,000 12/16 D.D.&L. Forms/C/2118/14

WAR DIARY
or
INTELLIGENCE SUMMARY

Army Form C. 2118.

John F. Passed Lt Col R Awle
OC 130 (St John) Fd Amb ee

Place	Date	Hour	Summary of Events and Information	Remarks and references to Appendices
ESTAIRES	19/4/17		Capt C. KELLY RMC. RAMC reports + puts on Strength the day. Capt S. ROBERTSON RAMC reports (place) on Strength.	JSHR
ESTAIRES	20/4/17		Took over duties H of ADMS. Major General WALLACE CMG AMS Consulting Surgeon 1st Army visited Advanced Surgical Centre 136 Fd Ambee	JSHR
ESTAIRES	21/4/17		At ADMS. No event to report	JSHR
ESTAIRES	22/4/17		Bot Battn to Parade & Drill	JSHR
ESTAIRES	23/4/17		Handed over duties of acting ADMS to Lt Col Mulloch Blake CMG Inspection of lines ASC	JSHR
ESTAIRES	24/4/17		No event to report.	JSHR
ESTAIRES	25/4/17		Brigadier General S. George Thomas DSO 115th Bde A.C. inspects Advanced Surgical Centre 136 Fd Ambee	JSHR

Army Form C. 2118.

WAR DIARY
or
INTELLIGENCE SUMMARY.
(Erase heading not required.)

John B. Daniel W/Cr Rowe
OC 138 Fold Amb

Instructions regarding War Diaries and Intelligence Summaries are contained in F. S. Regs., Part II. and the Staff Manual respectively. Title pages will be prepared in manuscript.

Place	Date	Hour	Summary of Events and Information	Remarks and references to Appendices
ESTAIRES	26/10/17		Capt. SPITERI R.A.M.C. Struck off Strength then transferred to 39 Siberian Hospital	8Hq
ESTAIRES	27/10/17		Brigadier General G. GWYN THOMAS D.S.O. visited Site	8Hq
ESTAIRES	28/10/17		Capt. FAULKNER RAMC struck off strength & transferred to 24 B.W. at A.D.M.S. weekly Fold Ambce	8Hq
ESTAIRES	29/10/17		Nothing to report	8Hq
ESTAIRES	30/10/17		Capt. B. ROBERTSON R.A.M.C. to 13 R.W? to temporary duty. Capt. PAGE M.C. proceeding on leave. visits 54 C.C.S.	8Hq
ESTAIRES	31/10/17		Capt. C. NELLY M.C. R.A.M.C. to 15 R.W? to Temporary Duty to Manchester proceeding on leave	

John B. Daniel
W/C G. Rowe
OC 138(S) John Fold Amba

A. Mussrs Lt. Col
W/C F. M. S
138(S) John Fold Amba

Confidential

War Diary

of

130th (St John) Field Ambulance

1st January 1918

to

31st January 1918

Army Form C. 2118.

WAR DIARY
or
INTELLIGENCE SUMMARY.
(Erase heading not required.)

John E.N. Davies
Lt. RAMC
OC 130 (St.Pb.) Field Amb.

Place	Date	Hour	Summary of Events and Information	Remarks and references to Appendices
ESTAIRES L29 6.6	1/1/18		Nothing to report.	82nd
ESTAIRES "St Pb Fld Amb"	2/1/18		Changes in Personnel { A.D.M.S. — Capt H.Y. RIDDELL. R.A.M.C. (one of the hund.) Capt J.H. BANKES. R.A.M.C. instead of the hund. — ADMS Tunes 17/1/18	82nd
ESTAIRES	3/1/18		48071 S/Major W. STROUD. — Tuxpdf. Awarded D.S.O. (Tunes 2/11/17)	82nd
ESTAIRES	4/1/18		No Event to report.	82nd
ESTAIRES	5/1/18		D.D.M.S. visited Advanced Surgical Centre Nord/Ambc. Bot. preparats for 32 the section.	82nd
ESTAIRES	6/1/18	9 a.m.	Inspection Inspection of Unit in Shelters &c. — Rifle Inspection. A.S.C.	82nd
ESTAIRES	7/1/18		No Event to report.	82nd
ESTAIRES	8/1/18		Inspection Visits by O.C. 5th C.C.S. Officers (3) of American Medical Services	82nd
"	9/1/18		Capt. BURKE of this Unit proceeded for temporary duty to 122-132 R.F.A.	82nd
"	10/1/18		Conference A.D.M.S. Office —	82nd
"	11/1/18		No Event to report.	82nd
"	12/1/18		Bax. Inspection. Drill & Instruction.	82nd
"	13/1/18		O.C. 3rd Div. visits Fld/Ambc. also OC/ADMS DaDus.	82nd
"	14/1/18		Nothing to report.	82nd
"	15/1/18		Rifle Inspection. A.S.C.	82nd

Army Form C. 2118.

WAR DIARY
or
INTELLIGENCE SUMMARY.
(Erase heading not required.)

John Barard McKenna
OC 130 (S)Fd Amb

Place	Date	Hour	Summary of Events and Information	Remarks and references to Appendices
ESTAIRES	16/1/18		No event to report	SNR
L29 b 6.6	17/1/18		DADMS XV Corps visited SHQ	SNR
"	18/1/18		No event to report	SNR
"	19/1/18		Major Gen. Sir A A BENTLEY Consulting Surgeon 1st Army visited Advanced Surgical Centre, Gas Helmet Inspection + Drill	SNR
"	20/1/18		Inspection of Unit	SNR
"	21/1/18		Conference at ADMS' Office	SNR
"	22/1/18		ADMS visited and inspected Site; GOC 11th Brigade inspected hospital	SNR
"	23/1/18		S.M. W STROUD & three men proceeded to 5th C.C.S. Shock & Shrapnel	SNR
"	24/1/18		ADMS 12th Div visited Ambulance Site; Capt. MELLUISH + 1 OR proceeded for July	SNR
"	25/1/18		1st Army Clearing Depot BERGUETTE. DADMS XV Corps visited Site	SNR
"	26/1/18		Gas Helmet Drill, and Inspection.	SNR
"	27/1/18		Inspector of Pathology unit in Flanders Rt visited 5th C.C.S. Surgeon General WALLACE Consulting Surgeon 1st Army visited Advanced Surgical Centre	SNR
"	28/1/18		ADMS visited inspected Site;	SNR

WAR DIARY
or
INTELLIGENCE SUMMARY.

Army Form C 2118.

Place	Date	Hour	Summary of Events and Information	Remarks and references to Appendices
ESTAIRES L29.b.6.6	28/1/18		Visited LESTREM + inspected all sites likely to be of use as A.D.S. + Workers on Some	B#1
			KQRWS.	B#1
ESTAIRES	29/1/18		Orders issued and inspected Site	B#1
ESTAIRES	30/1/18		DADMS XV Corps visited site for station of Bahus & for accommodation of Staff	B#1
			Visited LESTREM and neighbourhood, and further report to advise in Lo/ issue to Site of new A.D.S.	B#1
ESTAIRES	31/1/18		Capt Hollman reports from Duty with Army Clearing St. 51	

John H. Daniel
Lt Col RAMC
OC 130" (St John) Field Amb.

John H. Daniel
Lt Col RAMC
OC 130" (St John) Field Amb.

Confidential

War Diary

of

130th (St John) Field Ambulance

From 1st February 1918

To 28th February 1918

Army Form C. 2118.

WAR DIARY
or
INTELLIGENCE SUMMARY.
(Erase heading not required.)

John N Dans
L/Col. R.A.M.C.
OC 130 (S.T.) Field Amb.

Instructions regarding War Diaries and Intelligence Summaries are contained in F. S. Regs., Part II. and the Staff Manual respectively. Title pages will be prepared in manuscript.

Place	Date	Hour	Summary of Events and Information	Remarks and references to Appendices
ESTAIRES A29.c.6.6.	1/2/18		No event to record.	
"	2/2/18		D.D.M.S. XV Corps, A.D.M.S. 38th Division visited Site, in reference to accommodation of Sick Cases	
"	3/2/18		Gas (Box Respirator) Inspection + Drill -	
"	"		Visited A.D.M.S. Office	
"	4/2/18		No event to record	
"	5/2/18		A.D.M.S. visited Site, + also inspected men recommended as unfit for forward area	
"	6/2/18		Capt. MELLUISH, R.A.M.C. of this unit to 1st Army R.A.M.C. School	
"	7/2/18		Visited Ambulance Site of 3/2 WEST LANCS 57th Div. at L'ESTRADE (A30.6.2.9)	
"	8/2/18		A.D.M.S. visited + inspected Ambulance Lieut MORGAN D.W. USMORC + Lt MOORE Z.J. USMORC attached for duty	
"	9/2/18		D.D.M.S. Inspected Site	
"	10/2/18		O.C. 2/2 WEST LANCS visited Field Amb - Inspection of whole unit by myself	
"	11/2/18		Conference G.D.R.ws Office OC 2/3 WESSEX visited site, Surg Genl WALLACE CMG visited Advanced Surgical Centre	
"	"		Advance party under Capt. Burke to Site of 3/2 WEST LANCS 57 Div at L'ESTRADE	
"	12/2/19		Advance party from 2/3 WESSEX Inspected, Lt MOORE Z.J. USMORC Proceeds to 54 CCS	
ESTAIRES / L'ESTRADE A30.6.2.9 Map 36	13/2/18	10 AM	Handed over Site at ESTAIRES to 2/3 WESSEX, + moved off at 10 A.M. to new Site - which had been taken over by Capt Burke at 10 AM. The new Site, an un-occupied Farm, No billet accommodation	

A6945 Wt. W11422/M1160 350,000 12/16 D. D. & L. Forms/C./2118/14

Army Form C. 2118.

WAR DIARY
or
INTELLIGENCE SUMMARY.
(Erase heading not required.)

John H Bernal
Lt Col OC 131 Field Ambulance

Instructions regarding War Diaries and Intelligence Summaries are contained in F. S. Regs., Part II. and the Staff Manual respectively. Title pages will be prepared in manuscript.

Place	Date	Hour	Summary of Events and Information	Remarks and references to Appendices
L'ESTRADE A30.6.5.9	13/2/18 (cont)		to form buildings for personnel. In front of these buildings, and two huts for patients, accommodation of 70 beds. — Carpenters still busy in front preparing good covered standing for motor cars	JSMD
"	14/2/18		D.D.M.S. XV Corps visited site and inspected. Arrived from No. M.B. & No. 164 Labour Company	JSMD
"	15/2/18		Lt Moore U.S.M.O.R.C returned to duty from 54 C.C.S.	JSMD
"	16/2/18		Capt MELHUISH of this Unit reported from 1st Army RAMC School of Instruction. Gas (Box-Respirator) Drill + Inspection	JSMD
"	17/2/18		A.D.S in S. inspected site. — Inspection Parade. Unit inspected by myself	JSMD
"	18/2/18		Reconnoitred area of Pont de Nieppe for suitable position for A.D.S. — reported to A.D.M.S. The BRASSERIE de L'ESPERANCE at B.23.6.6.0 what has large Cellar (2) one 40ft by 30ft. The Cellar is lofty, has a roof composed of girders concrete and brickwork several feet thick — on the ground floor above its cellars is another large room about 40 × 25 with cement floor, and roof composed of girders, brickwork, and cement	JSMD
"	19/2/18		Visited into A.D.M.S above referred to site	JSMD
"	20/2/18		Capt PAGE, M.C. of this Unit proceeded to 1st Army RAMC School of Instruction	JSMD
"	21/2/18		Conference ERQUINGHEM, A.D.M.S.	JSMD
"	22/2/18		Opened A.D.S. Pont de Nieppe, B.23.6.6.0., Capt Burke, 30 Other Ranks. to Pont de Nieppe	JSMD

Army Form C. 2118.

WAR DIARY
or
INTELLIGENCE SUMMARY.
(Erase heading not required.)

Instructions regarding War Diaries and Intelligence Summaries are contained in F.S. Regs., Part II. and the Staff Manual respectively. Title pages will be prepared in manuscript.

Place	Date	Hour	Summary of Events and Information	Remarks and references to Appendices
L'ESTRADE A.30.6.2.9 ADS PONT. L' NEPPE B.13.6.c	22/2/18		Box per Pr ader Driee Inspection	85M2
	24/2/18 25/2/18 26/2/18		Inspection OC. — ASC. Rifle Inspection. No going to report. Groomed Cases al Bn Rev Ends for W.B. — visited Pont de NEPPE A.D.S. L"MARKHAM Medical officer reports	85M2 85M2
"	27/2/18		visited A.D.S. — visited M.D.S., Major Carter Reports Prin beard	85M2
"	28/2/18		No event to report	

W/g Thompson S.
Col rapports
3/8

John D. Deroch
W. G. Rawe
OC 136(St John) Fd. Ambulance

140/2549.

130. Field Ambulance.

COMMITTEE FOR THE
MEDICAL HISTORY OF THE WAR
Date 12 MAY 1918

War Diary

of

130th (St John) Field Ambulance

From 1st March 1918

To 31st March 1918

WAR DIARY
OR
INTELLIGENCE SUMMARY.
(Erase heading not required.)

Army Form C. 2118.

Instructions regarding War Diaries and Intelligence Summaries are contained in F. S. Regs., Part II. and the Staff Manual respectively. Title pages will be prepared in manuscript.

John Str Rawe
W. G. F. Rawe
O.C. 136 (5h) Feld Amb

Place	Date	Hour	Summary of Events and Information	Remarks and references to Appendices
L'ESTRADE A30.6.5.9	MARCH 1st/3/18		1 N.C.O. 20 other ranks to 131st Field Ambce as "working party"	8343
"	2/3/18		Capt. Page M.C. returned fr' Army R.A.M.C. School	A921
"	3/3/18		Lt. Marklaw joined as N.O. 16.203, 1-shirts St Shirts	8944
"	4/3/18		Capt. Page M.C. posted 121st R.F.A. to relieve Capt. PALMER R.A.M.C. (proceeding on leave). Capt. MELHUISH to A.D.S. to relieve Capt. BURKE R.A.M.C. this day proceeding on leave. Major CARTER to SAILLY	92 MB
			(inspecting no. 100) School —	
"	5/3/18		Visited A.D.S. at PONT de NIEPPE, D.A.D.M.S. 12 Div visited M.D.S.	8943
"	6/3/18		Major CARTER R.A.M.C. one Staff Sergt. to 15 1st Army R.A.M.C. School of Instruction	92 MB
"	7/3/18		Lt. MORGAN US MORC. reported (from duty) with 64 R.F.A Brigade. Corps Commander XV Corps	
"			Visited inspected A.D.S. at PONT de NIEPPE	8943
"	8/3/18		Visited A.D.S. at PONT de NIEPPE	8943
	9/3/18		D.D.M.S. XV Corps visited M.D.S. no inspection	8943
	10/3/18		Conference ADMS Office — took over A.D.S. (from 131st) 35th Field Amb at HOUPLINES C26.6.8.1	8943
	11/3/18		WT 4/037249 Dr. ROBINSON, A.M. H.A.S.C. attd. wounded (Shrapnel R.O.L.) ARMENTIERS, sh ¼ Inspected 247th R.E. evacuated by 131.7A/6 574 CCS visited ADS at B2866.0	8942
	12/3/18		Visited 54 C.C.S., also ADSs at Copfront + B23.6.6.0	8942

WAR DIARY or INTELLIGENCE SUMMARY.

Army Form C. 2118.

ADS Dave & Rouse
O.C. 130 (S.W.) Fd Amb

Place	Date	Hour	Summary of Events and Information	Remarks and references to Appendices
L'ESTRADE A 30.6.2.9 ADS's at B 23.6.0 C 26.6.8.1	13/3/18		Visited ADS's at B 23.6.0. + C 26.6.8.1	JSHD
	14/3/18		Visited ADS's at B 23.6.6.0	JSHD
	15/2/18		A.D.M.S. visited M.D.S.	JSHD
	16/3/18		MOR reconnaissance of hospitals on both sides of Canal between ERQUINGHEM & PONT DE NIEPPE	
			2nd in Command departed on leave in relief to ADMS - visited ADS at B 23.6.6.0 "Cas.(S.)	
			Major CARTER R.A.M.C. reported from 1st Army Medical School	JSHD
	17/3/18		1st MORGAM US MORC to HOUPLINES ADS to relieve Capt BROOKS US. MORC	
	18/3/18		Capt. BROOKS US MORC to PONT DE NIEPPE to relieve Capt MELHUISH RAMC who returned to HQ's	JSHD
	19/3/18		Ordinary Duties - buses to evacuated Cases from HOUPLINES ADS to PONT DE NIEPPE ADS	
			From the later ADS. Cases evacuated direct to CCS. by MAC Car	JSHD
	20/3/18		No Events to report - Capt. Burke departed on leave. Capt. PAGE MC reported from 12th RFA	
	21/3/18		Visited both ADS's	
	22/3/18		M.D.S. visited & inspected by A.D.M.S.	JSHD
	23/3/18		Major Carter Rowe proceeded to No. 5. Convalescent Depot. "Shuncks St Strength of the hand	
			Attended daily course at Gas School	JSHD
	24/3/18		Capt BURKE RAMC evacuated to 51. C.C.S. - Promoted Act/Major as from 4/1/18.	JSHD

WAR DIARY
or
INTELLIGENCE SUMMARY

Army Form C. 2118.

(Erase heading not required.)

Place	Date	Hour	Summary of Events and Information	Remarks and references to Appendices
LESTRADE ADS at A30&29	25/3/18		Visited 51 CCS. - Capt PAGE M.C. RAMC to PONT DE NIEPPE ADS., ADS at HOUPLINES	
B23&6.0 C24.8.1			Conferred with Relay Post	
			Capt BROOKS U.S. M.O.R.C. posted to 90 HAB Struck off Strength of this Unit. 25/3/18	
			Lt MORGAN U.S. M.O.R.C. returned to M.D.S.	P.M.
"	26/3/18		7 O.R. Seconded to 51 CCS with Staff Car (W) -	P.M.D.
"	27/3/18		No Post to 9.30	P.M.D.
"	28/3/18		Visited ADS PONT DE NIEPPE, Relay Post HOUPLINES, R.A.P's C27.66.70 C26.6 Rel C7.a.9.4	
"	29/3/18		Took over the Collecting Post ERQUINGHEM, ADS VICTORY I.d.7.5 "Posts at Eq&Gi.4
			- I.c 6.3.8 from 131st Field Ambulance	
		2.30 PM	Attended Conference ADMS' Office. Received RAMC Order No 4th Corps No 2 29/3/18	
		11.50 PM	Advance Party 102 Field Ambulance reported to take over ADS.	
	30/3/18	12 Noon	ADS's at B23.6.0. I.d.7.5. H.c.3.6. Handover + all Posts in forward area	
			Handed over to 102 F.A. of 34 Div. -	
			Began withdrawn to move with 115th Brigade - via AQ 115th Brigade S.	
			Authorities Capt Mallinck - proceeded with Brigade - MDS tabenarea by 104 Field Amb.
	31/3/18	Our 8.45	Fallen - forces by road to MERVILLE	

Signed J.N. Duncan
Lt Col RAMC
Comdg 2/8 F.Amb.

Confidential

War Diary

130th (St John) Field Ambulance

From 1st April 1918

To 30th April 1918

COMMITTEE FOR THE
MEDICAL HISTORY OF THE WAR
Date —6 JUN. 1918

WAR DIARY
or
INTELLIGENCE SUMMARY.

(Erase heading not required.)

Army Form C. 2118.

Place	Date	Hour	Summary of Events and Information	Remarks and references to Appendices
LA VICOGNE	8/4/18		Inspected Camp & Sanitation of 12th R.E & 7th Welsh.	ASW
MOLLIENS	9/4/18		G.O.C. 111th Brigade visited S/O. A.D.M.S visited Eve	8 SW
"	10/4/18		Capt McEWAN. C.A.M.C. reported for duty and taken on Strength.	ASW
"	11/4/18		Attended Conference A.D.M.S Office.	8 SW
RUBEMPRE	12/4/18 9.0 am		Moved to RUBEMPRE, arriving 11.15 am, and A/C H.S Camp & location guide	8 SW
"	13/4/18		No Casual.	8 SW
"	14/4/18		Capt. PAGE (DCM) M.C. seconded to H.S.C.O.S, reported & lieut O.S.C	82 W
"	15/4/18		Visited FREVENT.	8 SW
"	16/4/18		Capt McEWAN. C.A.M.C. transferred to 2 Canadian General Hospital & Struck off Strength.	82 W
"	17/4/18		A.D.M.S visited B.H.Q. Advance Party to VADENCOURT to hold S/O. Conference ADMS Office	8 SW
"	18/4/18		No report	8 SW
"	19/4/18		Advance Party returned from VADENCOURT	8 SW
"	20/4/18		D.D.M.S. v Capt visited S/O. — today	82 W
"	21/4/18		Conference ADMS Office. — Inspection of lieut O.S.C	8 SW
"	"		Reconnoitred Sites for Ambulance at FIEFFES, and FRANQUEVILLE Reported on Same	
"	"		to A.D.M.S	8 SW

WAR DIARY or INTELLIGENCE SUMMARY

Army Form C. 2118.

102nd Brigade West T. Ramel

Place	Date	Hour	Summary of Events and Information	Remarks and references to Appendices
RUBEMPRE T.14.C.4.0	22/4/18		1 Officer + 30 Other Ranks (S.B's) proceeded to 129' Fd. Amb. for July. also 2 Horse Ambulances + 3 with Cars., 6 Miller James blocked Stretcher Cond. to 131	BJD
RUBEMPRE T.14.C.4.0	23/4/18		38 O.R. to 129 3rd Amb. for July. - visited WARLOY. DAQMG visited S/we Advance Party 1 Officer + 6 OR to HERISSART.	BJD JSMD
RUBEMPRE HERISSART T.10.A.4.4	24/4/18		Took over Site HERISSART. (T.10.A.4.4) Herd. held by 37 Fd. Amb. Visited RUBEMPRE - MIRVAUX.	JSMD JSMD
"	25/4/18		Remainder of S.B's returned from July, with 129' Fd. Amb.	JSMD
"	27/4/18		Visited A.D.M.S. Office + Gas Demonstration Parade.	JSMD
"	28/4/18		Inspection of Unit.	JSMD
"	29/4/18		With ADMS + DAQMG 3rd Div. visited + inspected site at DOMQUEUR	JSMD
"	30/4/18		Unit sent advance Party to DOMQUEUR	JSMR

John S. Rose Lt. Col. OC 130 (S.M.) Fd. Amb. 3/5/18

Confidential

War Diary

of

130th (St John) Field Ambulance

from 1st May 1918.

to 31st May 1918

Army Form C. 2118.

WAR DIARY
or
INTELLIGENCE SUMMARY.

(Erase heading not required.)

Instructions regarding War Diaries and Intelligence Summaries are contained in F.S. Regs., Part II. and the Staff Manual respectively. Title pages will be prepared in manuscript.

John J. Devey Lt Col RAMC

Place	Date	Hour	Summary of Events and Information	Remarks and references to Appendices
HERISSART T10a S16	1/5/18	8.30 PM	Marched via TALMAS, - NAOURS - WARGNIES - HALLOY - BERTEAUCOURT - ST. LEGER - DOMART - DOMQUEUR to its Chateau - LE PLOUY a distance of 23 miles - arriving 5.1+5. PM.	12 MD
DOMQUEUR (LE PLOUY)	2/5/18		Reconnoitred sites for Field Ambulance in area of HIERMONT - MAISON PONTAIEU St LOT, - BERNATRE - with OC Divisional Supply A.D.M.S. visited site	12 MD
DOMQUEUR LE PLOUY	3/5/18	2 PM	Marched via CRAMONT - CONTEVILLE, - HIERMONT, to St LOT, - of Snow, Ambulance Site - 50 O.R. detailed for duty as S.B's (31 13th 131 Field Ambs - S. Bearer Processes by Car.	12 MD 12 MD
ST LOT HIERMONT ST LOT	4/5/18 5/5/18		H.S. O.R. proceeded to Surg. as S.R.s b 131 - Visited ST. RIQUIET ABBEVILLE A.D.M.S. visited site, - & visited 2 CC.S returned to Beaurah Sick to this C.C.S - (2 m) Inspection of hunt - Visited HQ of 36 Div Divn arrangements for 2 Balen Carts of the Field Prefer HIERMONT - MAISON - PONT AIEU	12 MD
ST LOT	6/5/18		Visited CRAMONT (field Cashier)	12 MD

WAR DIARY
INTELLIGENCE SUMMARY

Army Form C. 2118.

John S.H. Frank
Lieut Col. R.A.M.C.

Place	Date	Hour	Summary of Events and Information	Remarks and references to Appendices
ST LOT Lens II.4.7.S.	7/5/18		No Sgd	32W2
"	8/5/18		30 O.R. to 131st Field Ambulance for duty	85W2
"	9/5/18		Inspection visit to OC Wing & Cookhouses, Latrines &. DDMS Cav Corps (he visited) Site Weeks (Lt/Col Morgan CMG Lab. Actual	
"	10/5/18		48072 L/Cpl BRENNAN J - G.S.W. L.Thigh (any fracture femoral down) Lt A/R.M.L.Stores) 48199 Pte THOMAS A.J G.S.W. R.Thigh L.Toe and (Feet) 48076 Pte ALLEN T (M.M.) G.S.W.shell upper arm L.Thigh - Shock St Marys to	25W2
"	11/5/18		0 Visits C.C.S. + Saw above Casualties - The follow Casualties also occurred 48738 Pte JENKINS W. - 4659th Pte WARD J.W. Shell(s)(wound) Blue (Room) Shock St Marys to	85W2
"	12/5/18		Forward of the Lunch, attached to D.122 Brigade R.F.A. reported "Killed" in action" by or 8/5/18 - Visited Wing - Cookhouses - Latrines of Lunch.	25W2
"	13/5/18		No Sgd	45W2
"	14/5/18		Visited AUXI-LE-CHATEAU - reported DDMS Cav Corps. (Late adjusted Bus also arranged for use of baths by 38 Div Amg. + also arranged use of FODENS	85W2

WAR DIARY or INTELLIGENCE SUMMARY

Army Form C. 2118.

(Erase heading not required.)

Place	Date	Hour	Summary of Events and Information	Remarks and references to Appendices
ST. LOT Sheet 11 A.17.b.5	15/5/18		Revisits A.D.M.S. Office.	ADMS
"	16/5/18		Disposes HIERMONT.	ADMS
"	17/5/18		Inspected MAISON-PONTIEU	ADMS
"	18/5/18		A.D.M.S. Inspected Site. Examined men unfit for duty in forward area	ADMS
"	19/5/18		No event	ADMS
"	20/5/18		25 O.R's reported from Duty in forward area, from 131st 2nd Amb	ADMS
"	21/5/18		D.D.M.S. visited Site. Attended Conference of OC's Fd Ambs at ADMS' Office	ADMS
"	22/5/18		No event. Orders issued to move to TOUTENCOURT	ADMS
"	23/5/18	16.40	M.T. Transport proceeded by road to new site. Personnel left 10.30 for site at TOUTENCOURT. in 3 W.D.6R Lorries arrived 2.P.M. took over site by 13th from 10.30 and	ADMS
TOUTENCOURT U.1.d.3.1 Sheet 57 D	24/5/18		Conference ADMS Office. Reported HQ 114th Brigade. Reconnoitre of bearers reported from 129th Field Amb CLAIREFAYE - Capt A.H.TOWERS, RAMC inspected station on Sheep Pen Post 8/7/51. Visits 139th Field Amb.	ADMS
"	25/5/18	6.30 a.m	Reconnoitred forward area, + selected spot for WWCP at U.10.d.8.5.	ADMS

John O'Donnell
W.Gt Rawd D.C. 135 ? for Forces

Army, Form C. 2118.

WAR DIARY
or
INTELLIGENCE SUMMARY.
(Erase heading not required.)

Instructions regarding War Diaries and Intelligence Summaries are contained in F. S. Regs., Part II. and the Staff Manual respectively. Title pages will be prepared in manuscript.

Place	Date	Hour	Summary of Events and Information	Remarks and references to Appendices
TOUTENCOURT U.1.d.3.1.	25/5/18		61249 Pte ELLIOTT J awarded Burnisnal - Distinguishes Conduct Certificate.	App 1
"	26/5/18		A.D.M.S. visited Site	
"			Repeated O.D.M.S. Office - 46297 Pte CHAVE RAMC that twice "Mentioned" in Despatches.	App 2
"	27/5/18		Re Refresher Parades by G.O.C 114th Brigade, 51 Brigade.	App 3
"	29/5/18		Lecture by Col GRAY AMS CB on Spleen at 131st Field Amb.	App 4
"	29/5/18		Inspection of Brigade by Corps Commander V Corps. ADMS visited Site	App 5
"			Lecture by Col GRAY AMS CB at the Site, on Spleen, to - Officers of SC2 & and RA)	
"	30/5/18		A.D.M.S. visited Site - Recognitions area - RAINCHEVAL - ARQUEVES - for Site, Selected N788	App 6
"	31/5/18		N.C.O's & men, attended Gas Officers Parade, and Box Respirators tests	App 7

W.D. Davies
Lt. Col. RAMC

W. D. Davies
Lt. Col.
OC 130 Infy Fd Amb

Confidential

War Diary

of

130th (St John) Field Ambulance

From   1st June 1918
To   30th June 1918

Army Form C. 2118.

WAR DIARY
or
INTELLIGENCE SUMMARY.
(Erase heading not required.)

John Davies
L/Sgt RAMC 80130 KWS Fd Amb

Place	Date	Hour	Summary of Events and Information	Remarks and references to Appendices
TOUTENCOURT U.id.2.1	1/6/18		Visited 148 F Amb - Inter-Divisional Gas Guide at CLAIRFAYE and arranged to take over this site on 5/6/18.	JSMD
TOUTENCOURT U.id.2.1	2/6/18		No general to report.	JSMD
TOUTENCOURT	3/6/18		Officers 148 F.Amb & 150 F.Amb & 63rd Divn visited site, 38 DRS St LOT. landed over to 131st Field Ambce	JSMD
TOUTENCOURT	4/6/18		Bivouacked from St LOT reported 6 P.M. - Convoy of 15 148 F Amb - Inter-Divisional Gas Guide proceeded.	JSMD
TOUTENCOURT CLAIRFAYE	5/6/18	1 PM	Handed over site to 150 F Amb - Took over site CLAIRFAYE O.29.c.5.6 from 148 Fd Amb 2.35PM	JSMD
			ADMS visited site	
CLAIRFAYE O.29.c.5.6	6/6/18		Visited HQ 107th 108th Field Ambce regarding W.W. site.	JSMD
"	7/6/18		Gas OR's inspected, was unfit for forward area - Visited site of 38 Divn Field Ambce ACHEUX.	JSMD
			reported as to suitability for Inter-Divisional Gas Guide -	
"	8/6/18		No total	
	9/6/18		The following U.S.M.O.R.C. Officers reported and taken on strength: - Lt CASSELL	JSMD
			1st Lieut BANTON, 1st Lieut ACKERMANN.	
	10/6/18		Visited Transport lines	JSMD
	11/6/18		Capt TOWERS R.A.M.C. of this unit to 13th R.E.F. for temporary duty in place of Capt.	JSMD
			ROBERTSON, R.A.M.C. attached SCR	

WAR DIARY
or
INTELLIGENCE SUMMARY.
(Erase heading not required.)

Army Form C. 2118.

War Diary
A.D.M.S.

Place	Date	Hour	Summary of Events and Information	Remarks and references to Appendices
CLAIRFAYE O2e.g.65.6 Gas Course	12/6/18		A.D.M.S. visits S.16	
	13/6/18		DDMS. visits - inspects 12th San. Sectn.	
	14/6/18		ADMS. inspected new recreation hut (for General Coxe) Capt. MELHUISH Raised S.I.B.W.14	
			Lecture Lt. LEIGH R.A.M.C.	
	15/6/18		Lecture to Permanent Nursing Other St Louis	
	16/6/18		Gas Parade, Respects of Box Respirators + Drill	
	17/6/18		Inspection of Anti- Clothing Infestation	
	18/6/18		Clothing Infestation Centres inspected Capt. MELHUISH relieving from 13 Aparl 12th	
	18/6/18	12 Non	Took over Existing Crowded Billeting Post from 51 F.A.N.B. 1st Div.	
	19/6/18	9/1.00	Conference ADMS	
	20/6/18		Handed over temporary Command to Major BURNE CAMC — took on duties	
			of ADMS during G.E. Thompson absence on Leave	
	21/6/18		Bearers (4 HP) returned from duty with 129 Field Ambulance	
			AD.M.S. examined men referred for PB2as	
	22/6/18		D.D.M.S. Corps visited San Centre, Anti- Malaria Bombing for Infantry	
	23/11		Inspection of Anti- tuberc Tripled 131 Field Ambulance with ADMS 16th	

WAR DIARY or INTELLIGENCE SUMMARY

Army Form C. 2118.

Place	Date	Hour	Summary of Events and Information	Remarks and references to Appendices
Clarfayes	24.6.18		Lt. Barton attached for duty with 129 Field Ambulance at Hesdinville	
	25.6.18		Lecture on splints by Col. Gray Consulting Surgeon 3rd Army. S.M.S.P.B. All Army and 2 Corps Medical Officers attended	
	26.6.18		Without incident. Weather fine	
	27.6.18		Med'l Inspected J.A. detacht. Sergeants in series of a more Kit inspection B	
	28.6.18		A.D.M.S. visited and examined men unfit for work in forward area & D.M.S. 3 Corps noted rise	
	29.6.18		A.D.M.S. visited site. Capt. Belcourt as Divisional Gun officer proceeded to No 3 C.C.S. for 8 days instruction in Gas Regional treatments Inspection by O.i/c	
	30.6.18		[signature] Lt Col R.A.M.C. O/c	

Confidential.

War Diary

of

130th (St John) Field Ambulance

From 1st July 1918

To 31st July 1918

WAR DIARY
or
INTELLIGENCE SUMMARY.
(Erase heading not required.)

Army Form C. 2118.

Place	Date	Hour	Summary of Events and Information	Remarks and references to Appendices
Camp Sibly	1.7.18		A.D.M.S. 3 Corps visited 16 L.Corps passed through to W. Post 11 Hrs 2 to 3.30	
"	2.7.18		Visit to 2 Bn Watches 134 Field Ambulance for duty	10
"	3.7.18		Visit to F.B. Warders 124 2nd Ambulance for duty	11
"	4.7.18		Nothing to report	11
"	5.7.18		Arrival of infected new proposed sight for forward area D.A.D.M.S. 2nd Div visited site	11
"	6.7.18		A.D.M.S. inspected collapse with Barn building by CHIPPAYE CHATEAU as a suitable Site	8Hrs
"	6.7.18		Visit A.D.S of C.W.W.P.	
"	7.7.18		Hanging over Buket Pi Wattous to A.D.M.S. looks over 138 Sigs Camb.	8Hrs
"			Officers Mess, both A.D.M.S visited Reserve Gird Post, Map Ref. P 31C.20 Observ.	8H.D.
"	8.7.18		Casualty Station. 3 Army Sir Wilmot HERRINGHAM C.B. visited Gas Centre	8H.D.
"	9.7.18		Conference A.Div's Office	8H.D.
"	10.7.18		33 O.R. k. Dt. 132S Outlift. H.Q. O.P. from 131 Inf Camb Hypts Sugar	
"	11.7.18		All Officers Neds train were for Inspection for one hour 1.30-2.30 Asst.	
"	11.7.18		Handed over to Major Burke	8H.D.
"	12.7.18		A.D.M.S handed full a/c instructions for next for forward area	11

Army Form C. 2118.

WAR DIARY
or
INTELLIGENCE SUMMARY.
(Erase heading not required.)

John Wyethe
Major RAMC

Place	Date	Hour	Summary of Events and Information	Remarks and references to Appendices
Chocques	12.7.16		DDMS 1st Corps visited site	App
	13.7.16		Visited ADMS as a autok before noon	App
	14.7.16		Visited all 6 but Field Ambulances (including)	App
	15.7.16		ADMS visited site	App
	16.7.16		Conference ADMS Office	App
	17.7.16		Conference ADMS Office	App
	18.7.16		Move of to Interview Officer in charge of working party behind to run Sa Col site	App
Vieille Chapelle	19.7.16		ADMS visited site	App
	20.7.16		Visited 114 Brigade at Lockingwart and 113 Brigade Headqrs and RMO's	App
			to arrange for collection of sick dentes chapelle Bois Line	App
	21.7.16		Bombing by Enemy Air Craft in vicinity	App
	22.7.16		Nothing to report	
	23.7.16		Raining all day	App
	24.7.16		Conference ADMS Office. had spells of a	App
	25.7.16		Conference of heads of Officers with ADMS at Rifle Handbombing	App
			of La Croix Blanche arrangement to be Collecting Post to 64th Field Ambulance	App

WAR DIARY
or
INTELLIGENCE SUMMARY.

Army Form C. 2118.

Place	Date	Hour	Summary of Events and Information	Remarks and references to Appendices
FOUNTEGHEM	27/7/18		ADMS visits C.in.C. and inspected men held for Duty by forward Cdo. Returned from Leave	
	28/7/18		Bn Respirator Drill. Inspection of men, clothing, respirators, rifle, inspection O.S.C.	8 NCO
	29/7/18		Men went sports — ADen.S visited file	8 NCO
	30/7/18		NCO'n (3) to RAINCHEVAL to train witness room for B.ne 33 Fd Amb	
	31/7/18		No. 5 wel. 15 posted	

J. Sinclair
Lt Col RAMC
OC 130 (S) Fd Amb Fd Ambulance

Confidential

War Diary

of

130th (St John) Field Ambulance

From 1st August 1918

To 31st August 1918

… Major [Ross?]
… [signature]
OC 130 [Field Amb?]

WAR DIARY
or
INTELLIGENCE SUMMARY.
(Erase heading not required.)

Army Form C. 2118.

Place	Date	Hour	Summary of Events and Information	Remarks and references to Appendices
TOUTENCOURT U.1.d.3.1	1/8/18	1.45 AM 2/15 am	1.45 AM Enemy bombed TOUTENCOURT, visits one of the craters course in HERISSART. TOUTENCOURT R.d. at 2.15 P.M. - and with Corp. of the Unit, and other [ranks?] This hit Officers were on duty at the time, went into village to see if R.A.M.C. aid required. Owning doing found portion of head face, nose + scalp with long black hair of one wounded - boy of about 14 years and both of man of 60 years. The calls Lung Cos by S88 [Stretcher bearers?] and others. 5. OR slightly wounded, came to the [Fd?] Ambulance, one returned to be relieved. Visited site of 52 FIELD Amb at U.8.d.4.3 where a party of 1 Sergt + 26 O.R. were employed making road (Entrance).	
TOUTENCOURT U.1.d.3.1	2/8/18	am	A.D.M.S. visited site, and examined men unfit for duty in [Divisional?] area	
TOUTENCOURT U.1.d.3.1	3/8/18	am	With Major [Bosanack?] visited ADS at HEDAUVILLE and with the OC [Parks?] of the St Field Ambulance visited the RAPs at MESNIL Q.26.c.6.3. BOUZINCOURT W.13.a.4.6 Q.31.d.2.0. Q.32.c.4.0. also [Relay?] Car post at Q.31.b.8.5. Q.32.a.4.2 Q.32.6.9.1	

WAR DIARY or INTELLIGENCE SUMMARY.

Army Form C. 2118.

John 2nd ADS
War Rand

Place	Date	Hour	Summary of Events and Information	Remarks and references to Appendices
TOUTENCOURT	3/9/18		Divisional Sports. Championship of Division (Just Silver bugles presented by G.O.C.	
U.id 3.1			Major General T.G. Cubitt CMG, DSO.) going to R.A.M.C. 16 pounds 2nd 15 Welsh	
			Into 8 pounds - The heat won 1st 100 Yards (L/Cpl Nicholas) 1st Long Jumps	
			17ft 8 in (L/Cpl Nicholas) 16-13½ 1st ¼ mile 1st ½ mile 1st 2 mile	RAM2
			1st in Wheel barrow race, 16. 129' 2" in Obstacle Race.	
TOUTENCOURT	4/9/18		1 N.C.O. & 13 O.R. to A.D.S. HEDAUVILLE to assist line party to O.C. 51. F² Amb	
U.id 3.1			O.R. detailed the W.S.L. lunt - Rfle. Inspection A.S.C. H.T	51F²A
			Divisional horse show races - wrestling	
			"Sacred concert" by 130th Field Amb. in kamper to 114th Boxpart	
TOUTENCOURT	5/9/18		2 Officers 90 Other Ranks to HEDAUVILLE to take over line from	
U.id 3.1			51 Field Ambee to J/c RAMC upon change Custards 2 stops on Over Country Run	51F²A
	5PM		wearing 1ee, 15 Welsh - who won - 26 points Rex	
			taking over Completed. Avenue Park. 53 Field Amb so reported	53F²A
TOUTENCOURT	6/9/18 2 PM		Hand over W.S.L to 53 Field Amb 2 PM. Took over W.S.L 027.6 & 9 from 131 Field Amb	131F²A
U.id 3.1			60 troops, 2 Serjts, 3 Cars of 131. Quadlas for Duty	
			G.O.C. 38 Div. - G.O.C. 114 Brigade visited site to say Good bye	38D.H.Q
O.27.5.8.9	7/9/18		69 O.R ranks of 129th Field Ambee reported for duty. Cpt. Boxing Competition Commenced 2F²A	

Army Form C. 2118.

WAR DIARY
or
INTELLIGENCE SUMMARY.
(Erase heading not required.)

Army Form C. 2118.

Place	Date	Hour	Summary of Events and Information	Remarks and references to Appendices
O27b 8.9	8/8/18		Conference ADMS Office	12MD
"	9/8/18		Visited ADS. roll Pol on Pot of line ADMS Visited IC site	TBMD
"	10/8/18		Visited Dressing Station at the turn at TOUTENCOURT and USD Coal w. 3 Bde	TBMD
"	11/8/18		O.C. Inspection DDMS visited Site MDS	8MD
"	12/8/18 Fr		M.T., A.S.C. Stak	8MD
"	13/8/18		Visited ADS - men roots on L of line. MESNIL.	8MD
"	14/8/18		O.D.M.S. visited O.D.S. HEDAUVILLE. Conference ADMS Office 8MD	8MD
"	15/8/18		Conference ADMS' Office	8MD
"	16/8/18		Visited ODS HEDAUVILLE, visited ADS's	8MD
"	17/8/18		Box Respirator Drill - Visited ADS's	8MD
"	18/8/18		OC's Parade. Visits. Lieutg Parker at TOUTENCOURT & D&d.	8MD
"			Lieut BANTON USMORC John reported from July with 38 M.G.C	8MD
"			Major Burke relieved Major Basework at ADS HEDAUVILLE	8MD
"	19/8/18		Conf ADMS Offce. 1st ACKERMAN, USMORC Relieved Lieut CASSELL	8MD
"			at HEDAUVILLE. Forward visited forward area and formed	8MD
"			forward ADS at BOUZINCOURT, DDMS Visited MDS & ADS with J HEDAUVILLE	

Army Form C. 2118.

WAR DIARY
or
INTELLIGENCE SUMMARY.
(Erase heading not required.)

Instructions regarding War Diaries and Intelligence Summaries are contained in F. S. Regs., Part II. and the Staff Manual respectively. Title pages will be prepared in manuscript.

J/C 2/1 Field Amb
W51 R.A.M.C. 2nd Bn/Sen. Jan 24th

Place	Date	Hour	Summary of Events and Information	Remarks and references to Appendices
MDS OUTREBOEUF M'IEALVILLERS ADS HEDAUVILLE forward ADS BOUZINCOURT	20/6/16		Visited ADS forward ADS. Took over ADS ENGLEBELMER from Field Ambulance of 21st Div	Sketch 2
ADS ENGLEBELMER	21/6/16		INCO (Sept) - 36 S.B.'s to 115th Bgde at Beaumont INCO Sept 36 S.B.K 114 Bgde.05. r113 Bgde.23. Visited RAP's HANEL, MESNIL & in AVELUY Wood. Repaired & improved communication across R. ANCRE at Q24a.	03#0 Sketch
"	22/6/16		Visited all ADS's. - Inspected roads to AVELUY, MARTINSART, MESNIL	Sketch
HEDAUVILLE	23/6/16	6 AM	Arrived HQ to HEDAUVILLE. Coln ADw3 visited ADS BOUZINCOURT, ALBERT R'd & W-7 Centre. We were shelled on our return with Gas Shells. (W.W. admitted in Distance 7th.)	Sketch
HEDAUVILLE	24/6/16	12 noon AM	Colo ADw3 visited ADS's AVELUY, MARTINSART. DDw.3 visited MDS. ADw3 visited, orders to move forthwith to MARTINSART to Rev Walking Wounded (elbows 3rd) (W.W. admitted 127)	
HEDAUVILLE MARTINSART LA BOISELLE	25/6/16	1.30 3 AM	Moved HQ to MARTINSART, opened WWCP. +ol Same hour Major BURRE visited forward ADS. at LA BOISELLE. Closed ADS BOUZINCOURT. (W.W. admitted 92) Visited Battlefield OVILLERS- LA BOISELLE. LA BOISELLE and just outside POZIERES.	
MARTINSART LA BOISELLE ADS CONTALMAISON	26/6/16	1 PM	Opened ADS CONTALMAISON, moved MDS, WWCP to LA BOISELLE. Visited Battlefield. (W.W admitted 137)	
LA BOISELLE CONTALMAISON ADS BAZENTIN LE GRANDE	27/6/16		ADS moved forward to BAZENTIN-LE-GRANDE HQ to CONTALMAISON - DDw3 visited HQ - Visited New ADS. (301 W.W. admitted) 5 PM Visited HQ 11A T15 HIGHWOOD, forward Rev. r RAP's	

A6945 Wt. W14422/M160 350,000 12/16 D. D. & L. Forms/C/2118/14.

WAR DIARY
or
INTELLIGENCE SUMMARY.
(Erase heading not required.)

Army Form C. 2118.

John Paroil
Lieut Colonel
OC 130' St John Field Amb

Place	Date	Hour	Summary of Events and Information	Remarks and references to Appendices
MDS VAN BOUSSEN 28/8/18	28/8/18	5 A.M	Visited A.D.S. BAZENTIN-LE-GRAND + R.A.P's in HIGH WOOD (WW from through 58)	61170 HARE W. G.S.W. Knee L
MDS CONTALMAISON				Casualties in R.A.M.C 180'
MDS BAZENTIN LE GRAND				#02320 DAWKINS W. GSW Hd
MDS BAZENTIN LE GRAND	29/8/18	9 A.M	Pushed up A.D.S. to LONGUEVAL (S.11d.3.0) and later to GINCHY T13 Central C.8.9	#8366 POWELL R.L GSW Arm
ADS GINCHY				#8181 RIDGEWAY W.J GSW leg (Sh)
			BAZENTIN-LE-GRAND (12 noon) S16a.2.8 — Visited 12 R.A.P's at HIGH WOOD and instructed M.O to	SM1286. PRATT L.W.C R.A.M., P. GSW Leg
			keep in touch with Batt's troops. Aid Posts up. Bat. A.D.S. WDI slightly shelled.	S.1919 WARBURTON GSW Shdr
			Cases passed through M.W.C.P. 70. Major BADCOCK to A.D.M. to below Major BURKE	also MDS & WWCG
MDS. BAZENTIN LE GRAND	30/8/18	7 A.M	with A.D.M.S. to A.D.S at GINCHY and reconnoited GINCHY - LES BOEUFS road to point T3d S5.2	
ADS GINCHY			also inspected old C.C.S. site at T14.A.6.8	
		1.30 P.M	Area around ADS heavily shelled. The following R.A.M.C. casualties severe	
			46563 L/Cpl PHILLIPS I G.S.W.L Chest After Severe	
			46559 L/Cpl NICHOLAS T.J G.S.W R Arm wounds of Both } 130' Field Amb	
			46130 Cpl. HOLMES A.D G.S.W L Hip " " "	
			Major BADNOCH relieves from ADS, Major BURNE-K ADS	
		4 PM	ADMS visited ADS.	(accidently wounded 155)
MDS BAZENTIN-LE-GRAND	31/8/18	6.30 A.M	To ADS with DADMS - Proceeded along road, taking Ford Car as far as T4.C.5.4 on GINCHY —	
ADS GINCHY			LES BOEUFS Road - to Cross Roads of Sunken Roads inspecting site of old CCS on the way at	
			T.14.a.6.8. — Suitable site for 131st MDS. Then proceed on foot to point T4C.8.8	

Army Form C. 2118.

John H. Bassel Lt Col
Rank
OC 130th (St John) Field Amb.

WAR DIARY
or
INTELLIGENCE SUMMARY.
(Erase heading not required.)

Place	Date	Hour	Summary of Events and Information	Remarks and references to Appendices
MDS BAZENTIN-LE-GRANDE POSTS GINCHY	21/9/16 (continued)		From this point T+C.8.8 along LESBOEUFS – MORVAL Road (reflecting on our Right at T.10.b.4½.8½ & CCS side) as far as T.10.g.5.5. Here we found parties of 13th & 14th Welch, who informed us, that heavy machine gun fire exists in wood (scrub) above the point in front of MORVAL and such was heard by us. DADMS inspected trolley lines, and found toller in order.	

John H. Bassel
Mor. Raw.
OC 130th (St John) Field Amb.

Confidential

War Diary
of
130th (St John) Field Ambulance

From 1st September 1918.

To 30th September 1918.

Army Form C. 2118.

WAR DIARY
or
INTELLIGENCE SUMMARY.
(Erase heading not required.)

John H. Parsons
Lt Col R.A.M.C.
O.C. 130 S. Sit. Bn. Fd Amb

Place	Date	Hour	Summary of Events and Information	Remarks and references to Appendices
MDS T+B BAZENTIN-LE-GRANDE	1/9/18	4.14.5 AM	Attack on MORVAL by 114th B.Ts.	
ADS GINCHY		7 AM	With D.A.D.M.S visited MORVAL. - Visited ADS van R.A.P's	
		10 AM	Attack on SAILLY - SAILLISEL. Large number of wounded through ADS GINCHY	
A.D.S	2/9/18	7.30	Visited ADS GINCHY. Opened up forward ADS at T.10 b.5.9. - MORVAL - LES BOEUFS Rd, with 2 M.O's Capt McMillan in charge, and nursing Staff	
			Inspected the Field Amb Site at C.C.S. at LES BOEUFS - Site at time Shelled. - good dugouts (T.4.C.2.6)	
			A number of beds - good Site -	
			Visited R.A.P's - Conference A.D.M.S Office -	
T.13.C.8.9 ADS GINCHY				
ADS MORVAL LES BOEUFS Rd T.10.d.2.4.	3/9/18	7 AM	Opened ADS. at T.4 d.2.4, and later advanced to Opened ADS at HEBUT U.13.a.4.6	
		2 PM	Conference A.D.M.S Office - MDS & GINCHY	
			2 horse Ambulances attached to 114th Bts Regps in truck with advance	
HB 6 U 306.8 SAILLY-SAILLISEL	4/9/18		front of MDs. formed ADS at U.6.C.4.1. moved from U.13.a.4.6 L.T.S. found HQ & M.O.R.C. at Rear person ADS side, ADS formed GOVERNMENT FARM, side poor dugout, huge Constant Observation of enemy Sketches Shells the morning, - Stretcher bearers in Slack 2/ts Car to MR PETRIPORT and MANANCOURT ADSed 2/Lt Stn called in reference Stacking arrival 40C Beavers 65 Fd Amb & Lieut J ACKERMAN U.S.MORC to 13 W.Sch	

WAR DIARY or INTELLIGENCE SUMMARY

Army Form C. 2118.

John H Bazel
W. Br. R.A.M.C. DC. 13th Div

Place	Date	Hour	Summary of Events and Information	Remarks and references to Appendices
Colmrie	3/9/18		In place of Lt Leiteh R.A.M.C wounded in action - Lt Ackerman Shick St. showing the ADS formed at OP.D.2.B. on Sailly-Saillisel - Mesnil - En - Arrouaise By H.R	
ADS SAILLY SAILLISEL Gas GOVERNMENT Farm MESNIL RD	5/9/18		Handed over all sites to Field Amb's of 21st / 17th Div. - MDS to 63rd 2nd Amb, and ADS's due to 65th Field Amb.	
SAILLY SAILLISEL U8C.2.10		4 PM	Moved to V.Corps Gas Centre. BEAULANCOURT N10C.2.3 - Taking over from 129 Field Amb. JSHR	
HQ Gas Centre BEAULANCOURT	6/9/18		DDMS visited S10 - Conference ADMS Office - Reconnoitred for site for DRS - and suggested site N15A.9.6 - old amb site.	
			Lt Cassell USMORC Shuck St Sheriff, and posted to 131st Field Amb. 19 ORS sent to 21 C.C.S. to relieve same number 129. Jas' April AMR	
BEAULANCOURT	7/9/18 9.30		Visited ADMS Office Corps Commander VC visited site, - DDMS visited Site, inspected T.A. Cubbitt & CMS BIO hutt, and personally thanked officers, NCO's & men for their good work - made nice little speech to them, which was much appreciated - Cheers for general ADMS	
		3PM	Became acting ADMS	

WAR DIARY or INTELLIGENCE SUMMARY

Army Form C. 2118.

Place	Date	Hour	Summary of Events, and Information	Remarks and references to Appendices
BEAULANCOURT	8/9/18		D Brs visited site — 1 NCO + 16 OR to N18 9.9.6 to prepare site of D.R.S	
"	9/9/18		D Brs visited site — and with Major Bunn inspected new site for Cor Cyp Cas	
			Arrived at O 23 d 2.14 — advance party sent to get this site in order	
	10/9/18		Moved to new site, Opens Sen Beatty at N33 site BUS (O 23 d 2.4) 12 hours	
BUS O 23 d 2.4			D.D. inf. visited site — Remains SB's & 129 returned to their units	
			Capt HORNER R.A.M.C. taken on Strength of this unit —	
			48536 L/Cpl IEUAN PHILLIPS R.A.M.C. (base) wounded 11/9/18 of Six Boles Artillery 130 Field Amb	
			48151 L/Cpl W.J KENDALL R.A.M.C.	
			M699516 Pte GEORGE CAPP A.S.C. attached to 130 Field Ambulance	
			Awarded Military Medal for acts of Gallantry — immediate reward	
BUS	11/9/18		10 A.S.C. car drivers reported for duty 129. also D Brs	
			D Brs visited site	
BUS	12/9/18		Capt MELHUISH + Lt BANTON of this unit attached for duty & 129. D Brs visited site	
			Military Medal Award (Immediate reward) 15 48150 Pte TIM RICHARDS 130 Field	
			Ambulance for acts of Gallantry —	

Army Form C. 2118.

WAR DIARY
or
INTELLIGENCE SUMMARY.
(Erase heading not required.)

Army Pres? VIII Army

Place	Date	Hour	Summary of Events and Information	Remarks and references to Appendices
BUS	13/9/18		Visited D.R.S. L/. BANTON reported from 129 F.Amb. S.C.R.	JSMD
	14/9/18		D.R.S Spencer DDMS visited Gas Guide -	JSMD
	15/9/18		DMS, DDMS, ADMS visited site - Capt. MELHUISH returned from 129 F.Amb	JSMD
			Visited 64 Field Amb.	
	16/9/18		Visited D.R.S - 3 N.C.O. + 40 O.R. to 129th F.Amb.	JSMD
	17/9/18	AM 2:30	Violent hurricane + thunder storm lasting early an hour, which blew + lifted roofs of most of the huts - one casualty only Scouts H.Q.? staff were carried some distance by hurricane	
			Capt MELHUISH R.A.M.C	
			D.D.M.S visited site and shelter specially -	
			20 O.R returnes to 131st Field Amb.	
			Visited D.R.S.	JSMD
	18/9/18	8:30am	Scene bombward by D.W - Bmgc.D? picked 2. Officers 7 men	
			DDMS visited Gas Guide,	
			following hon of hut awarded M.M. 48074 Corp. TRIGG W. R.A.M.C	
			48197 Pte THOMAS. D.A. 48222 Pte HARRIS. W.	JSMD

Army Form C. 2118.

WAR DIARY
or
INTELLIGENCE SUMMARY.
(Erase heading not required.)

Army Form C. 2118.

Place	Date	Hour	Summary of Events and Information	Remarks and references to Appendices
BUS	19/9/18		D.D.M.S. visits Gas Cauldie. Number of cases admitted up to date. Visits ADMS & Officers	
"	20/9/18		A.D.M.S. inspects men unfit for duty in forward area, and visits D.R.S.	
			& Bearers attached to 75th Costa's Batteries —	
"	21/9/18		D.R.S. handed over to 139th Field Amb.	
			M.M. awarded to 48153 Pte F.T. MARTIN of this unit —	
			Heavy shelling surrounding area — this site	
			O.C. Gt Bradley, 15 Field Amb. this second in Command Major McCriec (killed)	
			by direct hit on Hq — Ort — The Ambulance assumes us.	
			O.C. with Major Bostwick, Capt Mathews, attended funeral of the above Officers	
			named —	
			ADMS visits site	
"	23/9/18		P.M. Snowfallier to Sylvenas body "Serjt. Powell" to S.W.B.	
			M.C. Our wounded pleased of — to MAJOR JOHN BURR RAMC of this unit	
			D.C.M. awarded pounded of — to 48124 Serjt T.G. HOPKINS MM RAMC	
			of this unit.	

WAR DIARY
or
INTELLIGENCE SUMMARY.

Army Form C. 2118.

Place	Date	Hour	Summary of Events and Information	Remarks and references to Appendices
BUS	24/9/18		Visited ADMS Office — DDMS visited this Stn, also ADMS 33 Div. A large number of Gassed Cases (MUSTARD) about 200. Passed thro' this centre from the 33rd Div.	
"	25/9/18		Corps Foth. temporarily resumed — DDMS visited Stn. Visited 3 & 34 CCS	
"	26/9/18		ADMS inspects Stn	
"	27/9/18		Conference G.H.Q. DDMS visits. v Corps Gas Cases. Conference ADMS Office Major Burke-Roure — Capt Nathwick Roure + 54 O.R.S 15 114th Personnel	
"	28/9/18		Bath Band of 114th Personnel reported for duty, who Field Club	
"	"		DD m S visited Stn, Reconnoitred for New Site, fixed Same at V12c 1.9	
"	29/9/18		Closed Stn. Staff an Ambce at O23d 2.4 3 P.M. Opened New Site FINS V12c 1.9 Same hour	
BUS FINS V12C 1.9	30/9/18		45. Gassed Cases (Mustard) 23 Drunken 14th WELSH Stilly annoying U	

A. J. Thompson Col
ADMS. 38th Div.

John W Barrett
Lt Col. R.A.M.C.
DC 130 G (John) DADMS

John W Barrett
Lt Col. R.A.M.C.
DC 130 G (John) DADMS

1076/91

COMMITTEE FOR THE
MEDICAL HISTORY OF THE WAR.
Date 12 JAN 1919

130 r. 7. a.

Oct 1918

Army Form C. 2118.

WAR DIARY
or
INTELLIGENCE SUMMARY.
(Erase heading not required.)

Instructions regarding War Diaries and Intelligence Summaries are contained in F. S. Regs., Part II. and the Staff Manual respectively. Title pages will be prepared in manuscript.

Major Daniel McGrane OC 1st Field Ambulance

Place	Date	Hour	Summary of Events and Information	Remarks and references to Appendices
FINS	1/10/18		D.D.M.S. inspected Sub. ADMS. visited site	8/MO
V.M.C.1.9 Sheet 57C	2/10/18		Visited B Section at W.H.T.B.S. a Nr HEUDECOURT. Major BADENOCH proceeded on leave (A-18), 8/MO - 8/MO	8/MO
	3/10/18		ADMS visited Site 1 & See Annex. B Section moved forward to F & a 3.7 Start 6.2 C - Major BURKE M.C.	8/MO
	4/10/18		DDMS visited Site - B Section on Tour (6"-20").	
	5/10/18		Proceeded on leave. Capt McMillan RAMC OC MO 38 Bn M.G.C. reported for temporary duty. DDMS inspected site.	8/MO
	6/10/18		Visited ADMS Office.	8/MO
	7/10/18		Reconnoitres for site for Car Cake in forward area.	8/MO
	8/10/18		No Scout to Report	
	9/10/18		To AUBENCHEUL - Out Bois with OC W.W.C.P. (Lt BENTIM R.A.M.C) & Surg Bm ADMS Index Party	8/MO
FINS, AUBENCHEUL AUX BOIS	10/10/18	10 AM	Site - Unit moved forward to AUBENCHEUL-AUX-BOIS. Capt MELHUISH RAMC 1/10/18 & Capt BARNES 1/10 F.AMB - Lt MOORE RAMC - WK 12 & Lt BARNES 25 HQ Temporary duty to 13 F AMB. L/Cpl BARNES to 64 Field Amb for temporary duty - from 11th Brigade	
AUBENCHEUL AUX BOIS MALINCOURT	11/10/18	8 AM	Unit moves via VILLERS-OUTREAUX - to MALINCOURT arrived 9.45 am - GSR up Site Sh. map location T.15.b.5.2.	8/MO

Army Form C. 2118.

WAR DIARY
or
INTELLIGENCE SUMMARY.

(Erase heading not required.)

John Dawson
Lt Col. R.A.M.C.
O.C. 13th Fd. Amb.

Instructions regarding War Diaries and Intelligence Summaries are contained in F. S. Regs., Part II. and the Staff Manual respectively. Title pages will be prepared in manuscript.

Place	Date	Hour	Summary of Events and Information	Remarks and references to Appendices
WAINCOURT & BERTRY	12/10/18	7.30 Bn. 9.30	Divided BERTRY, and Reconnoitred for site. Unit moved via WALINCOURT, SEVIGNY, CLARY to BERTRY. Unit arrived at 7h. Centre opened Site P. & S.6.	13th Fd. Amb.
BERTRY P. & S. 6	13/10/18		Refugees to collect. Sgt. Burhan — nearly 2000 civilians in village, all family succeeded to work, food and great number suffering from some Influenza. Complexions with bronchitis and Pneumonia. All in extremely bad conditions. Many of the 10,000 people were all living in overcrowded cellars and obliterating cleans and in horrid condition with sunken eyes and very wasted and very anaemic bones. Its youngsters children and almost without colour. They shew their true. Collected and carried them in blankets to allow before it is late to "Caves" — so busy butler etc, will take ages — all live from houses taken off. Everything — adult flocks previous — volatile have collapsed. Houses thrown about damaged and destroyed. The whole village in a most insanitary condition — cabins turned off. Visited A.D.M.S. Office.	13th Fd. Amb.
			Visited A.D.S. Shelter at TROISVILLES, and inspected town — a very large number of Civilian Sick — suffering from Influenza, Pneumonia, Bronchitis, bodily food values	13th Fd. Amb.
BERTRY P. & S. 6	14/10/18			

WAR DIARY
or
INTELLIGENCE SUMMARY

Army Form C. 2118.

(Erase heading not required.)

Place	Date	Hour	Summary of Events and Information	Remarks and references to Appendices
BERTRY	15/10/18		Conference A.D.M.S. Office. Visited New Site D.V. Hosp. No D.S. MONTIGNY - has to the village where our forward A.D.M.S. Gt. Thompson Cmg. D.O. two Forces Prisoner Officer Commanding a Post Evidence they visited a large number of sick civilians leaving been attacked with influenza but 5 no majority of the cases show signs of rapid improvement with good air ventilation. But two old people Sister Monchilt v Prainnes dying of pneumonia.	
BERTRY	16/10/18		No truck to report - Stretcher bearer v Sister Gabain above visited the Schlosser see Classes B Thompkins abortion. G.O.C. visited site.	JGHD
	17/10/18		No truck to report - dits	
	18/10/18		Conference A.D.M.S. Three.	
	19/10/18		Village bands, Stables Committee of Sudden v Civilian killed or buried in Action. Others to the people from having knowledge of first aid Sergt J.R. Dawes Sergt J.R. Dawes R.A.M.C. of this Unit words Distinction of great value - Sergt J.R. Dawes buried in DeCroix Corpl WALKER R.A.M.C. buried [illegible] in following day Brown Stove Jnr Civilian buried	JGHD
"	20/10/18		Conference A.D.M.S. Office	JGHD
"	21/10/18		No truck to report	JGHD
"	22/10/18		No truck to report	JGHD
"	23/10/18		Conference A.D.M.S. Office	JGHD
"	24/10/18		A.D.M.S. Office moved to R.S.d. Camel.	
"	25/10/18		A.D.M.S. Office moved to R.S.d. - R.A.M.C. Dsn No 71. Personel D.R.S. Syrne This side 38" Dsn Malinois 33" Dsn	JGHD
"	26/10/18		D.D.M.S V Corps Visited This Side A.D.M.S Visited This Side	JGHD

Army Form C. 2118.

WAR DIARY
or
INTELLIGENCE SUMMARY.

(Erase heading not required.)

Lt Col N Razal
Lt Col Rauno OC 136 Field Amb

Instructions regarding War Diaries and Intelligence
Summaries are contained in F. S. Regs., Part II.
and the Staff Manual respectively. Title pages
will be prepared in manuscript.

Place	Date	Hour	Summary of Events and Information	Remarks and references to Appendices
BERTRY	27/10/18		Large number of Influenza Cases, Complicated with Bronchitis & Pneumonia admitted	
"	28/10/18		No Event to report	ASC 9/10
"	29/10/18		Reported for Orders when turfit for forward area	82nd
			G.O.C. 38th Divs. inspected site	82nd
"	30/10/18		D.D.M.S. V Corps inspected site. A.D.M.S. inspected site	
"	31/10/18		No Event to report	

Lt Col N Razal
O.C.

CONFIDENTIAL

WAR DIARY OF

130ᵗʰ (Sᵗ. JOHN) FIELD AMBULANCE.

FROM 1ˢᵗ NOVEMBER 1918 To 30ᵗʰ NOVEMBER 1918.

WAR DIARY or INTELLIGENCE SUMMARY.

Army Form C. 2118.

J.W.2 A Dorsel
War. R.A.M.C. 136 Field Amb.

Place	Date	Hours	Summary of Events and Information	Remarks and references to Appendices
BERTRY	1/11/18		No event.	
"	2/11/18	14.00	Conference A.D.M.S. Office, RICHMOND FOREST.	89WD 89WD
"	3/11/18		Advance party consisting of Major BURKE M.C. + 30 other ranks proceeded to MOULIN D'HARPIES. ENGLEFONTAINE is taken over from 131st Field Ambulance. The Clearing of the line - 1 Officer + OR from 131st proceeds as advance party to take over D.R.S. BERTRY.	89WD
"	4/11/18		Reconnoitres roads in forward area	89WD
BERTRY MOULIN D'HARPIES	5/11/18	09.00	Unit marches to MOULIN D'HARPIES with full packs, convoy 1300 1st. with Major BURNE Accommodates ENGLEFONTAINE and forward area HECQ, GRAND PATURES, LOCQUIGNOL. MAJOR BURKE with 30 other ranks, and 5 cars proceeds to SASSABARAS to perform 19th Field Ambulance D.B.S.	89WD 89WD
MOULIN D'HARPIES	6/11/18	05.00 09.00	Unit marches in direction of LOCQUIGNOL (FORET-DE-MORMAL) lies up by Chateau in roads. Bivouacs for night in forest. in passing down in teeming rain in the forest outside SASSABARAS.	89WD
FORET DE MORMAL BERLAIMONT POT-DE-VIN	7/11/18	16.45	A.D.S. opened. POT-DE-VIN (Dqt 8.4.) Unit HQ. moved to BERLAIMONT. + (U26 6.4.) Took over S.O.S. of 19 Field Amb.	89WD

(37092). Wt. W14859/M1293. 75,000. 1/17. D. D. & L. Ltd. Forms/C.2118/24.

Army Form C. 2118.

WAR DIARY
or
INTELLIGENCE SUMMARY.
(Erase heading not required.)

Place	Date	Hour	Summary of Events and Information	Remarks and references to Appendices
BERLAIMONT ADS POT DE VIN	8/11/18		Visited ADS + RAP's of 114 Bgde, also on HQ's 113 -114 Bgades. Visited RAP's of 13th RWF 14th RWF 16th RWF. Reconnoitred roads in forward area as far as DOURLERS.	82 MD
BERLAIMONT POT-DE-VIN	9/11/18	12.00	Mule marched to new HQ at POT-DE-VIN arriving 1500 hrs. ADS moved to WATTIGNIES-LA VICTOIRE D.D.M.S. ADMS visited S/E BERLAIMONT also ADuS 19th Div	82 MD
WATTIGNIES LA VICTOIRE W.30.b.1. (A.D.S.)				
POT-DE VIN HQ WATTIGNIES LA VICTOIRE ADS	10/11/18	12.30	Mule marched to new HQ WATTIGNIES-LA VICTOIRE arriving 1530. Open hospital in School. Reconnoitred roads to DIMONT + DIMACHEUX. Major BURKE [to consolidate?] Hospital (German) site at SOIRE-LE-CHATEAU but found that this was in 1st Corps Area.	82 MD
WATTIGNIES HQ	11/11/18	0630	News of Armistice received. Notifies sent at 0900 hrs [that hostilities would] cease at 1100 hrs. G.O.C. 38th Div with ADMS visited ADS	to FD
WATTIGNIES	12/11/18	0900	Conference ADMS Office — Visited 114th Bgade — Instruction [Instructions?] [with] to other water supplies in Village, and has [same] labelled Clothing the Anglican. — Visited M.O.S. 14th RWF	[unit]
WATTIGNIES	13/11/18	0900	DIMACHEUX Capt. D.A. POWELL R.A.M.C. Roberts 16 R.W.F. to BANTON U.S.M.O.R.C. Ponds WELSH of DIMONT + 16 RWF at DIMONT + Shock of that Unit this day	82 MD

Army Form C. 2118.

WAR DIARY
or
INTELLIGENCE SUMMARY.
(Erase heading not required.)

J.D. Dadd
L/Col, France
O.C. 130 (St John) Fus Bn (?)

Instructions regarding War Diaries and Intelligence Summaries are contained in F. S. Regs, Part II and the Staff Manual respectively. Title pages will be prepared in manuscript.

Place	Date	Hour	Summary of Events and Information	Remarks and references to Appendices
WATTIGNIES	14/11/18		Quarters in 113th Brigade Troops. Flag of Cameroon Wattignies by Germans — G.O.C. 38 Divn. visited site	1/2 MO
WATTIGNIES	15/11/18		Holding party sent to site, presumably occupied by the end of BERLAIMONT.	9/MO
WATTIGNIES	16/11/18		Visited 14th RWF, 16 RWF of DAMOUSIES, and OBRECHIES, to inspect Saunders. Visit MO's arrange about Collection of men Sick.	8/MO
WATTIGNIES	17/11/18		No Sick to Report	
WATTIGNIES	18/11/18		Football Match Rugby v 139 Bde H.Q. won. 2 24th to Bride 83rd	
WATTIGNIES	19/11/18		Brigadier General I.E. of R.A.S. PRYCE CMG DSO handed over Command of 113 Bde to Brigadier General CARTON DE WIART VC CMG DSO.	
			Took over duties as A.D.M.S. 38th Divn — handed over Command of the 2nd Battn RWF.	85 M(?)
WATTIGNIES	20/11/18		to Major J. BURNE M.C. — Football Match Rugby v. 131 Bde won 24 pts nil	29 MO
do	21/11/18		Transcription of Honours Ribbons by G.O.C. 35th Division	205 MO
do	22/11/18		Nothing to report	
do	23/11/18		Moved to BERLAIMONT	
BERLAIMONT	24/11/18		A.D.M.S two medical aids (?)	
do	25/11/18		Played 19th Welsh Rgt at Rugby by another Divisional Company	
do	26/11/18		Medical Inspection of minor officers and men	

Army Form C. 2118.

WAR DIARY
or
INTELLIGENCE SUMMARY.
(Erase heading not required.)

[Signature] Major Raine

Place	Date	Hour	Summary of Events and Information	Remarks and references to Appendices
BERTANCOURT	27/11/18		Medical Inspection of 113 Bde numbers also those of Pioneers.	
do	28/11/18		O.C. attended a G.O.C. 130th Divisional conference from Leave, assumed duties as O.C. 130th Divisional Signals. A/Bn.S. returned from Leave.	
do	29/11/18		Played 1st Welsh Regt (3rd time). Won by 2 tries (6 pts) to nil. 3 runners for Bde Rowe, W.J. Duggan, A. Philip approved for training.	
do	30/11/18		Cross Country Race.	

30/11/18.

[Signature] Major Raine
O.C. 130th Divisional Signals

Confidential

War Diary

of

130th (St John) Field Amb.

From 1st Dec. 1918
To 31st Dec. 1918

COMMITTEE FOR THE
MEDICAL HISTORY OF THE WAR
Date 6 MAR. 1919

Army Form C. 2118.

WAR DIARY
or
INTELLIGENCE SUMMARY.
(Erase heading not required.)

Instructions regarding War Diaries and Intelligence Summaries are contained in F. S. Regs., Part II. and the Staff Manual respectively. Title pages will be prepared in manuscript.

John M Dawson
Lt Col RAMC
OC 13 D (old [?]) 2nd Aust.

Place	Date	Hour	Summary of Events and Information	Remarks and references to Appendices
BERLAIMONT	1/12/18		To see O.i.c. 16 inspect site for D.R.S. at QUERRIEUX near AMIENS. - The Cousins of very large Chateau devoid of every kind of furniture, the in the grounds of which are a number of huts - both require stoves + oil. Sen for lorries. Chateau which require stoves + oil sen for lorries. Went on to Amiens. on unable to return hadnight - stayed at #1 Stationary Hospital went on 16 Dec. Lt Col H Julie-Roberts CMG it/c DC.	JBHD
"	2/12/18		Car broke down Amiens Station. Returned in Car of 129 Fd Amb. Garage. S.M. Interpreter + St Clair-en-Caux behis. Called at workshop exchanged for spare D/car 23 pts burst RAMC v 38 MGC - Final of SE Comp - Won Rugby.	JBHD
"	3/12/18		On Command Stopped 1 Officer + 70 OR from each Fd Gets Ambulance lined Roads to be hansed by the Propetie the King - the king walked past at 1115 [?] for Great Ovation - Called out - by King. who shook hands r Capitals Secured great Ovation for hard work of RAMC of Division. he on football of RAMC of Division.	JBHD JBHD
"	4/12/18		No Sport Cross Country RAMC v 36 MGC = won by MGC - the Nithan Division Southern leech	85 PD
"	5/12/18		Semi final for Divisional Rugby - RAMC v 13 RWF won by RAMC 23/6 & nil 8HD Group Association football. RAMC v 38 Divl HQ Signals won by RAMC 2 Goals Neutral	8HD
"	6/12/18		No Sport	8HD JEHD
"	7/12/18		14 Divers left next for Inverness Final of Sport Association football	
"	8/12/18		Final of Divl Rugby RAMC v 19 Welsh won by RAMC 2 (Penaltys)	JEHD
"	9/12/18		a Drw Various Nil RAMC v 14 Welsh Drawn Game.	85 HD
"	10/12/18			85 HD

WAR DIARY
INTELLIGENCE SUMMARY

Place	Date	Hour	Summary of Events and Information	Remarks and references to Appendices
BERLAIMONT	11/12/18		Major Bastwick proceeds to Eng. On 7 days leave. Shrapnel Fuel Divisional Rugby. RAMC v 14 Welsh — Won by draws.	9 S/H/D
"	12/12/18		Took over duties of ADMS. 20 miners proceeded to England	ASMS
"	12/12/18		Took over from Col. Jones DSO	
"	13/12/18		Rugby football final v 14th Welsh Regt. Won — R.A.M.C./Proxs malaria 9/0	
"	14/12/18		Nothing to report. 9/0	
"	15/12/18		Attended parade. 9/0	
"	16/12/18		Renewals in men. 45 three cases to England. 9/0	
"	17/12/18		Thirteen reinforcements arrived. Four H.S.L.S. drivers arrived 9/0	
"	18/12/18		New H.T. Ltd driver arrived. 9/0	
"	19/12/18		ADMS malaria 9/0	
"	20/12/18		Nothing to report. 9/0	
"	21/12/18		ADMS malaria 9/0	
"	22/12/18		Nothing to report 9/0	
"	23/12/18		Conference ADMS office. 9/0	
"	24/12/18		Extra fee nothing to report. 9/0	
"	25/12/18		Xmas Day. G.O.C. Division malaria. Men knee down feed. 9/0	
"	26/12/18		Army malaria 9/0	

Army Form C. 2118.

WAR DIARY
or
INTELLIGENCE SUMMARY.

(Erase heading not required.)

John Burke
Major Name

Instructions regarding War Diaries and Intelligence
Summaries are contained in F. S. Regs., Part II.
and the Staff Manual respectively. Title pages
will be prepared in manuscript.

Place	Date	Hour	Summary of Events and Information	Remarks and references to Appendices
BERLAIMONT	27.12.18		Nothing to report.	
	28.12.18		do.	
	29.12.18		ADMs visited Unit. Nothing to report.	
	30.12.18		Unit moved to Bavaria by march. Transport	
	31.12.18		moved by train with Brigade to Monday.	

John Burke
Major Name
O.C. 130th (ST. JOHN) FIELD AMBULANCE.

CONFIDENTIAL

38 DIV

WAR DIARY

OF

130 (ST JOHN) FIELD AMBULANCE.

FROM - January 1st, 1919
TO - January 31st, 1919.

Army Form C. 211

John Burtle
Major R.A.M.C.

WAR DIARY
or
INTELLIGENCE SUMMARY.
(Erase heading not required.)

Instructions regarding War Diaries and Intelligence Summaries are contained in F. S. Regs., Part II. and the Staff Manual respectively. Title pages will be prepared in manuscript.

Place	Date 1919	Hour	Summary of Events and Information	Remarks and references to Appendices
ENGLEFONTEIN QUERRIEU	Jan 1		Unit moved with 114 Brigade to INCHY	
	2		Entrained with Brigade for QUERRIEU.	
	3		A/Adms visited site.	
	4		Nothing to report.	
	5		D.D.M.S. V Corps visited	
	6		A/St Maj. Sam R.A.M.C. notified of his award of D.S.M. by A/Adms B	
	7		Reconnoitred for new site, none to be got nearer by Donnowal H.Q. 2 1/6	
			from one now occupied.	
	8		nil.	
	9		nil.	
	10		nil.	
BUSSY	11		moved to BUSSY. Tent & Equipment erected.	
	12		nil.	
	13		nil.	
	14		D.D.M.S. V Corps visited site.	
	15		nil.	
	16		R.A.M.C. winners of Divisional Association Football Competition	
			Semi-final beating 105 F.A. 7.B. 5 - 1.	

Army Form C. 2118.

WAR DIARY
or
INTELLIGENCE SUMMARY.
(Erase heading not required.)

John Burke
Major R.A.M.C.

Instructions regarding War Diaries and Intelligence Summaries are contained in F.S. Regs., Part II. and the Staff Manual respectively. Title pages will be prepared in manuscript.

Place	Date 1919	Hour	Summary of Events and Information	Remarks and references to Appendices
BUSSY	Jan 17		Capt Horner M.O.R.C.S. U.S.A. reported KB	
	18		A.D.M.S. visited KB	
	19		NIL KB	
	20		NIL KB	
	21		NIL KB	
	22		G.O.C. 38th WELSH DIVISION visited KB	
	23		Funeral Drowned A footballer R.A.M.C. 2 sols 124 R.F. 2 18 and B	
	24		NIL KB	
	25		NIL KB	
	26		Capt Arundel returned to 131 Field Ambulance KB	
			Lt Kerr R.A.M.C. taken on strength KB	
	27		No sgd. - fall of snow	
	28		Major Burke M.C. attended Aviary Board at DHQ gHD	
	29		Returned from leave, took over from Major Burke acting OC 92 HO gHD	
			Visited A.D.M.S. + DHQ. gHD	
	30		No sgd. gHD	
	31		Lt. Major Burke attended Aviary Board. - reported ADMS office 9 AD KonZA Brasel gHD Raune	

WJ Humphrey Col
JBurke LtCol

No. 180 Field Ambulance

Army Form C. 2118.

WAR DIARY
or
INTELLIGENCE SUMMARY.

(Erase heading not required.)

Instructions regarding War Diaries and Intelligence Summaries are contained in F. S. Regs., Part II. and the Staff Manual respectively. Title pages will be prepared in manuscript.

HQ 2nd Bassd
HQ Royal 2nd Cumberland
(3rd S. July 1906)

Place	Date	Hour	Summary of Events and Information	Remarks and references to Appendices
BUSSY	FEBRUARY			3
	1		No Secret.	JBHQ
"	2		No Secret.	JBHQ
"	3		G.O.C. 3⁴ Bde. visited hut. into A.D.M.S.	JBHQ
"	4		No Secret — #. 6 L.D., 5 H.D. Y. Horse taken off. strength.	JBHQ
"	5		No Secret —	JBHQ
"	6		A.D.M.S. visited Ste	JBHQ
"	7		No Secret	
"	8	11 A.M.	H.R.H. the Prince of Wales walked over from QUERRIEU with the G.O.C. and inspected the Ambulance Ste, and spoke to a large number of NCOs & men of the Unit — visiting also the Bakaha. — Transport &c	
		1 P.M.	Information to all Officers that W.O.'s Daughter of P.O.'s at his invitation was introduced to all Officers at W.O.'s. Dr THRESY Thomas, U.P.A: Dr THRESY Thomas U.P.A: He also consented for the money of the Chateau — should it be forsaken. — should be turned into	JBHQ
			DE THRESY	
	9		Ambulance match. Semi final V Oxfos. Postponed. DaPaul called.	JBHQ
	10		8. H.D Horse Z clerk taken off. strength	
	11		Col. A.C. Thompson A.M.U.S. 3⁴ Div on tour to R.D.s VIII Corps area inspected and approved the Units and said Farewells	JBHQ

WAR DIARY
or
INTELLIGENCE SUMMARY.

Army Form C. 2118.

Place	Date	Hour	Summary of Events and Information	Remarks and references to Appendices
BUSSY	Feb 13th		Visited Div HQ Quarters – Semifinal Corps Association. Range 36 Div Kit V Corps R.E.	
	14th		Visited Corps Association – RAMC 36 Div v 1st R. Yorks 2.5. Div 1(2)	
	15		Wrestled by 3 goals & nil – 3rd cup & silver medals	
			The runners up receive Cohen's cup – two of whom belonged to this Unit v. ug	
			Lieut HARBOTTLE, R.J. PRITCHARD, W NESBITT, G.H DAVIES	
			E. VANN. All Rowe –	
			The Team 36 Div. 2.151 Div Composite. 50 v. Pay. Liverpool another	
			Round Wesleyan Army Sunday with Rowing Rivers.	
			GOC returned.	
			No Event – 2 horses. 1 HDY – 1 LD-Y – Sent to proposed stables	
			No Event –	
BUSSY	16th		No Event	
	17th		V Corps Final Rugby 36 Div v 21 Div. 36 Div won 32ft 2nd	
	18th		The following from the Ambulance played in Burrowed –	
	19th		Rain. 1Capt T.J. Nicholas. Pte W. BATCHELOR –	
	20		A.D.M.S visited Protocols S.JE	
	21		No Event	
	22		No Event	
			Visited D.H.Q. g.p.c.	

Army Form C. 2118.

WAR DIARY
or
INTELLIGENCE SUMMARY. John H Basnet
Lt. Col. R.A.M.C.
(Erase heading not required.)

Place	Date	Hour	Summary of Events and Information	Remarks and references to Appendices
BUSSY	February 23		Not set	
"	24	2.30 PM	Conference OC's Field Amb's M.O. o/c Div. S. Subjects. Precautions and treatment Venereal Disease. — Blue Room. Lecture to Units. — Influenza. Method of — Sanitations. — bathing — clothing.	85 HQ 85 MD
"	25		4 R.D. 4 L.D. stores 5A strong Ko, thro' Iny	95 MD
"	26		Not set	
"	27		Lecture on Venereal Disease to Unit. (very well attended) by 82 RD Major Burrg M.C.	
"	28		Not set. OC 3d Div Visit this unit 85 HQ	

John H Basnet
Lt. Col. R.A.M.C.
O.C. 136 Field Amb.

140/3551

17 JUL 1919

1305 F.A.

Aug 1919

Army Form C. 2118.

WAR DIARY
or
INTELLIGENCE SUMMARY.
(Erase heading not required.)

John H. Stansel War Raune
OC 130 St John B gds Amb 35 38 th Div

Place	Date	Hour	Summary of Events and Information	Remarks and references to Appendices
BUSSY March	1/3/19		ADMS visited Site.	
"	2/3/19		No Event.	
"	3/3/19		" "	
"	4/3/19		No Event.	
"	5/3/19		Trucks taken to Site at Chateau LA MOTTE, BREBIERE, Bisports & Equipments sent to Cage Parts at GLISSY	
"	6/3/19		3 R. & 2 L.D. Stores Balances. — 2 Horse Ambulances, 1 GS Wagon, 1 Water Cart to Cage Park/R	
"	7/3/19		1 Horse Ambulance, 2 Limbers & German Cooker to Cage Park	
"	8/3/19		G.O.C. Visited Site.	
"	9/3/19		No Event.	
"	10/3/19		Acting ADMS	
"	11/3/19		" "	
"	12/3/19		2 H.D. 2 L.D. (2nd) horses to Sale at Amiens	
"	13/3/19		G.O.C. 3rd. Div & A.D.M.S. Visits Ambulance & to say goodbye.	
"	14/3/19		Took over from ADMS. as SMO	
"	15/3/19		G.O.C. & ADMS. left Division — 1 N.C.O. & Private Shuckcliff sent to	
"	16/3/19		Proceeding to Army of Occupation Rhine.	
"	17/3/19		Took over charge X from OC who is acting A.D.M.S.	
"	18/3/19		One Turning horse to Corps Horse Cards.	
"	19/3/19			

Army Form C. 2118.

WAR DIARY
or
INTELLIGENCE SUMMARY.
(Erase heading not required.)

Instructions regarding War Diaries and Intelligence Summaries are contained in F. S. Regs., Part II. and the Staff Manual respectively. Title pages will be prepared in manuscript.

Place	Date	Hour	Summary of Events and Information	Remarks and references to Appendices
Bussy-les-Daours	20.7.19		Nothing to report	
	21.7.19		Three horses left Corps Horse Camp.	
	22.7.19		Nothing to report	
	23.7.19		do.	
	24.7.19		do.	
	25.7.19		do.	
	26.7.19		do.	
	27.7.19		do.	
	28.7.19		do.	
	29.7.19		do.	
	30.7.19		do.	
	31.7.19		do.	
			Moving to Corps Front	

116/3550

130 to F.O.

Op. 1919

WAR DIARY
or
INTELLIGENCE SUMMARY.

Army Form C. 2118.

John B. Dawson
Maj. R. Ruff
O.C. 130 (S) Fd. Amb.

Place	Date	Hour	Summary of Events and Information	Remarks and references to Appendices
BUSSY-LES-DAOURS	1/4/19		Acting D.D.M.S. visited Field Ambulance	85 F.A.
"	2/4/19		G.O.C. 38th Brigade visited Castre.	83 F.A.
"	3/4/19		Roll call	
"	4/4/19		Capt. T.W. MELHUISH R.A.M.C. to 141 Stationary Hospital, struck off strength	85 F.A. / 89 F.A.
"	5/4/19		Capt. ["Major] BURNE M.C. R.A.M.C. proceeded to Dispersal Station and struck off strength	85 F.A.
"	6/4/19		Capt. ["Major] to The Chateau - LA MOTTE BREBIERE	85 F.A.
"	7/4/19		Lieut. Thomas ley route march	
LA MOTTE BREBIERE	8/4/19		No event	85 F.A.
"	9/4/19		No event	85 F.A.
"	10/4/19		Handed to Ordnance This day - 13 mules surplus to Castre w/ 1 Horse Ambulance 185, 1 Limber	
"	11/4/19		1 Mule Can S/ Bn Castre Association mules Raw O broken by DAC 2 foresland	82 F.A.
"	12/4/19		Semi-final	
"	13/4/19		No event	85 F.A.
"	14/4/19		Equipment examined by Ordnance Officer	
"	15/4/19		Mules R.Q.S.C al business - Ear. Ambulance below to R.S.C. 87th	
"	16/4/19		No event	85 F.A.
"	17/4/19		130 reported down to Castre strength 85 F.A.	
"	18/4/19		Ambulance below to R.S. 85 F.A.	
"	19/4/19		No event	
"	20/4/19		82nd F.A. + Field Amb. Fld.Pd. & L. Amb Pound W.120 - To TREPORT. 85 F.A.	

Army Form C. 2118.

WAR DIARY
or
INTELLIGENCE SUMMARY.
(Erase heading not required)

Instructions regarding War Diaries and Intelligence Summaries are contained in F.S. Regs., Part II. and the Staff Manual respectively. Title pages will be prepared in manuscript.

Place	Date	Hour	Summary of Events and Information	Remarks and references to Appendices
WARLUS BREFERT	21/4/19		Capt. T.W. MELHUIST RAMC from 85 Labour Coute. Reported to take over Command of Capt. 130. 380 Coy/ce. Visited SWO & Capt. Packer at LONGPRÉ. Visited D.H.Q.	
"	22/4/19		Handed over duties of SWO. by Capt SPROULE 131st Batt Cam, and Capt. 130 Batt Cam to Capt T.W. MELHUIST. Took over command of 130. Field ambulance from T.W. Melhurst Visit from S.M.O. 4 W.13. 14 Divns N.Z.O. Capt. Park O.C. 13a Field ambulance Started checking unit equipment very carefully	
"	23.		continued "	
"	24		" " "	
"	25		" " "	
"	26		" " "	
"	27		" " "	
"	28		" " "	
"	29		nothing of any importance	

No. 130 Field Ambulance

WAR DIARY
or
INTELLIGENCE SUMMARY.

Army Form C. 2118.

T.W. Melhuish. O.C. 130 Field Ambulance
Capt. R.A.M.C.

Instructions regarding War Diaries and Intelligence Summaries are contained in F.S. Regs., Part II. and the Staff Manual respectively. Title pages will be prepared in manuscript.

(Erase heading not required.)

Place	Date	Hour	Summary of Events and Information	Remarks and references to Appendices
LA MOTTE BREBIERE	1/5/19 2/5/19 3/5/19 4/5/19 5/5/19 6/5/19		Visited S.M.O.	
	7/5/19 8/5/19		Nothing to report	
			Visited S.M.O. Appointment of Capt. T.W. MELHUISH RAMC as O.C. 130 Field Ambulance (capt. attached under my orders DMS BT in A & T 50406/109 CAPT T W MELHUISH relinquish command of 130 Field Ambulance (capt. go home) received through S.M.O. that Field Ambulance would go home. This figures from	
	9.5.19		Visited S.M.O. who said he would give me the information as to my position under the order DMS BT in A & T 5046/109	
	10.5.19		Nothing to report	
	11.5.19 12.5.19 13.5.19		Entraining orders for the hill Cadre received for 14th inst. all waggons loaded orders being that on departure of 130 F.A. Capt T.W. MELHUISH RAMC should hand over command to Capt J.L. SPROULE R.A.M.C.	
			The two remaining horse waggons/motor ambulance + H.Q. after taking water Cart to Gray Wagon Park sent to C.R.C. for disposal. Imprest account.	
		4.30		
	14.5.19		Orders received through S.M.O. 38 Div. that 130 Field Ambulance but address not shown would be broken up on Return	

Lt Col Newman
Lt Col R.A.M.C.

130 Field Ambulance
T.W. Withnall, Capt
Capt RAMC

Army Form C. 2118.

WAR DIARY
or
INTELLIGENCE SUMMARY

(Erase heading not required.)

Instructions regarding War Diaries and Intelligence
Summaries are contained in F. S. Regs., Part II.
and the Staff Manual respectively. Title pages
will be prepared in manuscript.

Place	Date	Hour	Summary of Events and Information	Remarks and references to Appendices
LA AIRE BRESIERE	16.5.19		Under instruction from S.M.O. B.OR's mtls to 14 WELSH Regt. 14 WELSH Regt. Jr. Jr. no Runs with 8 OR's handed to SAVEURSE for demobilisation 5 OR's handed to SAVEURSE for demobilisation	
			Three drawing of RAMC. D.C.L. Quartermaster. 5 RASC (HT) to guard equipment 1 RASC (HT)	
	17.5.19	9 am	Instructions received through S.M.O. that this unit "Returns to Depot" Visit from S.M.O.	
			2 O.R's attached to 14 WELSH Regt for demobilisation Visited S.M.O. in the afternoon with O.C. 129 F.A.	
	18.5.19		Nothing to report	
	19.5.19		The remainder of 131 F.A. (10 OR's) then demobilised kits and that 131 F.A. War Diary were handed over to me by Capt J. SPROUGE RAMC	
	20.5.19		Waiting to return	
	21.5.19		Nothing to report	
	22.5.19		Pay received by Capt A.T.C. DAVIES OC. 12 F.A. through as my ...... acct to date D	
			The remainder of 131 F.A. (9 O.R's) proceeded to SAVEURSE for demob. Capt A.F.C. DAVIES RAMC on the through ...... of his unit came to live here.	
			Visited BB Division Headquarters	
	23.5.19 24.5.19 25.5.19 26.5.19 27.5.19 28.5.19		Nothing to report	

T.W. Withnall
Capt RAMC

160/308-
Consul

18 AUG 1919

130r. 7.9

June 1919

WAR DIARY
or
INTELLIGENCE SUMMARY.

Army Form C. 2118.

T.W. Mulhurd
Capt Trans
O.C. 170 F.A.

Place	Date	Hour	Summary of Events and Information	Remarks and references to Appendices
LA MOTTE BRIBIERE	1/6/19 2/6/19		Nothing to report.	
	3/6/19		(1 Dec) Instructions from 38 Division regarding to return equipment (tools) equipment of POULANVILLE	
	4/6/19		Medical Stores removed equipment to POULANVILLE and got possible to Mem	
	5/6/19		Veterinary chest at MONTIÈRES	
	6		Visited A.D.M.S. 3rd Corps. Panelleys 4 O.Rs R.A.M.C.	
	7		Details instructions from A.D.M.S. of area to discharge unit.	
	8		Visited H.Q. AMIENS Sub area.	
	9		Nothing to report.	
	10		Unit partly disbanded. R.G.S.(M)'s VET. GALLON (H.T.) to R.A.S.C. 38 Div Train R.A.M.C. to 4th Stationary hospital	

T.W. Mulhurd
Capt Trans

www.ingramcontent.com/pod-product-compliance
Lightning Source LLC
Chambersburg PA
CBHW080841010526
44114CB00017B/2349